ADDITIONAL PRAISE FOR *BUILDING WINNI* *ALGORITHMIC TRADIN*

"This is a great book to get a much better understanding of what in really involved in system development and help on your journey from someone with a lot of real-life trading experience. For those already working with systems, it may challenge some of the approaches you use and help you to become a better system developer and trader. From my perspective, the chance to look over Kevin's shoulder and see the concepts and full code from some systems he has been using in his own trading alone would be of far more value than the cost of the book."

—Tim Rea, Proprietary systems developer/trader; 1st place winner, World Cup Championship of Futures Trading® 2011

"Part *Reminiscences of a Stock Operator* and part *Market Wizards,* Kevin Davey has written a superb book for the modern trader. Not only does Kevin provide a step-by-step plan on how to develop algorithmic trading strategies but he actually reveals the strategy he used to win The World Cup Championship Of Futures Trading® along with two additional euro currency systems. I have no doubt this will become a popular and often referenced book amongst traders. Readers will find Kevin's humble and engaging voice easy to follow and grasp. They will also find his personal journey from aerospace engineer to beginner trader, to a championship winning trader and finally to a full time professional trader insightful, entertaining, and inspiring. Wiley should also be congratulated for recruiting a real trader who trades real markets with real money to write a trading book for people aspiring to become real traders. I highly recommend this book to anyone who is serious about developing a successful and sustainable trading career."

—Brent Penfold, professional trader and author of *The Universal Principles of Successful Trading* (Wiley 2010)

"Few trading books on the market today are written by those who actually make their living from trading and those that are frequently suffer from being unintelligible to the layman. Kevin Davey has the authenticity of a real trader and the ability to distill complex ideas into a format that is easy to read and, at times, brutally honest. For those aspiring to trading success, Kevin gives a step by step guide on how to approach systems development as well as outlining many of the pitfalls to avoid and throughout the book he provides a wealth of information and tools that will prove invaluable to novice or expert alike."

—Michael Cook, Founder, Katmai Capital Advisors; World Cup Championship of Futures Trading® 2007

"Of all the trading books that I've read, this book takes the cake. Kevin Davey brings us a realistic perspective in an industry full of dreamers. I suggest that all traders drop what they're doing and read the incredibly valuable lessons summed up in this book. This book is the quickest path for a new trader to stop dreaming and start succeeding."

—Peter Hagen, Citracado Capital, LLC

Building Winning Algorithmic Trading Systems

The Wiley Trading series features books by traders who have survived the market's ever changing temperament and have prospered—some by reinventing systems, others by getting back to basics. Whether a novice trader, professional, or somewhere in between, these books will provide the advice and strategies needed to prosper today and well into the future. For more on this series, visit our Web site at www.WileyTrading.com.

Founded in 1807, John Wiley & Sons is the oldest independent publishing company in the United States. With offices in North America, Europe, Australia, and Asia, Wiley is globally committed to developing and marketing print and electronic products and services for our customers' professional and personal knowledge and understanding.

Building Winning Algorithmic Trading Systems

A Trader's Journey from Data Mining to Monte Carlo Simulation to Live Trading

Kevin J. Davey

WILEY

Cover Design: Wiley
Cover Image: © iStockphoto/Emilia_Szymanek

Published by John Wiley & Sons, Inc., Hoboken, New Jersey.
Published simultaneously in Canada.

Davey, Kevin, 1966-
Building algorithmic trading systems, + website : a trader's journey from data mining to Monte Carlo simulation to live trading / Kevin Davey.
1 online resource. — (Wiley trading)
Includes index.
ISBN 978-1-118-77891-3 (pdf) — ISBN 978-1-118-77888-3 (epub) — ISBN 978-1-118-77898-2 (pbk.)
1. Futures. 2. Portfolio management. 3. Investment analysis. 4. Monte Carlo method.
5. Electronic trading of securities. I. Title.
HG6024.A3
332.64′2028567 — dc23

2014014899

Printed in the United States of America

To Amy, Owen, Kathryn, Andrew, and Guardian Angel Anthony—
My love, my children, my life

CONTENTS

panded the daily downside limit. For my account size, having a "locked limit" down even with one contract was extremely painful.

A week later, after three days of a locked limit down market—where I could not exit at any price—I was finally able to liquidate, with a $5,400 loss.

This was about seven times the maximum loss I had expected, and as a percentage of my account, it was brutal. Not the end of the world, but it really made me wonder. Was the past month just the start of a prolonged losing streak, both in trading and in life? What was I doing trading anyhow, after all the recent emotional hits to my psyche? And trading on a whim, a hunch? When was I going to stop such destructive behavior? Could I stop such destructive behavior and finally turn into a winning trader? Could this series of unfortunate events provide the impetus to rise from the ashes, to turn my trading around? So many questions—ones I had no answer for.

As it turns out, as bad as this trade was, mad cow disease probably saved my trading life. This book documents that trading story, warts and all. Along the way, I got better and better at developing mechanical trading systems, and later in the book I show you the process I use to develop winning algorithmic trading systems.

Who Can Benefit from This Book?

Regardless of the type of trader you are, or your experience level with trading, I think you'll find something in this book that resonates for you.

For beginner traders, I hope this book is an eye-opener for you. I can't, and I won't, fill your head with thoughts of trading profits raining down from the sky. Anyone who tells you trading is easy is flat-out lying to you. Sure, you can make lots of money trading, but you also need to be prepared for a lot of losing, a lot of drawdowns, and a lot of risk. Whenever someone tells me trading is a piece of cake, I always suspect that they are half-baked. My story, as painful as it is at times, is a realistic journey for many retail traders. Of course, as I tell all beginners, read what I have written, but then read books by other traders, too. Keep an open mind to everything. After a lot of reading, you'll be able to make solid judgment calls on what is correct, what is BS, and what you like and don't like. The amount of misinformation about trading is staggering, so all beginners must be wary.

For intermediate or slightly experienced but struggling traders, maybe your failures up until this point aren't a result of psychology or confidence. Many trading books nowadays put a lot of emphasis on the mental aspect, but all the mental preparation in the world won't help you if you are developing strategies incorrectly. If you've ever lost money after you started trading a strategy right after optimizing it, then you probably realize you were doing something wrong. The process detailed in this book should be right up your alley, since it will steer you in the right direction.

For expert traders, most of what I present here you'll have already seen before in some fashion. Certainly, there are many great trading books that discuss many of the issues and problems that I address here. But there is always something new to learn, a different approach to try, and a different way to think. You probably find many items in this book that are different from your current method, and you'll likely benefit from incorporating these new ideas in your trading.

Although the book is designed around algorithmic or mechanical trading, which is what I primarily do, discretionary traders can benefit from the concepts detailed in this book. Maybe there are parts of your discretionary approach that can be statistically tested. For example, let's say your discretionary entry consists of a moving average crossover, combined with your intuition. It might be impossible to test your intuition, but a moving average crossover can be walk-forward tested and gently optimized. Or perhaps you want to evaluate breakeven or moving stops for your exit. There are many wrong ways to test this, but only a few correct ways. You'll learn a correct way in this book. Therefore, utilizing the concepts in this book, you can improve your discretionary approach a great deal, all because you'll know how to properly design and test a trading system. Whether it is a 100 percent mechanical strategy, or a part mechanical and part discretionary system, putting actual performance numbers to entries and exits can only give you confidence and make for a better trading approach.

I have organized *Building Winning Algorithmic Trading Systems* into seven parts. In all seven sections of the book, you'll see me use certain terms interchangeably:

Strategy or trading system—the approach used to trade. This can be rigid rules, general guidelines and principles, or flat-out random guessing. The net result is your strategy or trading system.

Mechanical or rule-based trading or algorithmic trading—a style of trading in which all the rules are defined 100 percent. There is no discretion involved, no decisions to be made by the trader.

Hybrid or mixed trading system—a style of trading that includes aspects of algorithmic trading, along with discretionary trading. An example would be a mechanical system that gives entry and exit signals, but gives the trader the option to accept or reject the signal.

In Part I, I walk you through my trading history. I think my early ups and downs—mostly downs—are pretty typical of new or beginning traders. I paid "tuition" to the market for many years. But I was able to persevere, winning the World Cup Championship of Futures Trading® in 2006, and finishing second in 2005 and 2007. After those successes, I reached the point all part-time, hobby shop, retail traders dream of: I was able to leave a promising career and live the dream of trading full time.

In the second part of this book, I tell you how I currently do things. From evaluating trading systems to designing new trading systems, I lay out my process. It is not perfect, and it is ever evolving, but it contains crucial information that I wish I had when I started out. Even if you just follow bits and pieces of what I do, you should be able to save thousands in market tuition.

In Parts III-VII, I build a trading system, from concept to live trading. It is a good trading system, but by no means the Holy Grail (which, by the way, does not exist). I also discuss in this section what I think is the closest one can get to the Holy Grail—diversification. Finally, I discuss how I monitor my strategies in real time, with a real-time diary of my trading progress through a number of months.

I hope that by reading my story, you'll be able to avoid my mistakes and learn from them. Trust me because, as you'll see, I've made a ton of them.

PART I

A Trader's Journey

CHAPTER 1

The Birth of a Trader

It was 1989, and I was California dreamin'. Actually I wasn't dreaming, I was already in California, living a young single man's dream. A year or so out of college, I was residing in sunny Manhattan Beach, California, with a small apartment three blocks from the soft white sand so wonderful that they used it to help create Waikiki Beach in Hawaii. I had graduated the year before, summa cum laude, with a bachelor's degree in aerospace engineering from the University of Michigan, a top-tier engineering school. Then I had turned my back on Massachusetts Institute of Technology (MIT), California Institute of Technology (Cal Tech), Stanford University, Purdue University, and Michigan, all of whom had accepted me in their aerospace master's degree program. I turned down those great schools to live and work in sunny California, a lifelong dream.

I still remember the precise moment I made that fateful decision. On a bitterly cold winter's day in Ann Arbor, Michigan, I was walking down South University Avenue to one of my final-semester classes. The wind was blowing so hard in my face that I actually leaned into the wind to see if it would keep me up. At that point, falling face-first onto the ice-covered sidewalk would not have been much worse than feeling the stinging wind in my face. What seemed like a gale-force wind kept me upright, and then I knew—I did not want, or need, to live where it was cold in the winter when aerospace engineering graduates like me were flocking to jobs in sunny southern California. My mind was made up. Sun and sand it was.

A few weeks after graduation, I packed up my belongings, and with my sister Karen as my driving companion, drove cross-country to warm and sunny Los Angeles.

One year later, I was settled in. I had a close group of friends, most of them Midwestern transplants like me. We'd while away the weekends playing beach volleyball, usually capping the day off with a few drinks at a local pub. I loved beach living and all the entertainment it provided. Driving around the beach cities in my little red T-roof sports car, life was pretty good.

But something was missing.

I couldn't put my finger on it, but I knew this wasn't the life for me. Well, beach life certainly agreed with me, but my choice of career was the wrong one. Sure, designing future fighter airplanes and working on secret government projects was fulfilling to a degree. But I just didn't feel like it was my future. I could not see myself doing that kind of work for even 5 years, much less a career of 30 or 40 years. I needed a jolt to wake me up. That jolt came in the form of junk mail that appeared in my mailbox one day, and it changed everything.

The junk mail booklet was from Ken Roberts, a futures and commodities trader. Or at least that is how he presented himself. Looking back on it, he was definitely more of a salesman than a trader. With a nice, folksy smile and a cowboy hat, Ken laid out the riches that awaited anyone brave enough to trade futures, or commodities, as they were more commonly referred to back then.

He had a compelling story in that little booklet of his, and I'll admit I was quickly hooked. Looking at a chart of sugar, as shown in Figure 1.1, seeing all the potential profit just waiting for me, how could I not be?

At that point, words like *drawdown, risk of ruin,* and *emotional control* were not in my vocabulary. But *massive profits, easy money,* and *simple trading* suddenly were! And with a money-back guarantee, how could I go wrong? It was a risk-free entry pass into a world of unlimited profit potential—or so my naive self-thought. So I sent a check and dreamed that night about all the riches that would soon be flowing my way.

A few weeks later, I received the full trading course. It was a hefty manual, full of charts with profitable examples. Initially, I was duly impressed. But then I started to

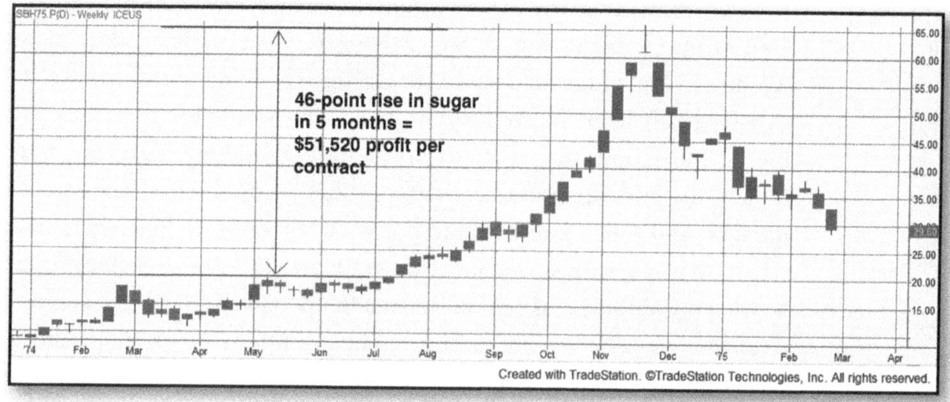

FIGURE 1.1 Sugar Skyrocketing = Unlimited Profits?

FIGURE 1.2 Good Head and Shoulders Pattern or Just a False Signal?

look a little closer at the details. Turns out the whole course was primarily based on the 1-2-3 head and shoulders pattern. As most traders and investors know, this pattern is a classic chart pattern, as shown in Figure 1.2. It is easy to find on just about any chart you look at—you can find a profitable example or two on most any chart, any instrument, and any time frame.

The problem is that the head and shoulders pattern gives a lot of false signals and usually looks good only in hindsight. Of course, I did not know that at first. I only knew I could look at a chart, pick out the head and shoulders pattern, and see how well it worked.

I eventually found out I was missing two key pieces of the puzzle. First, when you look at a chart with a head and shoulders or any other pattern in it, it is easy to see the winning trades because you are looking at both the pattern and the outcome of that pattern. If you try hiding the outcome of a pattern, it becomes much more difficult to find the good patterns.

The second key I was missing is that the existence of a pattern, by itself, doesn't necessarily mean a trade should be taken. If you take every single head and shoulders trade you see, you will soon be broke, as shown in Figure 1.3. Of course, the naive wannabe trader in me was oblivious to this fact.

After a month of dutifully following and paper trading all the head and shoulders signals, and finding most of them to be unprofitable, I sent all my trading records, along with the manual, back for a refund. True to his word, Mr. Roberts refunded my money.

My dream of trading riches was shattered, at least temporarily. On the bright side, I now saw futures as the way to go—I just realized head and shoulders patterns were not going to be the way. Once I abandoned the get-rich-quick idea with the 1-2-3 head and shoulders patterns, I did what many scientific, numbers-oriented people do: I looked to mathematical formulas to help me in my decision making. And I started where many people do: moving averages.

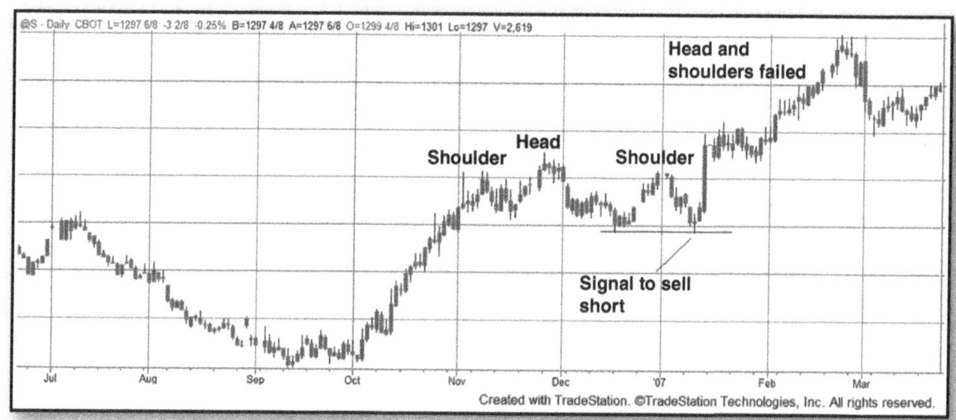

FIGURE 1.3 Many Head and Shoulders Look Good but Eventually Fail

■ My Moving Average Debacle

I'm sure every trader or investor has seen or used moving averages at some point in their trading career. Moving averages are a great way to see the general market direction, simplifying sometimes chaotic price action. But it comes at a price—lag. Moving averages will always lag whatever their calculation is based on, which can be a major problem.

There are many ways to trade with moving averages. In the simplest method, you simply buy when the price is above the moving average, and sell (or sell short) when price is below the moving average. This scheme works very well during prolonged trends, but gets absolutely hammered during trading range price action (see Figure 1.4).

Early market technician pioneers rectified this by employing two, or even three, moving averages. By using more moving averages, the idea was to filter out some of the trading range whipsaw trades, and leave the long-term, profitable trend trades.

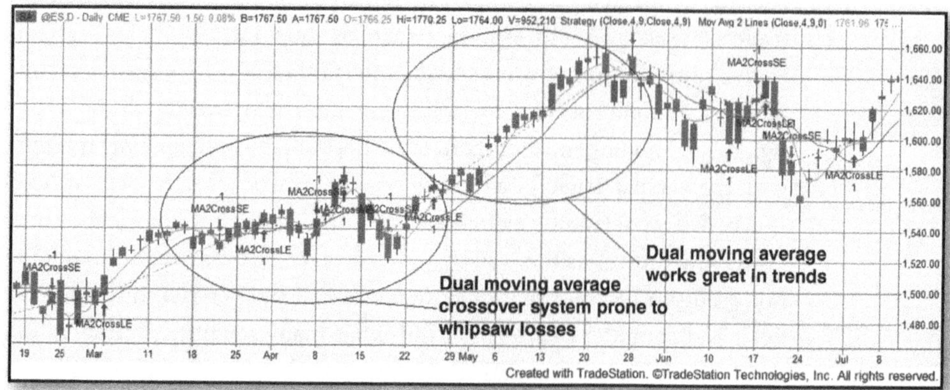

FIGURE 1.4 Great in Trends, Moving Averages Fail in Trading Ranges

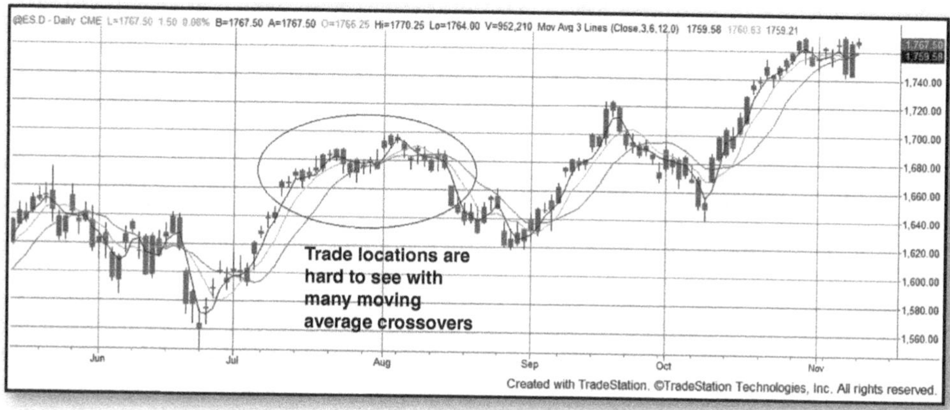

FIGURE 1.5 Triple Moving Average Crossovers Can Be Deceiving

After my unsuccessful foray into futures with chart patterns, I was struck by the apparent awesomeness and simplicity of the triple moving average. Looking at a chart, it was easy to see the profitable trades, while the unprofitable whipsaw trades were much harder to detect (see Figure 1.5). During the whipsaw periods, the moving average lines were very close together, and seeing crosses of lines was exceedingly difficult. Obviously, I had learned little from my head and shoulders experience, where what I saw on the chart was deceiving me.

I quickly became a convert to the whole moving average concept, and after a few quick successful tests (I did not understand the need for testing over hundreds of trades at this point, so 10 or 20 trades, computed by hand, were good enough for me!), I decided to fund my first account. Even though I had recently purchased a condo in expensive southern California, which took most of my savings, I was able to scrape together $5,000 to open an account. Naturally, I was nervous beyond belief. This was my nest egg, at the mercy of moving averages. In retrospect, the insanity of this is obvious, but at the time profits were all I could see.

I decided that my triple moving average system would work perfectly with live hogs, as the contract was called back then. I don't recall if this was the result of testing, where hogs looked the best, or if it was based on margin requirements, with hogs requiring relatively small margin. I suspect the latter. I liked the lower volatility of hogs, too, especially when compared to other agricultural products like soybeans and pork bellies.

With my trusty calculator, the daily newspaper, and a sheet of paper with five columns on it, every morning before work I'd record the date, closing price, and calculate the 4-, 9-, and 13-day moving averages. Then, once I got to work, I'd call my broker and place any necessary trades.

The first few days and weeks of my first trading system went fairly well. I lost more than I made, and I learned firsthand about slippage, broker's errors, and the general inefficiency of phoning in orders. But I was surviving, which I thought was the most important thing.

Then disaster struck. I was long hogs, and one morning, I was up $400. I was feeling great—this was my ticket to riches! At lunch, I spent a half-hour trying to convince my ultra-conservative and risk-averse engineering coworker Dave that speculating in commodities was easy for a technical-minded person. Just a few calculations, some simple math (no calculus required), and poof! Money would just add up in my account. He wasn't buying it, and I wondered why.

After lunch, I found out why. I checked hog prices right after lunch. I went from up $400 to down $800. A $1,200 swing in an hour or so. Twenty-five percent of my account vaporized, just like that. I was numb. And I still had the position open since my system hadn't given me a close signal yet.

A few days later, and a few quick whipsaw losers after the big loss, I totaled the damage: $1,500 in losses—30 percent of my account. Never in my wildest dreams had I expected that outcome. Panic set in. I stopped trading temporarily. Thank goodness I avoided the urge to double or triple my size to avenge my losses (such misguided dalliances would come later in my trading journey).

I took the weekend to regroup, and figure out my next steps. Clearly, I mistakenly thought, after a handful of trades, it was obvious that my triple moving average system was no good. If that system was terrible, my money-losing-addled mind reasoned, then the opposite system would be the answer, right? Sort of like the episode of *Seinfeld* where George Costanza flourishes when he begins to do the exact opposite of what he has always done before.

It was a *eureka* moment for me—if my first system was so bad, then the opposite system had to be just as good! Plus, I did not even need to test or evaluate this plan. All I had to do was add $1,500 to my initial account balance, instead of subtract it (for some reason, commission and slippage losses somehow became money makers in my twisted reasoning, but that is another story). Sunday night I went to sleep, in my mind thinking I had made $1,500 with my reverse trading system, when in actuality I had lost $1,500 with the original system. I was excited and happy. Monday morning, I was ready to jump in with both feet.

Fast-forward a few weeks, and hogs finally hit a great trend. It was a trend that a triple moving average system picked up perfectly. If only I were trading the original method! Of course, with the "opposite" method, big trends were a killer, and that is exactly what the market provided me—a huge losing trade. After that losing trade, my account was now down $3,000, a 60 percent account loss brought on by the triple moving average and reverse triple moving average systems. I had had enough. I raised the white flag, called it quits for a while, and decided I needed more education.

CHAPTER 2

Enough Is Enough

Before I continue with my saga of losing money trading futures, you might be asking yourself, "Why was it so tough for this guy? I see ads every day for futures and forex trading, and it seems like any half-brained nitwit can make money easily. Why is this Kevin guy such a loser?" Good question, but let me ask it a different way: "Assuming trading is that easy—that you can spend five minutes a day entering orders on your computer, while relaxing on a white sand Caribbean beach—why isn't the person selling you this miraculous system for $99 doing the same thing? Why is he spending his time practically giving away his secrets, instead of just trading his own ever-growing mountain of money?"

The answer should not surprise you: trading is tough, even for the so-called gurus, most of whom are not gurus in any sense of the word. I'd estimate that over 90 percent of the trading systems for sale are junk (and I am being generous here—the actual number might be closer to 99 percent), marketed by people who figured out that selling to newbie traders was far easier, and far more lucrative, than actually trading. The statistics you hear about 80 or 90 percent of traders losing money is no lie, and the reason is that trading is really, really difficult. I hope that by reading about my trading journey and later learning about my trading process, you will get a sense of how challenging it is. At the same time, you'll come to realize that success in trading is possible but that there aren't any shortcuts.

Research

After my quick and disastrous initial foray into futures trading, with my subsequent 60 percent loss in account value, I was scared to trade again. I also realized there was much I did not know, and that if I wanted to succeed in the trading "wars," I needed to bring more weaponry than just a simple moving average crossover. So I delved into just about any trading book I could find. I read the classics like *Reminiscences of a Stock Operator* (George H. Doran Company, 1923) and *Market Wizards* (New York Institute of Finance, 1989), and newer get-rich-quick books by authors who probably never even traded. But regardless of the book, I kept an open mind and just soaked it all in. After reading probably at least a dozen books, I was very confused. Here is some of what I learned:

- Stop-losses are a must. Stop-losses are only for losing traders.
- Entries are all that matter. Exits are all that matter.
- Aggressive money management is the key to riches. Aggressive money management leads to account failure.
- Trend following is the best way to trade. Trend following is dead.

I could go on and on, but you get the idea. For every trading "principle" espoused in one book, another book would claim the exact opposite was true. Which was right? Which was wrong? My head was swimming. But I kept on reading, gathering more information. Eventually, I concluded that all the books were right, and all the books were wrong. For example, for certain styles of trading, stop-losses were a great idea. But, for other methods, stop-losses would only stop you from making money. A light bulb went on over my head with this concept: there is no one right way to trade. What is important is to properly evaluate the way I wanted to trade, whatever that might entail.

After this "aha" moment, I went out and bought a database of daily futures prices and got myself some programming software. Rather than use an expensive piece of trading software (in the early 1990s, trading software was not very popular and it was relatively expensive), I decided to create my own back-testing software, using Microsoft Excel and Visual Basic. I'll spare you the details, but suffice it to say that I had no trouble developing terrific-looking trading systems. Creating nice-looking equity curves turns out to be a trivial task when you neglect commissions and slippage. It is also easy to do when your system has 10 variables and you run 1 million iterations with various combinations of those variables. Typical newbie mistakes, and I was repeating each one of them over and over. The only thing that saved me was that the results were so good, and profits were so astronomically high, even I did not believe them. I assumed it was bad data or my software was faulty, but that wasn't the root cause. The main problem was that I was testing incorrectly.

Because I felt my homemade systems were just "too good to be true," I luckily did not put any money into live trading these "Holy Grail" systems. Thank goodness I did not. Instead, I decided to abandon my testing and head off in a different direction. This was all because of a book that said I could not lose in trading. Naiveté at its finest!

You Can't Lose—Or Can You?

The book that temporarily took me away from methodically testing trading systems was *You Can't Lose Trading Commodities* (R. F. Wiest, 1988), by Robert Wiest. At the time I read it in the early 1990's, the book was already over five years old, and I remember its being prominently displayed in a local bookstore. I assumed this meant it must be a legitimate money maker to still be around after five years. This book was all about scale trading. The concept is that you find a commodity that is trading near a multiyear low, find a fundamental reason for it to go up in the near future, and then buy on a scale down and sell with a small profit. Here's an example: let's say wheat is currently at a 10-year low of 300 cents per bushel. You also hear forecasts the next wheat crop is going to be much smaller because of bad weather. Your analysis indicates that over the next 6 months, wheat is likely to go up. So you buy wheat at 300 cents, hoping to sell it at 305 cents ($250 profit per contract). If the price falls to 290 cents, you buy a second contract, hoping to sell that at 295 cents. You continue to add to your position every 10 cents down, with a profit target 5 cents above the corresponding entry. Ideally, the price will fall a bit, allowing you to buy three or more contracts, before it rises to 305, letting you exit with a profit on each contract. Then, if the price fell again, you'd just repeat the process, scaling in and scaling out.

The author claimed something like 90 to 95 percent wins with this method, which is entirely possible. But winning percentage is really meaningless. What matters is the return on account, and the drawdown. And, when done correctly, scale trading produces fairly low rates of return (10 to 20 percent), with fairly high drawdowns (20 percent or more). This is because you need a lot of capital to keep buying on the way down. If you don't have enough capital, you won't be able to continue buying. Then you won't be able to cash in on the lucrative oscillations in price. Eventually, if the situation gets dire enough, you'll be hit with a margin call, and your scale trading will likely abruptly end.

Even with the drawbacks in the approach, scale trading appealed to me on an inexperienced trader level. All I had to do was find commodities near multiyear lows and set up scales to trade them. I knew I would not be satisfied with only 10 to 20 percent return, so I had to make some adjustments, the main one being trading with a much smaller than recommended account size. This worked great the first year I did it. I ended the year with about 90 percent annual return, all from scale trading.

They say early success in any field leads to eventual disaster, and that is what happened to me with scale trading. After a 90 percent annual return that first year, I concluded I had this trading thing all figured out. Losses would be small and infrequent, but the cash register would keep ringing as I cashed in scale-trading winner after winner. Of course, the market slapped me around, and slapped me hard, for thinking this way. I don't even recall which commodity was the source of pain—it might have been wheat, corn, cotton, or coffee—but one of my second-year scales went terribly bad. I lost all my first year's profits, and most of what was left in my account. For me, the book title *You Can't Lose Trading Commodities* should have been "When You Ignore Simple Directions, You Can Lose a Ton Trading Commodities!" Needless to say, I was done with scale trading.

Averaging Down—Adding to Losers

Although I abandoned the scale-trading approach, I was intrigued with the idea of adding to my position as the price went against me. When this occurred, which was frequently, I could buy even more at a cheaper price! Then, when I was inevitably proven to be correct in my market analysis, I would gain even more profit. I had already done the same thing with mutual funds through automatic investments; I'd buy more shares as the price fell, getting a better deal on the asset.

The whole approach sounded too good to be true, and of course it was. Adding to a losing position works with mutual funds because (1) over time, mutual funds almost always go up eventually, and (2) mutual funds are not leveraged. With futures like wheat (my personal favorite for the adding-to-losers strategy), the price doesn't necessarily have to go up over a 5- or 10-year period. Price could stay depressed for a long time, leaving you with a pile of open, losing trades. Plus, for every wheat contract you purchase, you need extra margin, and eventually even small price moves become huge swings in your equity. That is what happened to me.

The year was 1998. For some crazy reason, I was convinced that wheat was due for an increase. In mid-1998, wheat was at a five-year low (see Figure 2.1).

Based primarily on that fact, along with some cursory fundamental analysis, I decided that wheat was on its way up to mid-1996 highs. So I bought wheat. The price went down. I bought more wheat. The price went down some more. This went on from May to September, and every time I bought another contract, I dug myself deeper in a hole.

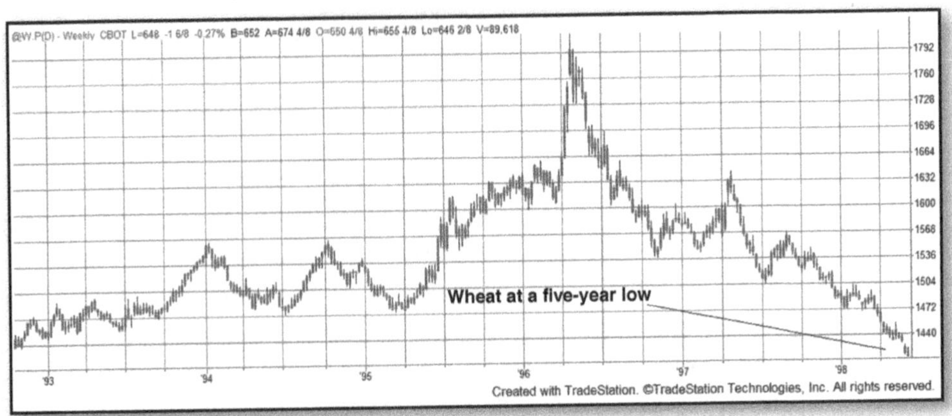

FIGURE 2.1 In 1998, Wheat Was at a Five-Year Low

If the price of wheat kept falling, I knew it wouldn't be long before the margin calls would start arriving. Psychologically, I couldn't accept that, so instead I'd run to the bank at lunch once or twice a week, and have $1,000 to $5,000 wired to my trading account. Somehow, I thought this was a better option than getting a dreaded margin call. I did this so many times—skipping lunch, speeding to the bank, speeding back to work—that I had my own personal wire transfer lady at the bank. Her name was Cookie, and in those many trips to wire money, I learned a lot about her family, her grandkids, and her life. I even gave her little gifts and toys for her grandkids. At this point, alarm bells that should have been screeching were silent—wasn't it strange that I thought this constant wiring of money to a drowning trading account was a good idea?

Luckily, starting in the beginning of September 1998, the price of wheat began to rebound. No more wire transfers! In fact, by mid-October, I was getting close to breakeven. I started buying more contracts on the way up, further leveraging myself. I was convinced, though, that the low was in, and if that were true, shouldn't I be buying? All told, I was down about $20,000 on the trade now, which was huge considering my account size. But the price was up, and I was looking to be king. Then came October 13, 1998 (see Figure 2.2).

I remember October 13, 1998, for good and bad reasons. I was in Seattle on business, and after the market closed, I saw that wheat had gone up 6 points! Plus, my hometown baseball team, the Cleveland Indians, were in the American League Championship Series against the dreaded New York Yankees. I watched Game 6 from my hotel room, and in the fifth inning, Jim Thome of the Indians hit a grand slam. Things were looking up, I thought. My Indians are going to win, and wheat is going up. Somehow, my mind linked the fate of wheat and the Indians together.

Of course, you can guess how this story ends. The next inning, the Yankees scored three runs, and the Indians lost and were therefore eliminated from the postseason. Wheat also slowly and surely fell in price, and with the extra contracts I bought during the previous up leg, even a small correction was a killer. By the beginning of

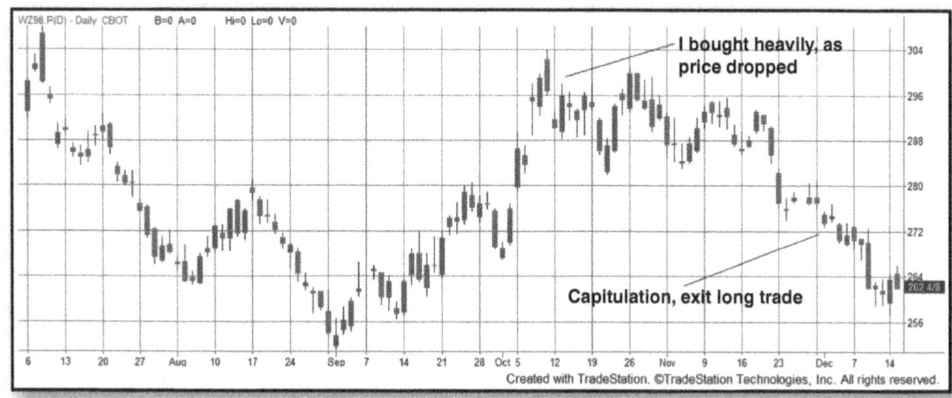

FIGURE 2.2 My Last Gasp with Averaging Down in Wheat

December, I was down about $70,000 on that trade alone and out of funds I could wire to my account. Cookie would have to get toys for her grandkids from someone other than me, because I was done trading. At least for a year or two.

The Wild Man Emerges

After my averaging down approach miserably failed, I spent the next couple of years doing only minor trading, focusing on rebuilding my trading funds. When I had enough spare capital, I turned to what I call the "wild man" approach. With this approach, I did not need to test or evaluate any idea before trading real money with it. If I got a brilliant idea that coffee should go down, I'd sell it. If OPEC was discussing stricter quotas, I'd buy crude oil. No real rhyme or reason to my method—just crazy trading based on whatever rumor I heard or whatever thought floated into my brain. I tried to keep losses small and winners big, but for some reason doing things the other way around was psychologically much easier. Plus, I still employed some tricks from my earlier trading, such as adding to losers. I'm sure my broker liked me, but my account equity did not. My account treaded water with this haphazard approach, but after a while I knew there was no future in it. Yet I still followed this approach, if you can call it that, until the fateful mad cow trade I discussed earlier. That trade and all the circumstances surrounding it were a cold slap in the face. I desperately needed to trade differently.

Time to Evaluate

As 2004 started, I was still licking my wounds from the live cattle/mad cow debacle. I took a long, hard look at my trading, and I did not like what I saw:

- Moving average crossover system—lost money.
- Reverse moving average crossover system—lost money.
- Tested thousands of systems—results too good to be true, never traded.
- Scale trading—lost money.
- Averaging down—lost money.
- Wild man approach—lost money.

Almost no matter what I did, I lost money at it. The deceiving part was that for a while many of these methods would work, giving me an extra boost of irrational confidence before the inevitable fall. The extra confidence really just made the resulting crash tougher, both emotionally and financially.

Yet when I looked at my history, I saw the one bright spot: I did have success developing, but not live trading, mechanical trading algorithms. The problem was that I did not know if it was because I actually had good systems, or if good results were the result of a flawed testing process (bad data, overoptimization, bad programming, etc.). I decided in early 2004 that this was my chance to become consistently profitable—I had to develop and test mechanical algorithms.

Most of the first half of 2004 was getting things in place—investigating trading ideas, looking at software options, determining how to do walk-forward testing manually. For my strategy, I decided to go with a simple X day close breakout; that is, if the close today is the highest close of the last X bars, then buy at the open of the next bar. For short entries, it was vice versa. For exits, I employed a simple stop based on average true range, a fixed dollar stop, a moving stop as profits accumulated, and a tightening stop that applied only when a big open profit occurred. It was a pretty simple system, but my initial results showed it worked well. Nothing earth shattering about this strategy's entries or exits—I am sure this approach was been applied by many people before. It is just a simple trend-following approach, and as long as some sustained trends develop, the system overall will make money.

Even though up until this point I had used back-test software I had developed myself, I decided that I did not fully trust the results. I obtained a copy of TradeStation software, which at the time was probably the best and most popular (many people say it still is the best, and I still use it as my primary tool, but there are many other excellent back-test programs available on the market today, too). In addition to making the testing easier, I had much more faith in the results. The only problem was that I wanted to utilize walk-forward testing (discussed in great detail later), and TradeStation at the time did not support that feature. So I was relegated to running optimizations on TradeStation, then computing results and manually performing a walk-forward analysis. It was tedious work, but at the same time it gave me a solid sense of how walk-forward testing actually worked (I suggest your first walk-forward test be done manually to increase your understanding.)

By the last quarter of 2004, I had a system I felt was ready to trade. I stuck my toe in the water, making a few trades with the system, and found that the results matched the back test pretty well. Full-size trading of my new system would begin in 2005. As 2004 ended, after more than 10 painful years of trying different approaches, and eventually failing with most, I finally saw the proverbial light at the end of the tunnel. Thankfully, it wasn't a train coming at me! I had a tested method that worked with real money, and I wanted to shout from the mountaintop, "I am a good trader!" Since I live in Ohio, where mountains are a rarity, I did the next best thing: I entered a public, worldwide trading contest. Actually, I had entered the contest in 2004, but I used a pseudo mechanical, mostly discretionary system that did well for a while, but eventually fell apart. But this time, I'd be armed with a good mechanical approach and hopefully not embarrass myself. With that fateful decision, my trading adventure continued.

CHAPTER 3

World Cup Championship of Futures Trading® Triumph

Based on the work I had completed in 2004, I thought I had a viable trading strategy. Of course, I wanted to share my "success" with the world but at the same time not give away the strategy. So I did the next best thing: I entered a public trading contest.

For those of you who have never heard of it, the World Cup Championship of Futures Trading, sponsored by Robbins Trading Company, is the premier worldwide, real money, year-long futures trading contest. It attracts some of the best and brightest traders from around the globe, all matching wits and pitting strategies against each other. It is a high-pressure contest, with results constantly posted for all to see (back in the old days, results were published monthly in trading magazines; now they are updated daily on the World Cup web site: www.worldcupchampionships.com). In 1987, legendary trader Larry Williams turned $10,000 into over $1.1 million in that contest. That gives you an idea of the caliber of traders who competed.

Once I had my mind set on entering the trading contest, I had to make sure my system was good enough. Looking at the performance of past winners, I concluded that I had a reasonable chance of finishing in the top three contestants, as long as I had an annual return of 100 percent or higher. That was actually my goal; it wasn't to win the contest, since I realized that at the upper end of performance, luck would play a role. I could not count on luck to win the contest; all I could do was set myself up to be near the top. To achieve 100 percent return over the course of a year, I knew I had to accept a very large maximum drawdown. I decided I would allow around 75 percent maximum drawdown, which would be ridiculous for any normal trader's account. But, as I'll discuss in great detail later, your goals and expectations should be based on the situation at hand. For a trading contest where the only success criterion was return on account, allowing a large drawdown makes sense. If, however, the contest were based on return and risk (say the winning contestant would have the highest Calmar ratio), I would have approached the contest completely differently. This will be discussed in detail later, but for now realize the goals and objectives I set at the outset dictated every subsequent step in the trading development process.

As previously mentioned, I had developed a decent trading strategy in 2004. It actually would have been good enough to finish in second or third place in the 2004 contest, but, of course, I wasn't ready to enter at that point. However, I was ready for 2005 with the following system:

Entry

Buy next bar after 48 bar high close (vice versa for short), as long as the 30-bar RSI was greater than 50 (less than 50 for short trades).

Exit

Calculate stop based on:

Fixed dollar value ($1,000)

Y * average true range from entry

Z * average true range from entry (profit target)

Other Rules (based on my psychology, I felt I needed these)

If last trade was a loser, wait 5 bars before entering next trade (minimizes whipsaws).

If last trade was a winner, wait 20 bars before entering next trade (be patient after wins).

The system utilized daily bars for all trading signals, which was perfect for someone with a full-time job, like me. Each night, I could simply review my charts, place any orders for the next day, and then not worry about the intraday variations. It was the ideal setup, as my time to check on my positions during the day was limited.

For markets to trade, I had a basket of nine futures that I looked at:

- Corn
- Cotton

- Copper
- Gold
- Sugar
- 5- or 10-year Treasury notes
- Coffee
- Japanese yen
- Nikkei Index

I selected these for their past performance, their relatively low margin requirements, and their general lack of correlation to each other. Looking back on this, though, I realize I made two pretty big rookie mistakes. First, when I tested my system, I tested over 20 to 25 different instruments. Then, upon seeing the actual performance, I simply selected the best performers. In other words, I optimized based on market! That is a big no-no for good strategy development. For my second mistake, I did not run any detailed correlation studies when selecting the portfolio. Rather, I simply guessed at what I thought the correlation should be ("Corn and the Nikkei Index are probably not correlated, so I can trade both."). At the time, this seemed reasonable, but my experience since that time has taught me that correlations sometimes are different than what common sense dictates, and should always be examined in a portfolio situation. Even then, it is important to realize that even noncorrelated instruments can become correlated during market panics. Thankfully, in spite of my rookie development mistakes, my trading approach still succeeded.

Since my capital was limited (I started each year with a $15,000 account), I could only trade one contract of each instrument. Occasionally, I had to skip a signal here and there, if I did not have enough available margin. At all times, I tried to trade as "fully loaded" as I could, using up as much purchasing power as I could while still avoiding margin calls. My plan was to take every signal and follow the system as best I could, within the constraints of my available capital.

Here is how I performed, and some of my thoughts, in each of the years 2005 through 2007.

2005

My equity chart for 2005 is shown in Figure 3.1. After the first month of 2005, I was slightly down. Huh? I was going to take over the trading world with this strategy, and yet I was losing money? It seems like this always happens to me—as soon as I start trading a strategy, it starts losing money. I was mentally crushed. I was down only

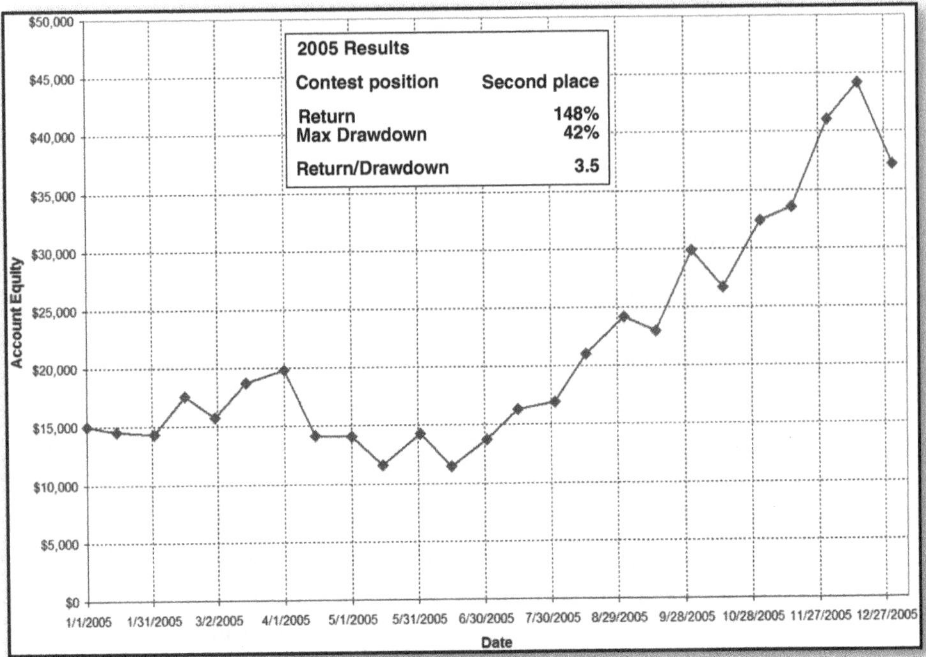

FIGURE 3.1 My Equity Chart, 2005 World Cup Contest Account

4 to 5 percent, but still it is always nice to begin the year with a bang. Thankfully, by mid-April things were looking up. I was now up over 30 percent for the year, which would translate into a 120 percent return for the year. I was on fire! Everything was working according to plan.

Of course, just like any Hollywood movie, the story has to have a dark period. For me, that was a four-month drawdown from mid-April to mid-August. Not only did it last a long time, but it also was severe—over 40 percent drawdown. At the lowest point, I had pretty much given up winning the contest or even coming close to winning. But I stuck to my plan. I was still trading the system as best I could, but I had to skip a few trades because of margin concerns. That summer was definitely a "bummer day 'round here" for my contest account.

Things started to improve in mid-June, and although it would take a few months to reach a new equity high, by mid-December I had almost tripled my account. A couple of nice trends in Japanese yen and copper in September 2005, and a coffee trend in November really helped the account take off. That is really how trend trading works—you can have months of flat to down performance, but catching a couple of trends can make your whole year. The problem, of course, is that if you miss the trend trade—let's say you give up before the trend shows itself because of the numerous false breakout losses, or you don't have enough money in your account to take every trading signal—your performance will be dismal. Because of this, trend trading is not for everyone, as it can be so psychologically difficult to follow.

When I hit my peak equity in mid-December 2005, I knew I was in good shape for the contest, for either second or third place. First place was out of the question, as the contest leader, Ed Twardus, was up over 250 percent for the year. With my confidence riding high, I did violate my system toward the end of the year, when I added on to a losing position in coffee. At the time, I was aiming for a 200 percent return, and apparently old habits die hard, since I was resorting to averaging down once again (will I ever learn?). So the last two weeks of December I gave back a chunk of equity. Lesson learned again: don't add to losers!

2006

After my success in 2005, I realized that I had a good strategy, and if I traded it correctly, without emotion, I'd probably do okay in 2006. The problem with a public trading contest, of course, is that it is embarrassing when one month you are in the top three finishers, and the next month you are out of the top three. Worse yet is when you find yourself right behind the lead trader. When that happens, it is very enticing to take a few flyer trades to catch that person. I tried that back in 2004, in an ill-fated attempt to catch eventual winner Kurt Sakaeda. Not that I had any chance, by the way: Kurt finished the year up 929 percent, a terrific performance. Yet he always remained very humble about his performance (a great characteristic for a trader).

As trading in 2006 began, I had high hopes, a solid plan, and a clear head. My performance in 2006 is shown in Figure 3.2. Unlike 2005, the first month of 2006 was great for me. I was up about 30 percent, and I felt great about my chances. Of course, whenever I feel great about my trading, a drawdown is right around the corner. That happened in February and March and brought me back down to breakeven. A couple of losing trades in yen and 10-year Treasury notes helped bring me back down to earth.

But in the midst of this drawdown, in mid-February, I would enter the trade that changed everything for me: I went long copper, as shown in Figure 3.3. I held that one trade (actually two separate trades, after accounting for rollover) from February 17, 2006, to May 1, 2006, and it produced a net profit of $28,875 per contract. It was one of those once-in-a-blue-moon-type trades, where the market just takes off, with me holding on for the ride. My account value on May 1 was $45,122, so that meant that one copper trade was responsible for over 95 percent of my profit for the year.

At the beginning of May 2006, being up 200 percent already in the contest gave me a euphoric feeling. Little did I know that was my peak for the year, and the rest

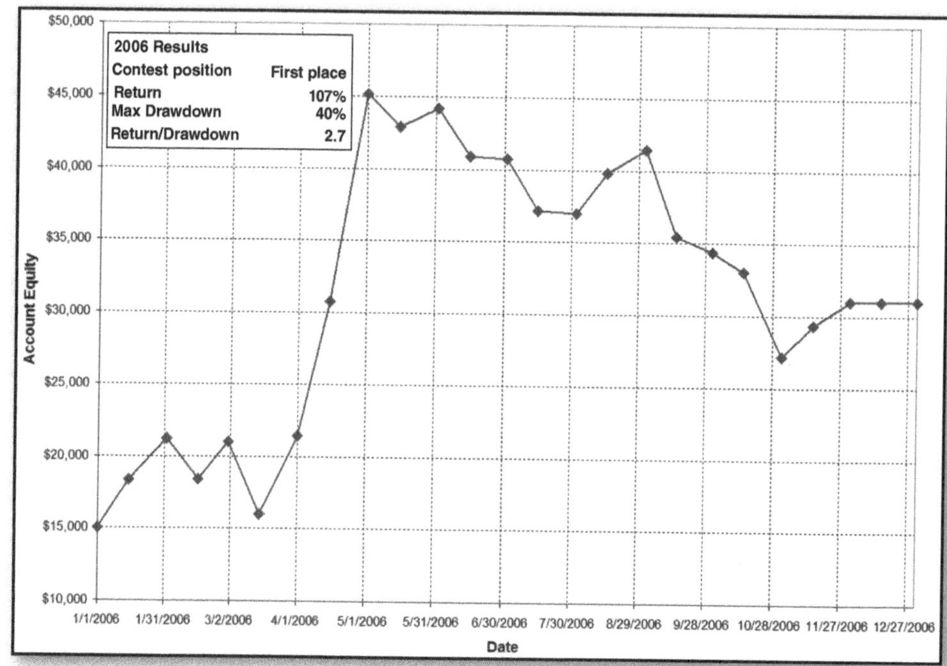

FIGURE 3.2 My First-Place Equity Chart, 2006 World Cup Contest Account

of the year would be a slow downhill slide. During the rest of 2006, I still traded the system as planned, and I still traded only one contract for each trade. I probably should have traded larger size, since my account had tripled, but part of me was scared that I'd give back my profit. That turned out to be a good decision, since most of the next seven months were net losers.

Toward the end of the contest, I also had to contend with Michael Cook, a worthy opponent in second place. Although I knew the guidelines about just focusing on your own performance and not worrying about the other traders, I

FIGURE 3.3 Copper Skyrocketed, and I Was Long

had heard how good a trader he was, and I was scared of falling behind him—so scared, in fact, that I shut my trading down at the start of December. Part of this was warranted (just look at the previous six months of poor performance), but part of it was because I thought I'd make Michael beat me, instead of me losing to him.

The ironic thing about my ceasing trading in the month of December, to preserve my eventual victory, is that that is not how I remember trading the contest years later. In my mind, I stuck to the system the whole year and traded per the plan up until the last day. I'm sure in public webinars and writings I have said the same thing—that I never stopped trading just to stay in first place. Yet that is exactly what I did! And that disturbs me now. No, not that I ceased trading, but that I remember a different reality. When that happens in trading, it is usually a bad thing. A good trader will remember things as they actually occurred, not as they fondly, but incorrectly, remembered.

Even with the six-month drawdown at the end, I was still able to finish in first place in the contest. I felt validated—all those years of struggle had finally paid off. Now the question was: could I repeat that performance in 2007?

2007

After finishing in second place in 2005 and first place in 2006, I somehow felt that I had broken through, and now trading would be easier for me. Of course, the lesson I learned was that trading is never easy, and it is always a struggle. An enjoyable struggle, sure, but a struggle nonetheless. As 2007 began, I began the contest with high hopes. Also, I decided to trade two contest accounts (one crashed and burned), and try some little modifications to my core strategy. After all, I was still a bit spooked by the last six months of 2006, wondering how long my original system would suffer.

Unfortunately, just like 2005, I started out in the wrong direction. My 2007 performance is shown in Figure 3.4. Losing trades in just about every instrument plagued my efforts, and by the end of March I was staring at a 50 percent drawdown. By mid-May, due to some nice trades in orange juice and lean hogs (markets I added as part of my modifications), I was back to breakeven, where I'd remain for the next few months.

In late summer and fall 2007, nice trends developed in Swiss franc and 30-year T-bonds, and I rode them according to my system's rules. By the end of the year, I was up over 100 percent again, which was good enough for second place. Michael Cook, the trader I had been watching in my rearview mirror the last part of 2006, raced past me in 2007, finishing the year up a whopping 250 percent.

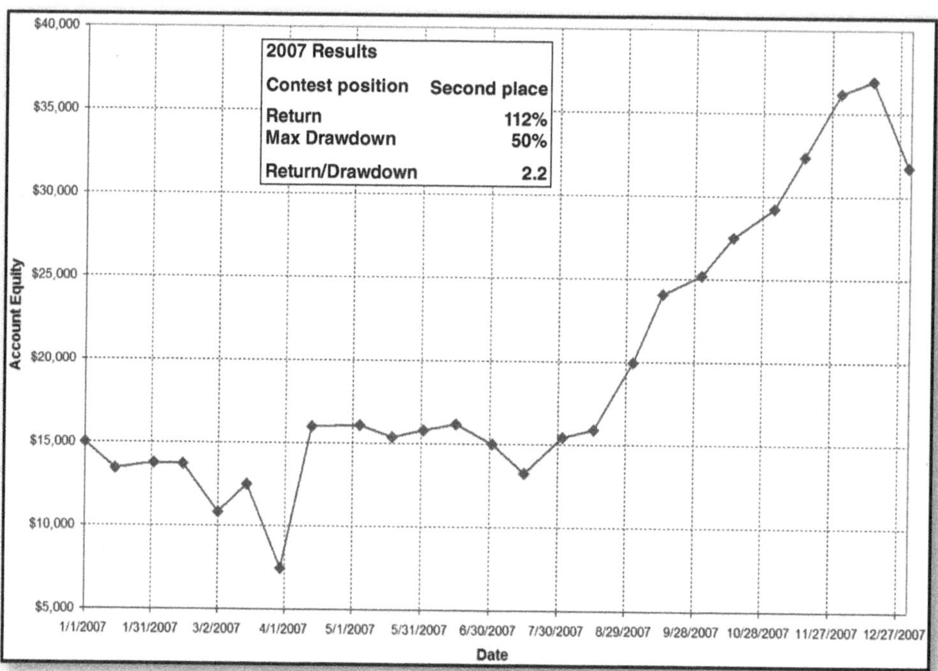

FIGURE 3.4 My Equity Chart, 2007 World Cup Contest Account

Reflections on the Contest

After finishing first or second three years straight in the World Cup of Futures Trading Championship, each time with over 100 percent return, I felt pretty good about my trading. To me, it did not prove I was a good trader, but rather it reinforced for me the importance of setting goals and objectives. Since I had developed my trading system to give me a chance to win the contest, I now realized that without goals and objectives established up front, the contest could just be considered gambling. As you will see later in the book, goals and objectives are a key part of what I do.

After my second-place finish in 2005, I wanted to let my informal mentor, market wizard Dr. Van Tharp, know of my success. I felt a bond to Van, as I had taken many of his home study courses and read most of his books. He was the closest thing to a mentor I had ever had. I was proud of myself, and I wanted to thank him. He was proud of my success, to be sure, but he also said this:

"And although Kevin has been trading and learning for 15 years, most people [who] win in trading contests are doing some very dangerous things with position sizing. So notice your reactions. Are you impressed with the people [who] win competitions? Or is your gut reaction to learn more about how to trade effectively in any market—and just stay in the game!"

It took me a long time to understand what Van meant by this comment, with my first reaction being anger ("how could someone not be impressed with my success?"). Eventually, though, I realized the wisdom in Van's words. The impressive thing is not winning a contest—luck, recklessness, and a host of other things can influence the final results. The impressive thing is to trade the contest effectively. For me, that meant following my system, the one developed specifically to average about 100 percent annual return. So don't be impressed with the performance itself. I'm certainly not. What I am impressed with is my discipline in seeing a goal, chasing it, and realizing it. That, to me, is the real success.

CHAPTER 4

Making the Leap—Transitioning to Full Time

It is the dream of every part-time, retail trader—one who loves all aspects of trading—to trade for a living, full time. At least that was always my goal, to live the dream. Trader Gary Smith wrote a book with just that title: *Live the Dream by Profitably Day Trading Stock Futures* (Advanced Trading Seminars, 1995). The dream, of course, is whipping the markets every day with your amazing strategies, taking as much money out of the market as you need (Want a new car? Simple—just double the size of your next trade!), spending your ample free time playing with your kids or doing volunteer work, or the typical stereotypical behavior: lounging on the beach, margarita in your hand, as bikini-clad women (or hunky guys, if that is your preference) stroll by on your private island.

The problem is that the dream is rarely, if ever, reality. The truth is that trading full time, as I tell many people, is in my opinion "the toughest way to make easy money." But that does not mean it cannot be done; it just means it is incredibly difficult. Anything great worth attaining is always difficult, right?

After about 15 years of part-time trading, quite a lot of unsuccessful trading, I had 3 consecutive years of contest-winning performances. As 2007 ended, I began to seriously consider trading as a full-time profession. After all, if I could not succeed at it, after all I had been through and all I had accomplished, who actually could? So in early 2008, I decided to take the plunge, and trade full time for a living. I thought I had it figured all out when I started trading full time. Boy was I wrong! I jumped into full-time trading doing some things, some things wrong, and many things I'd do differently if I had to do it over.

Confidence

Even though you need many things to succeed at trading (capital, strategies, computers, etc.), self-confidence will influence your long-term success in full-time trading more than most other things. It took me a long time to figure out that most of my trading success and failure wasn't due to having the fastest computer or having the Holy Grail of strategies. Rather, the confidence in my trading abilities, the confidence in my strategy development, the confidence in my never failing optimism in the face of harsh drawdowns would help me survive as a trader. Obviously, confidence alone will not get you there—regardless of what some trading gurus might say—but at some point, you'll need confidence to weather a trading storm. Be it a major drawdown, many failed strategies, or an inability to develop new approaches, sooner or later confidence in your abilities will be required to get you through the tough times. After three years of trading contest–winning success, I felt I had confidence to succeed. After all, staring each day at three trading trophies (Figure 4.1) helped me feel like I was invincible.

What I Did Right

I had enough confidence to think I could succeed at full-time trading.

What I Did Wrong

I probably had too much confidence when I began trading for a living. After all, winning a trading contest is nice, but did it really mean I could trade full time? Now, I of course realize this. Back then, I equated contest success with full-time success. That was a dangerous way of thinking.

Capital

I'm sure you've heard the stories of people who started with $1,000 and parlayed that into a lucrative full-time trading career. I'm equally sure that for every one of those people, there are probably 999 who started with that amount and failed. After

FIGURE 4.1 My Contest Trophies

all, as I'll demonstrate in a later chapter, being undercapitalized is the easiest road to ruin, whether or not you have a great trading strategy. Even a breakeven strategy will lead to ruin if your bankroll is smaller than your opponent's. The excellent book *Chances Are ... Adventures in Probability* by Michael and Ellen Kaplan (Viking Penguin, 2006) describes this very well:

> Let's imagine some Buddhists opened a casino. Unwilling to take unfair advantage of anyone, the management offers a game at completely fair odds: flip a coin against the bank and win a dollar on heads, lose a dollar on tails. What will happen over time? Will the game go on forever or will one player eventually clean out the other?
>
> One way to visualize this is to imagine the separate moment when the gambler is down to his last dollar. Would you agree that his chance of avoiding ruin is exceedingly small? Now increase the amount you imagine in his pocket and correspondingly reduce the bank's capital; at what point do you think than gambler's chance of being ruined equals the bank's? Yes: when their capital is equal. Strict calculation confirms two grim facts: the game will necessarily end with the ruin of one party—and that party will be the one who started with the smaller capital. So even when life is fair, it isn't. Your chances in this world are proportional to the depth of your pockets—the house wins by virtue of being the house.

Of course, you might protest, "But I have an edge, therefore I'll win in the long run." While that is true, remember your edge is likely small, and it probably will not last forever. Over time, it will likely regress to breakeven, and that means your account size becomes critical. Can you outlast your opponents?

What I Did Right

I started full-time trading with a low-six-figure account, although I kept some of that out of trading accounts, effectively "in reserve." I felt I was reasonably well capitalized.

What I Did Wrong

Based on my starting capital, I had to make 50 to 100 percent annual returns just to pay living expenses, taxes, and slightly increase my trading account. Wow! Looking back on that, I realize I was insane and started with about 10 times less than I should have. Another full-time trader friend once told me that every successful trader he knew started with $2 to $3 million before embarking on full-time trading. As crazy as that amount sounds (I would have scoffed at it six years ago when I started full time), I now believe it is reasonable. After all, you want your trading account to grow over time, and you want to draw living expenses from it, and at the same time you need to survive the inevitable drawdowns. It is nearly impossible to accomplish all three on a shoestring-sized account.

Living Expenses

When I started full-time trading in 2008, I was fortunate enough to have three to five years of living expenses saved up. That savings was not part of retirement, and was not part of my trading capital. I think those are the key issues to living expenses when embarking on full-time trading. Trading is stressful enough without worrying about where your next meal or mortgage payment is coming from. You need to feel secure that your expenses are covered, even if you hit a drawdown right from the start (which always seems to be the case for me!).

What I Did Right

Due to years of saving money, and a lucrative change-of-ownership agreement I had at work, I could easily cover living expenses for quite a while, even with a growing family. Knowing that allowed me to focus on my trading 100 percent.

What I Did Wrong

Nothing. I think having three to five years of living expenses in reserve was a great decision.

Family Support

I am probably in the minority, but I had (and still have) a loving spouse who was totally on board with my dream of trading full time. For us, this meant my giving up an upper management position in the aerospace industry, where the sky—no pun intended—was the limit. But she realized that my heart just was not in giving up my soul to a ruthless corporation, that I was destined for better things. My children also support my trading, and since they are young, it is really the only "job" they have ever seen me do. They understand when it is playtime, and when Dad has to work. It does seem to them—and to me, too—that it is a lot of the latter and not enough of the former.

What I Did Right

I married the right person, someone who understood and supported my trading 100 percent. Now, after six years of full-time trading, she is still fully committed to my journey, and so are my three children.

What I Did Wrong

I pretty much nailed this right on. I shudder to think how much more difficult full-time trading would be without a supportive spouse and family.

Home Office Setup

To save on expenses, I decided to trade right out of my house, in a dedicated home office. The distractions are many, especially with three young children now running around. Sometimes my work gets buried in a pile of crayon drawings, and sometimes an overeager child will accidentally close a spreadsheet without saving it first. Plus, my oldest even placed a few mini S&P trades on my open trading platform. At least his trades made money! Overall, though, I can't complain, when rush hour traffic for me is merely needing to dodge a few Legos on the stairs.

What I Did Right

I created a dedicated office for my trading business.

What I Did Wrong

I probably should have established firmer boundaries, such as no touching Dad's computer. But most of the time, intruding children are no problem.

Trading Strategies

When I started full-time trading, I had about three to five strategies I felt comfortable going live with. Unfortunately, I did not have any extra strategies waiting in limbo, ready for trading when some of my first group of strategies lost their performance edge. Back then, I naively thought I could trade the same strategies forever. Now I realize that some strategies burn bright, like stars in the sky, for a long time. Others, though, are more like shooting stars—you need to stop trading them before they crash to earth.

What I Did Right

I had multiple strategies to trade. Even from the beginning, I knew it was a bad idea to rely on just one particular method.

What I Did Wrong

If I were starting full-time trading today, I'd make sure for every strategy I took live, I had at least one good strategy ready to take its place. Plus, I'd make sure I had a long list of potential strategies to test and evaluate.

Brokers

Just like any other aspect of trading (computers, Internet connections, strategies, etc.), it is crucial that you have a backup for your broker. I don't mean having a backup phone number for the trade desk (which you definitely should have handy, by the way). I mean having multiple accounts at multiple brokers, ideally having different clearing firms. Brokers do fail from time to time (I was a victim of Refco's bankruptcy and of PFG Best's corrupt owner), and by having multiple accounts, you can still trade even if one broker goes down. Since I trade multiple strategies, it also makes bookkeeping a bit easier, since many times I'll dedicate one strategy to one specific account.

What I Did Right

I had multiple brokers, which used multiple clearing firms. So I think I was pretty smart in this regard.

What I Did Wrong

I've experienced two broker failures over the past 15 years, and some warning signs were evident with each of them—warning signs I missed or ignored. I assumed the system would make me whole, and that indeed happened in the Refco case. But I am still waiting for most of my money from the PFG Best case. That really irks me, which you can see firsthand by seeing my interview on Fox Business Channel (go to www.foxbusiness.com and search for "davey" and you'll see my interview).

Free Time

Ahh, the days of working with the evenings free. That was life in the corporate world, for the most part. But now, working full time at home, I feel the need to check the markets at all times of day and night. Trading ideas pop into my head, and immediately I run downstairs to program and test them. Now most of my waking life is thinking about, or working on, trading. I have become too one-dimensional in my pursuit of making a living full-time trading. I think my wife believes that my trading computer is actually now part of me, since I seem to be attached to it so much.

Of course, for many people who leave a job and start trading, the opposite could be true. All the free time, with no boss and no rules, lead many would-be traders to a life of laziness. It is sometimes hard to stay motivated and continue developing new trading strategies, especially when your trading account is in a drawdown. Motivation can really be an issue, and while that might not hurt performance today, it can affect performance down the road.

What I Did Right

I have always been disciplined enough to keep working and never stop trying to improve my trading.

What I Did Wrong

I probably spend too much time working on trading, and I'll bet many of these extra hours are not the least bit productive. A trader, like any other self-directed worker, needs balance. I need to work on that.

Taking the Plunge

Once I had all the foregoing items in place, at least to a point that I thought was acceptable at the time, I was ready to take the plunge. I took that full-time plunge in May 2008, and I haven't looked back since. Has it been easy? No way! Has it been fun? Definitely! Would I do it again if I had the chance? Of course, although I'd naturally be smarter the second time around. The main point here is that I had a goal, thought through all the details of it, and eventually took the gamble. If I—someone with no trading knowledge until I started reading some books and then trading—can do it, I think most people can. If your heart is in it, as mine always has been, the road to trading success is much easier. If you find all the talk of developing strategies to be burdensome, my suggestion to you is: walk away—trading probably is not for you.

As I look at my trading day, years after going full time, I find that most of my trading activity is not in placing trades or examining account statements. Rather, most of my day-to-day routine consists of developing strategies, looking for ideas, thinking about trading, and, of course, testing and evaluating potential strategies. Most of the rest of this book focuses on just that—how I evaluate, design, and test trading strategies.

PART II

Your Trading System

CHAPTER 5

Testing and Evaluating a Trading System

If you are going to design trading systems, it is critical that you know how to evaluate the performance metrics of a trading system. This is not always as easy as it sounds. To show you what I mean, take a look at Figure 5.1. This equity curve is for a futures trading system, typical of what you might produce if you tested strategies yourself, or one you might find publicly available on the Internet. This curve was produced with TradeStation software, but results from other popular programs, such as MultiCharts and NinjaTrader, are basically the same. All good trading software gives you a variety of important (and, in my opinion, many unimportant) metrics to review and examine. Most of the time, the equity curve and performance report bring up more questions than they answer. Are the results good or bad? Are the results believable? Do the results have any predictive value? Finally, how do you separate the wheat from the chaff? I'll answer these questions and more in this chapter.

The first point to realize and understand when looking at performance reports, equity curves, or trade data is the old adage "if it is too good to be true, it probably is." As a general rule, future performance of a trading system is almost never as good as its historical performance. In fact, the better a trading system tests historically, the less likely it is to perform that well in the future. Of course, there are exceptions to this rule, and after developing trading strategies for a while, these exceptions become easier to find.

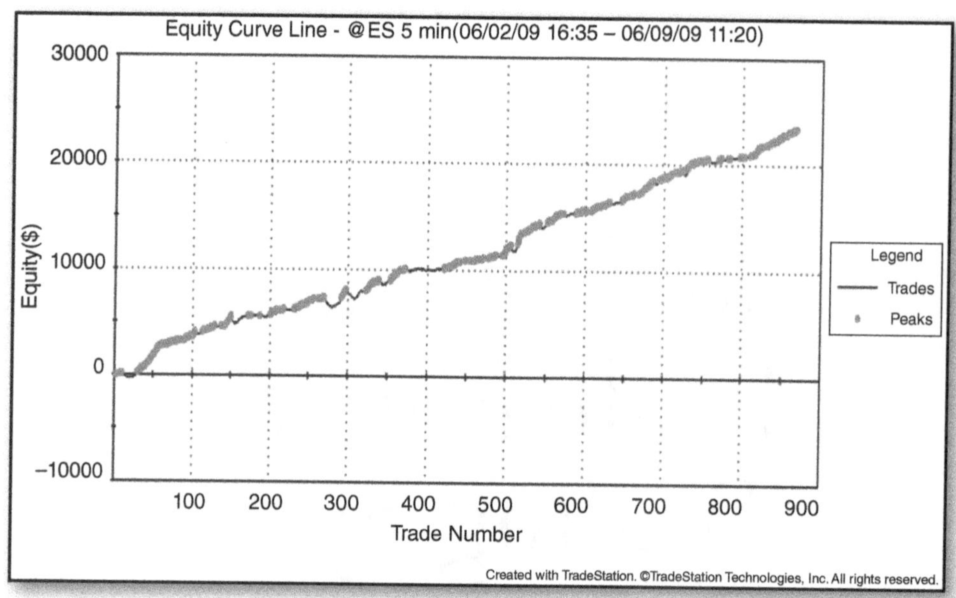

FIGURE 5.1 Trading System Results—Is This Believable?

Why do historical test results usually look better than future results? Some of it has to do with survivorship bias, meaning only the good historical trading systems are typically shown. Why would a vendor sell a system with poor historical performance? Why would you trade a poor system that you created yourself? The simple answer is that in both cases the bad results would be discarded, leaving only the remaining good results.

It is also possible that the historical test results are indeed valid and that the system developer has uncovered a true edge in the market. Over time, though, this edge may disappear, either due to others finding it, market changes, or a host of different reasons. The trading system will then revert to the mean, which would be a break-even strategy before commissions and trading costs.

Historical test results also can look better than future results due to the method of the historical testing. Most people test and evaluate systems incorrectly. Later in the book, you'll learn one correct way to test and evaluate systems, but for now just realize that the standard accepted way of testing is wrong. This faulty testing leads to overoptimistic results and trading systems that are sure to disappoint the end user. Of course, experienced traders know how to test systems. The question is: when looking at historical results, how do you know what to believe?

Figure 5.2 depicts what I call a "BS" meter for performance results. It gives you an idea of who, if anyone, you can trust with providing you trading results.

At the very top of the scale—the group with the most BS to sling—are trading system vendors. I put this group at the top, even though I have been part of this

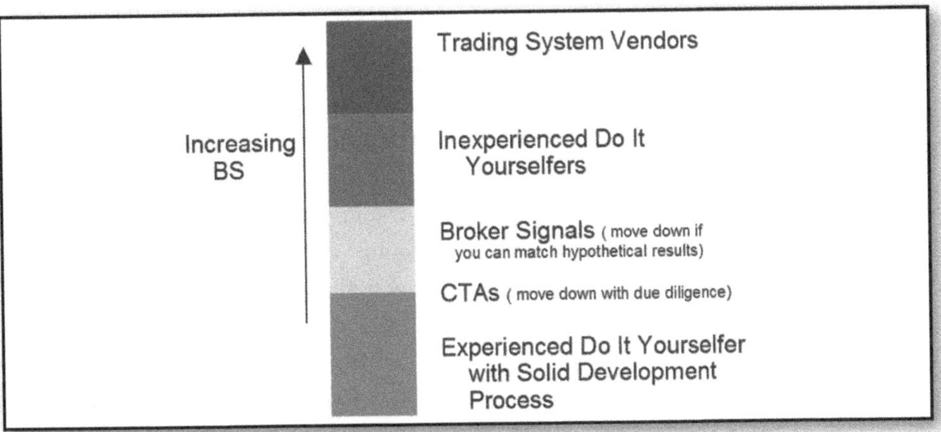

FIGURE 5.2 BS Meter for Trading System Results

group (although I trade my systems with my own money, unlike most in this group). In general, any performance information you receive from someone wanting to sell you signals, a black box system, a subscription, trading room, and so on should *not* be trusted. An excellent general rule is: don't believe any of it.

This approach is extreme, I realize, but given the probability of a vendor's selling a great trading system, as opposed to a vendor's selling you a good-looking but actually terrible system, this is sound advice. You will save a lot of money by avoiding anyone offering you a fantastic trading system. Anyone offering a great trading system for only a little money just doesn't pass my "smell" test—the vendor should be trading it himself, raking in the big bucks, not hawking the system on the Internet for pennies. That is why trading system vendors top the BS list.

Since trading system vendors typically provide worthless junk, you may be inclined to go the "do-it-yourself" (DIY) route. For the DIYers out there, there are dozens of trading platforms that will help you analyze, test, and optimize any type of trading system you want to create. On the surface, this seems to be a great way to go, relying just on yourself, your ideas, and the trading software. The problem, to be discussed in great detail later, is that developing trading systems is not as easy as the software vendors would lead you to believe. In fact, new developers following the approach suggested by the software will inevitably create an overoptimized, curve-fit trading system. Such a system will produce a great back test, but will almost never perform well in the real-time future. So novice DIY developers rank just below trading system vendors on the BS scale.

If buying from a vendor is fraught with hazard, and novice DIYers not much better, what options are left? If you are convinced that you have to have someone else provide you with a trading system or signals, using a broker-supplied system or a Commodity Trading Advisor (CTA) system is a much better approach. Let's take a quick look at what they offer, and the advantages and disadvantages.

Many futures brokers now offer what they call "Broker Assist" or "Follow the Signals"–type services. Two groups that offer these services are Striker Securities (www.striker.com) and World Cup Advisor (www.worldcupadvisor.com). (Full disclosure: I have in the past, or plan in the future, to offer signals through these two brokers. Based on my personal experience, I believe they are reputable.) For a monthly fee, you can "follow" trading signals from a signal provider. The signals provider will typically have an account at the broker and will be placing live trades. So the results shown are typically actual results, a *huge* step above the nonsense most trading system vendors show as "real."

Of course, just because the results provided by these services are from a traded account, it does not mean you will get the same results. Even real results should be treated as hypothetical. In fact, my general rule is that unless the results actually happened in your account, you *must* treat the results as hypothetical. As you well know, hypothetical leaves the door open for a lot of variation in actual results, which you should be prepared for. That is one disadvantage of the broker services.

Another possible disadvantage of a broker-supplied signal service is that something can go wrong with either the developer providing the signals to the broker or the broker itself. For example, if the developer uses a discretionary approach to trade, a personal crisis might throw his/her trading off, and a trading approach that was once good now becomes bad. On the broker side, a quick and sudden fraud, à la the PFG Best corruption and bankruptcy in 2012, might put your account at risk.

If you choose to follow a CTA, it is reassuring to know that the group is audited by regulators and accounting firms and that trading results shown are by-and-large accurate. Of course, some unethical bad apples always slip into the bunch, and they may produce stellar results for many years, before being destroyed in an explosion of fraud and deceit. Bernie Madoff and his firm, while not a CTA, is a good example of a trusted investment company actually being a complete fraud.

If you can't believe trading system vendors, with inexperienced DIY trading system developers not being much better, and brokers and CTAs being much better but not without risk, what can you do? What is the low group on the BS totem pole?

My opinion is that an experienced DIY trading system developer is the least susceptible to BS or otherwise invalid performance reports. I claim this for a few reasons. First, an experienced developer knows his trading back-test software and knows all the ways to fool it. He knows to avoid these software limitations, where many trading system vendors actively seek out these limitations and use them to produce their faulty, extremely good-looking performance reports.

A second reason an experienced developer, creating his own systems, is lowest on the BS scale, is that he is in charge of the process. He can eliminate many potential issues, such as faulty or missing market data, incorrect forward-looking rules, and overoptimization and curve fitting. Being in charge of the complete process is an enormous responsibility, but an experienced developer will be quick to fix issues, since he ultimately is solely responsible for his results.

Of course, just developing trading systems for many years does not make one an expert. The key is to develop systems and then verify the performance in real time. Over the course of a few years, a good developer will get better and better at producing historical results for trading systems that have a better and better chance of holding up in the future. Certainly, when done correctly, an experienced DIY developer can be pretty low on the BS scale.

At this point, a few readers are probably asking, "Why even bother testing? All it does is prove something worked in the past. It has no bearing on future performance." This is an argument that has some validity, up to a point. It is definitely true that "past performance is not indicative of future results," which is why the U.S. government requires this disclaimer when discussing trading system performance. But does it therefore mean that historical testing has *no* validity? I don't think so.

Here is a case in point. Let's say you want to build a model of the sun rising. Every day for a month, you get up before dawn, and wait for the sun to appear. Every day, it rises in the east. So, you build you model, run it for tomorrow, and it "predicts" the sun will rise in the east. Will it? Who knows for certain? Some strange axis switching or earth rotation reversing could occur overnight, and the sun could rise in the north, south, or west. Highly unlikely, yes, but so was the flash crash of 2010 or the financial crisis of 2008. Outlier and unexpected events can and do happen.

If such a calamity occurs, does it mean that the model is useless and never should have been built? No, but certainly you'd have to now take into account that the world you modeled has changed dramatically. It is the same for trading systems. Completely new market conditions could render your trading strategy useless tomorrow, or next week or next month, or maybe not at all. But I contend that having a model based on history is much better than completely guessing. With guessing, you are likely to be looking the wrong way when the sun rises tomorrow morning.

In evaluating trading systems and their performance report and equity curves, it is important to distinguish *how* the results were obtained. There are four main ways to produce results:

- Historical back testing
- Out-of-sample testing
- Walk-forward testing
- Real-time testing

Each of these is discussed in turn next.

Historical Back Testing

Historical back testing is the most common method of testing. It is also the easiest to perform, and the easiest to abuse and misuse. The developer simply enters the start date and the end date (usually today's date), includes any parameters to optimize, and then lets the strategy engine do all the calculations. The end result will be the best set of parameters for that period of time, which can then be used in real live trading.

Unfortunately, there is a major problem when performing a back test in this manner. Assuming that the results are not due to overoptimization—too many rules, too many parameters, and/or too many parameter values—the historical results are by definition going to look great. After all, those results come from optimizing! There is virtually no chance that the results in the future will be close to the optimized results. The results are just too "tuned" to the data used in the test.

A great example of this is shown in Figure 5.3. Looking at just the optimized results of a simple trading system, it looks like this is a viable system. But this is because what you see was optimized. Take any other set of parameters and the system will look worse. Going forward, which result do you think is more likely—the one optimized good result or the many poor results? I hope the answer is crystal clear: the poor results are a truer reflection of the actual system performance. The deceiving part in all this is that sometimes these systems perform well for a time after

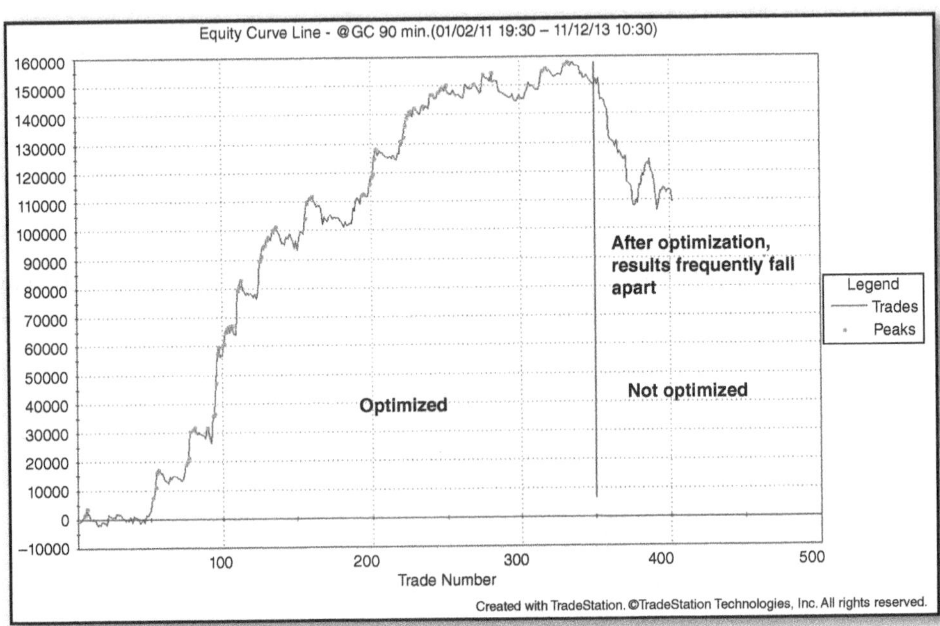

FIGURE 5.3 Optimized Results Frequently Fall Apart after Testing

optimizing. In general, though, the more optimization that is done, the less likely the system will work well going forward.

Out-of-Sample Testing

Only the most inexperienced and naive developers test and optimize their trading system over the whole historical data set. If that has been your approach up until now, this statement may make you mad. But odds are that your real-time trading results have not been good, or at least not consistently good. Much of that can be attributed to evaluating the strategy's performance on the same data it was optimized on. It is just not a very good practice. Trust me, I know—I used to do it all the time before the market told me, via taking money out of my account, that I was doing things incorrectly!

Some developers get around this by including an out-of-sample period. This is shown in Figure 5.4. An out-of-sample period will be 10 to 20 percent of the data reserved for review after optimization. Typically, the data left for out-of-sample testing will be the most recent data. I have, however, seen people apply it to data before their optimization data. The theory behind that alternative approach is that the optimization should include the most recent data, so the strategy is "tuned" to current market conditions.

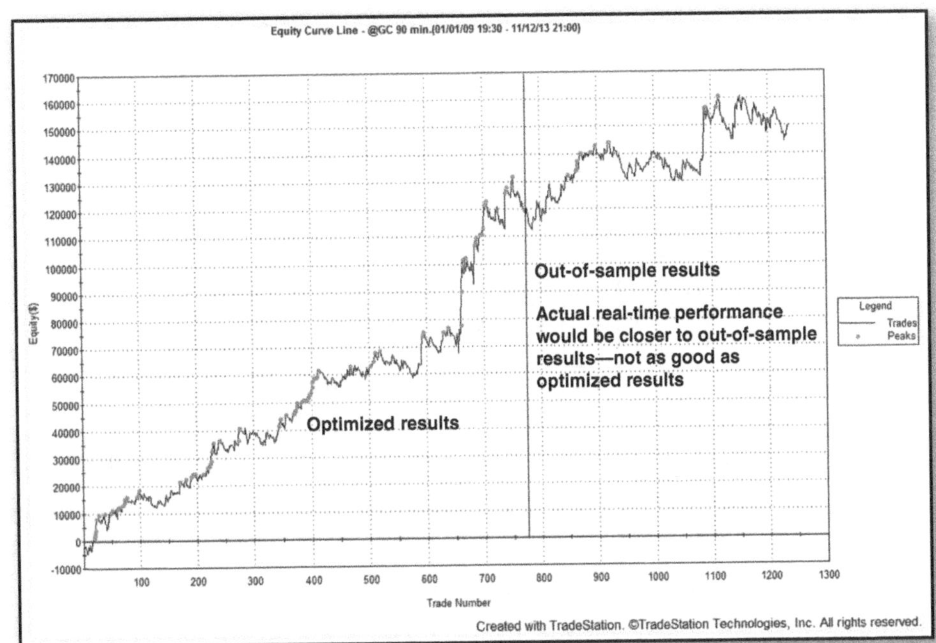

FIGURE 5.4 Out-of-Sample Testing Results

Conducting a test with out-of-sample data is a magnitude or two better than optimizing over all the data, especially if the out-of-sample period has a significant number of trades in it. If the optimized results look good with the out-of-sample data, there is much more confidence in the optimized results. It will likely perform better in real time.

One problem with the out-of-sample approach is that the optimized parameters are set forever. So, for example, if you optimize your trading system and get values X, Y, and Z as the best inputs to your system, those inputs should never change. But, perhaps due to changing market conditions, you do want the ability to change your input parameters, or at least check them on an ongoing basis. In this manner, the out-of-sample test idea can be taken one step further. The resulting analysis, walk-forward analysis, is much better, and much closer to reality.

Walk-Forward Analysis

Walk-forward analysis is much more cumbersome than traditional back tests, but the results are usually worth the effort. Walk-forward analysis can be done by hand, in conjunction with trading software optimization. This was the method I used to be a top finisher in the World Cup contest, and I encourage you to try it by hand a few times to fully understand the process. After that, many trading software packages now include walk-forward analysis in their available tools.

The idea behind walk-forward analysis is simple: the performance results and the optimized results are based on two different data sets. This can be seen in Figure 5.5.

	2001	2002	2003	2004	2005	2006	2007	2008	2009	2010	2011	2012	2013
In sample #1													
Walk-forward #1													
In sample #2													
Walk-forward #2													
In sample #3													
Walk-forward #3													
In sample #4													
Walk-forward #4													
In sample #5													
Walk-forward #5													
In sample #6													
Walk-forward #6													
In sample #7													
Walk-forward #7													
In sample #8													
Walk-forward #8													
In sample #9													
Walk-forward #9													

In-sample period: 4 years
Walk-forward (out-of-sample period: 1 year)

Walk-forward periods then combined into one continuous equity curve

FIGURE 5.5 Walk-Forward Analysis

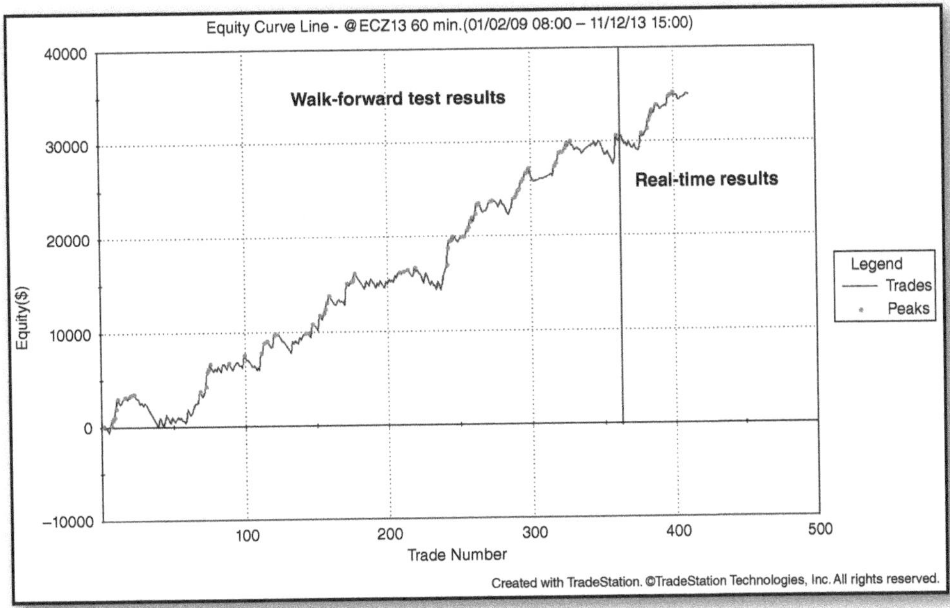

FIGURE 5.6 Walk-Forward Testing Results

Walk-forward analysis is simply the aggregate of many out-of-sample periods, stitched together.

Results of walk-forward analysis, when done correctly, can be much closer to reality than a simple optimized test. A sample of this is given in Figure 5.6, which shows that the walk-forward analysis, and the live results are pretty comparable. There is no dramatic shift in performance between live and walk-forward results.

Walk-forward analysis is a great tool when there are a lot of historical data to analyze. It is my recommended method. But in cases where there is not much historical data, the best approach may be to test and evaluate the trading system in real time.

Real-Time Analysis

Some very successful traders eschew all forms of back testing due to inherent conflicts and issues in such testing. These folks simply test strategies in real time, possibly even with real money. The obvious advantage to such a method is that fitting rules to past data and using hindsight bias is just not possible. One big disadvantage is that you can only gather data at market speed. It is impossible to gather statistics over many years until you have tested in real time for many years. Most people do not have the patience to wait for such a test to complete. Another disadvantage is that anytime the strategy is changed, the clock goes back to zero, and the evaluation starts fresh. This can really prolong the test period.

For the reasons cited, most people do not consider real-time testing, even with its advantages, as a viable solution. In the trading system development method shown later in this book, however, real-time analysis is used and provides useful verification of a trading system.

CHAPTER 6

Preliminary Analysis

Now that we have examined the primary ways to test a trading strategy and produce a trading performance report, I'll share with you what I think is important in these reports. A typical summary performance report is shown in Figure 6.1. A complete TradeStation-produced performance report spans at least seven pages and includes hundreds of calculated parameters, trade lists, and performance graphs. The amount of information supplied is frankly overwhelming. Most of the results, it turns out, are not all that important when time comes to evaluate the trading system. Maybe a performance metric for "drawdown—coefficient of variation" matters to some people but certainly not to me.

As with most aspects of trading, I try to keep my performance report analysis simple. A few numbers are typically all that I need to conduct a cursory review of any trading system. Once I find something I like, then I will delve deeper.

First, a few ground rules are in order. The performance report should be based either on live data or on a walk-forward test. Optimized back tests should not even be analyzed, as their results are bogus and misleading. Next, there should be multiple years of data, with a multitude of trades. A good rule of thumb is 5 to 10 years of data, and 30 to 100 trades for each trading rule in the system. Third, I usually review performance reports without position sizing applied. As you review many performance reports, it will be important to compare "apples to apples." If you look at one performance report based on single-contract trades and try to compare it to another report that uses multiple-contract-position sizing, a fair comparison is all but impossible. Plus, a bad strategy can be made to look appealing by position sizing. To keep it simple, I look at position sizing only after I feel confident the strategy is viable trading one contract at a time.

Finally, accurate assumptions for commission and slippage must be included in the report. Many times I see performance reports without these values added in, with the flippant response from the creator, "Those costs can be added in

TradeStation Performance Summary Expand

	All Trades	Long Trades	Short Trades
Total Net Profit	$34,932.50	$18,660.00	$16,272.50
Gross Profit	$88,760.00	$44,435.00	$44,325.00
Gross Loss	($53,827.50)	($25,775.00)	($28,052.50)
Profit Factor	1.65	1.72	1.58
Total Number of Trades	411	203	208
Percent Profitable	49.39%	53.20%	45.67%
Winning Trades	203	108	95
Losing Trades	208	95	113
Even Trades	0	0	0
Avg. Trade Net Profit	$84.99	$91.92	$78.23
Avg. Winning Trade	$437.24	$411.44	$466.58
Avg. Losing Trade	($258.79)	($271.32)	($248.25)
Ratio Avg. Win:Avg. Loss	1.69	1.52	1.88
Largest Winning Trade	$2,407.50	$1,620.00	$2,407.50
Largest Losing Trade	($442.50)	($442.50)	($442.50)
Max. Consecutive Winning Trades	8	8	8
Max. Consecutive Losing Trades	9	5	9
Avg. Bars in Winning Trades	4.79	5.09	4.45
Avg. Bars in Losing Trades	2.56	2.52	2.59
Avg. Bars in Even Trades	0.00	0.00	0.00
Max. Shares/Contracts Held	1	1	1
Total Shares/Contracts Held	411	203	208
Account Size Required	$3,522.50	$2,370.00	$2,565.00
Return on Initial Capital	34.93%		
Annual Rate of Return	6.29%		
Return Retracement Ratio	0.36		
RINA Index	5068.08		
Trading Period	4 Yrs, 9 Mths, 5 Dys, 5 Hrs		
Percent of Time in the Market	2.64%		
Max. Equity Run-up	$36,030.00		
Max. Drawdown (Intra-day Peak to Valley)			
Value	($4,160.00)	($2,792.50)	($3,052.50)
Net Profit as % of Drawdown	839.72%	668.22%	533.09%
Max. Drawdown (Trade Close to Trade Close)			
Value	($3,522.50)	($2,370.00)	($2,565.00)
Net Profit as % of Drawdown	991.70%	787.34%	634.41%

Performance Summary | Trade Analysis | Trades List | Periodical Returns | Performance Graphs | Trade Graphs | Settings

FIGURE 6.1 Sample Performance Report

later, no problem." Not including commissions and slippage, beyond being highly unethical—if not immoral—due to the way these costs impact a trading system, suggests that the developer doesn't really understand proper strategy development. It can easily be shown how testing without commissions and slippage leads one to select trading systems that trade more often, with lower average profit per trade. For example, if you optimize based on net profit or something similar, the optimizer will usually give you a best set of parameters that make you trade too much. Here is an example:

Without Slippage or Commission

Parameter Setting 1: Gross profit/trade = $25, 1,000 trades, gross profit = $25,000
Parameter Setting 2: Gross profit/trade = $50, 300 trades, gross profit = $15,000

The optimizer will select Setting 1 as superior.

With $25 Slippage and Commission

Parameter Setting 1: Net profit/trade = $0, 1,000 trades, gross profit = $0
Parameter Setting 2: Net profit/trade = $25, 300 trades, net profit = $7,500

The optimizer will now select Setting 2 as superior.

Which approach is better? Well, in the first scenario, such a system in the real world will churn the average trader until his account is depleted. It is definitely not as simple as "you can add commissions and slippage in later." The second scenario, however, produces a result that is far more realistic and believable. So, all other things being equal, optimizing with slippage and commissions is an approach much closer to reality and should always be used.

With these basic ground rules in place, the first number I look at is the total net profit. This seems self-evident, since if there is no profit, why bother looking at the report any further? It may be that the net profit shown is not worthwhile, either due to the time period involved or the drawdown that has to be endured, but there should be profit nonetheless. In my experience, with a walk-forward back test, the annual net profit should be $5,000 per year per contract minimum, preferably $10,000 or more. Any amount less than this will likely not be worthwhile on a risk-adjusted basis or will not have enough trades to be significant.

Profit factor is the next number I review. Obviously, higher numbers are better here. Many people say that only profit factors greater than 2.0 are acceptable, but I don't share this view. To me, anything over 1.0 has at least some merit, so I don't discard any systems between 1.0 and 2.0 just based on this number. I do find that profit factors below 1.5 generally have a hard time making it through the rest of the steps in the development process, though.

I always review total number of trades to ensure that enough trades are being taken during the test period. If, for example, the report contains only 5 trades, just how valid can the results actually be? I generally use a rough guide of 30 to 100 trades minimum per strategy rule. So, for example, if I have four strategy rules, I'd like to see at least 120 to 400 trades in the report. Obviously, the more trades the better.

Average trade net profit is the next performance number I look at. Since this number is after commissions and slippage, it is a great and easy way to compare trading systems. I generally like to see $50 or more per trade average, based on trading one contract. For average trade values less than $50, the system might still be viable, but the closer you ride to that $0 breakeven line, the less leeway you allow for errors, mistakes, slight changes in performance, and the like.

The next number I review is average losing trade, which I combine with the average trade net profit to calculate expectancy. There is a lot of confusion about expectancy and how to calculate it, so I will explain it here.

Many traders calculate expectancy in this way:

$$\text{Expectancy} = \text{average \$ winners} * \text{win \%} + \text{average \$ losers} * \text{lose \%}$$
$$= \text{average trade}$$

where average $ losers is a negative number

Note that this is also the average trade net profit. So calculating an expectancy using this equation does not provide any additional information beyond what is already known with the average trade net profit.

An alternative expectancy can be calculated as follows:

$$\text{Expectancy} = (\text{average \$ winners} * \text{win \%} + \text{average \$ losers} * \text{lose \%}) / (-\text{average \$ losers})$$

This metric is useful since it is a risk-adjusted value. It basically states for every dollar you risk, what is your expected return? So with an expectancy of 0.2, you'd expect to receive 20 cents in gains for every $1 you put at risk. This expectancy has been heavily touted by trading psychologist and educator Dr. Van Tharp, so to avoid future confusion, I will refer to this calculation as "Tharp Expectancy." To me, it is much more valuable than the first method of calculating expectancy.

For the Tharp Expectancy, I generally look for values greater than 0.1. Anything below this threshold will be difficult to trade and likely will demand too much risk for too little reward.

The next numbers I look at in the performance report are total slippage and total commission. If the numbers are $0, I immediately discard the report and ignore all other results I may have seen. There is no such thing as cost-free trading, so any performance report showing that is bogus. In general, I need to see $5 per round turn trade per contract for commissions. That is a typical value charged by a discount broker, after all exchange fees, National Futures Association fees, and so on are added in. Commissions can be less than this, especially if you do a lot of volume or if you are an exchange member, but the $5 figure is appropriate for most retail traders.

Total slippage is an even more critical number than total commission. Many developers, especially those who have never traded before, consistently underestimate the amount of slippage experienced in the real world. I define slippage as the difference between what the software strategy back-test engine gives for fills and what your actual fills are. For example, many strategy engines assume buy fills at the bid, when in real trading you'll buy at the ask. The difference is what I consider slippage. Based on my experience, I assume the following slippage values for heavily traded markets:

- Market orders: 1 to 2 ticks slippage per round turn.
- Stop orders: 1 to 2 ticks slippage per round turn.
- Limit orders: 0 ticks slippage.

The tricky part is that a typical trading strategy will have some mix of market, limit, and stop orders. In that case, if you can apply only one slippage value to each trade, what should it be? I find being conservative in this situation helps. I will generally apply 1.5 to 2.0 ticks of slippage per round turn trade for these mixed-order-type strategies. I find this generally a bit pessimistic, but it is better than underestimating the slippage costs and being disappointed with real-world results.

The final number I look at in the performance report is maximum drawdown. I have no set criteria for a drawdown limit, but if I see a $10,000 maximum drawdown for a strategy that produces only $15,000 net profit, alarm bells go off. In the back of my mind, I look at the drawdown knowing that I can expect to see an even larger drawdown at some point during live trading. If I can't handle the drawdown, I'll discard the system immediately. Otherwise, I know that high risk, low rewards will be tossed out during later steps, so I don't eliminate the strategy just yet.

There are arguably other important numbers in the performance report, to be certain. Many people, for example, put a lot of faith in winning percentage, or Sharpe ratio, or one of the hundreds of other metrics. The fact is that all metrics are important to an extent, and the developer should try to find ones he or she is comfortable with. Ultimately, any metrics relied upon should prove themselves by leading to successful real-time strategies.

Once I am done reviewing the performance report, I generally take a look at some of the trade graphs. I am interested in one chart in particular: the closed trade equity graph. If you are a visual learner, just looking at an equity curve—either a closed trade equity curve or a daily equity curve (shown in Figure 6.2)—might tell you all you need to know. Here are the main things I look for in an equity chart.

The first thing I look for in an equity curve is the slope. If the chart is not steadily going from lower left to upper right, it may not be a very good strategy. The problem is that the chart can be distorted by the scaling used. So it is also important to look at the end equity, and then divide that by the number of years in the curve. That will give you an annual average profit and a good indication of whether the strategy is at all worthwhile.

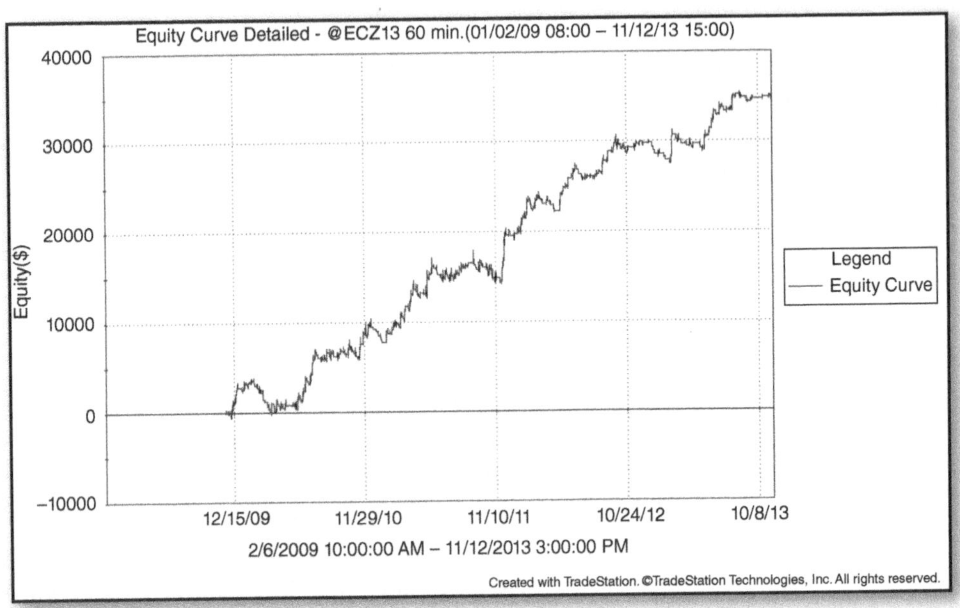

FIGURE 6.2 Sample Equity Curve

After the slope, I like to look for flat periods. Flat periods are obviously better than periods of drawdown, but many periods, punctuated by rapid rises, should be cause for concern. Such an equity curve suggests that the strategy may have caught only a few good trades, possibly because of curve fitting or overoptimization. Flat periods could also be caused by government intervention, for example the United States quantitative easing programs (QE, QE2, QE3) in the 2009–2013 time frame. In this case, it might be okay to assume that performance will improve when government intervention ends. Of course, when, if ever, will some sort of government intervention end, and who can predict it?

The third major item I look for is drawdown periods. How severe are the drawdowns, and how long does the strategy take to recover from these drawdowns? Answers to these questions will give you an idea of what to expect if you trade this strategy for real. Drawdowns in the future may be more severe, and may last longer—your position sizing and money management should assume that both of these things will happen—but you can at least get a sense of what to expect.

The absence of any drawdowns on the equity curve should also be cause for concern. I know of no real system, except for money deposited in a savings account, that has only a small or no drawdown. Again, the curve has to "look" realistic. Reward with no risk is not realistic.

A final item I review on equity charts is the "fuzziness" of the curve. This cannot be seen on a closed equity chart, but it can be seen on a daily equity chart. The fuzzier the curve, the more the daily results jump around, moving up and down short term, even if the longer-term trend is up. Curves that are very fuzzy are harder to trade, harder to position size, and harder to emotionally deal with. Think about it: if System A gains $200 on day 1, loses $200 on day 2, and gains $75 on day 3, is that preferable to System B, which gains a steady $25 per day? Both have the same end result, but the fuzziness of System A makes it less appealing than System B.

Obviously, just looking at an equity curve is by no means a very scientific or very rigorous way to evaluate a trading system. But it can be useful for preliminary analysis. There is no need to look at performance report details if you do not like the look of the equity curve. In those cases, you can save a lot of time by spending a few seconds staring at the equity curve and then rejecting a system you do not like.

The discussion thus far has focused on simple, quick numbers and methods to evaluate the performance of a trading system. Such analysis is useful in the early stages of development, where most strategies are junk, and a fast, cursory review can eliminate them, freeing up more time for you as the developer to create new systems. But, eventually, you will need to do in-depth analysis of performance results. That is a whole different animal.

CHAPTER 7

Detailed Analysis

As the development of a trading strategy progresses, the analysis also progresses, and the performance hurdles a strategy must meet to be considered viable get more stringent. My primary method of analysis at the later stages is Monte Carlo analysis. But before I explain how I run the analysis and what I look for in results, I'll first briefly describe the process.

What Is Monte Carlo Analysis?

Monte Carlo analysis, or simulation, sounds like a daunting topic, but actually it is not. With the Monte Carlo spreadsheet I created, which you can download for free (www.wiley.com/go/algotradingsystems), the analysis is pretty simple. But what is it actually?

Think about the individual trades in your strategy. These trades taken sequentially, in the order they occurred, yield the strategy equity curve. But what if the order of those was different? Could the drawdown become more severe? Could the end equity be different? These are the questions Monte Carlo analysis can answer.

In its simplest form, you can think of it this way: First, get a number of little pieces of paper, one for each trade in your strategy. Then, write down one trade result on each piece of paper. Once you have all trades accounted for, put all the pieces in a hat. Randomly choose one. That is your first trade. Record it, adding it to your initial equity, and then put the piece of paper back in the hat (this is referred to as random sampling with replacement). Then, pick another piece of paper, record its value, and add it to the existing equity curve you are building.

If you do this for a number of trades, you'll have a possible equity curve. If you perform the whole analysis many, many times, you'll have a family of equity curves. Each one represents a possible way that trades in your strategy could have occurred.

Using the family of possible curves, you can get statistics about your trading system. These statistics can help you evaluate a strategy, determine a position sizing approach, and give you realistic scenarios for what you might face if you actually trade the strategy live. Of course, this all assumes that the historically derived trades will be the same as the trades in the future. If your historical trades are based on flawed development, future results will be garbage.

Obviously, there are some potentially serious drawbacks to this analysis. First, the analysis assumes that the trades in your performance report are the only possible trades that can happen. This is obviously false, since when you start trading live, any result is possible for a particular trade. But, if the distribution (overall mean and standard deviation) of the trades is accurate, then the Monte Carlo approach can yield meaningful results.

A second drawback is that this analysis assumes that each trade is independent of the previous trade, a condition commonly referred to as serial or auto correlation. For most trading strategies, this is not an issue. However, if you have a strategy in which the trade results depend on each other, simple Monte Carlo analysis is not appropriate. An example of such a situation would be if the trade B signal is dependent on the outcome of the previous trade A. You ideally should check for it before using the Monte Carlo analysis. One method for checking for serial correlation is the Durbin Watson statistic. Although it is beyond the scope of this book, you can find details, examples, and spreadsheets on this calculation on the Internet.

If you find that your trades do exhibit serial correlation, the simple Monte Carlo analysis may not be appropriate to use. In such cases, you could try to use a Monte Carlo simulation that included serial correlation effects, or you could gather statistics from a method called "start trade analysis" or "moving start analysis." In this analysis, you simulate the start of trading at each trade, and gather the statistics for return and drawdown. For example, if you have 10 trades, $i, i + 1, \ldots i + 9$ in your sample, you'd first create an equity curve starting with trade i. From the resulting curve, you could get the drawdown d_i. Then, start the equity curve at trade $i + 1$. This curve would give you the drawdown d_{i+1}. If you continue through all the trades, you can analyze the set of drawdowns d. This method may be a bit more cumbersome than Monte Carlo, but it is a better way to analyze the data when you have serial correction, since trade sequence will be mostly preserved.

Assuming you can live with the drawbacks listed, Monte Carlo can help you answer the following questions:

- What is my risk of ruin for a given account size?
- What are the chances of my system's having a maximum drawdown of X percent?
- What kind of annual return can I expect from this trading system?
- Is the risk I am taking to trade this strategy appropriate for the return I am receiving?

Each of these questions will be addressed in the discussion that follows. To simplify the narrative, I will assume the reader is using my Monte Carlo spreadsheet. Any Monte Carlo simulator available to the public should be able to give the same results, although some of the terminology and assumptions used may be different. Therefore, whether you use the simulator or not, the discussion will still be useful for you.

Inputs to Monte Carlo Simulator

There are only a few required inputs to perform Monte Carlo simulation. These are listed below, and are shown in Figure 7.1.

Base Starting Equity. This is the starting amount of your account, in dollars.

Stop Trading if Equity Drops Below \$. This is the amount of capital below which you will cease trading. For example, if you enter \$3,500 here, once your equity, on a closed-trade basis, drops below \$3,500, you will not be permitted to trade anymore. Your account will be considered "ruined." At a minimum, this value must be greater than the initial margin for one contract of the instrument your system is trading. In the preceding example, you could trade only products that had an initial margin below \$3,500. If you wanted to trade a higher-margin instrument, such as gold (currently at \$8,800 initial margin), you would have to increase this minimum amount. As a rule, I never recommend trading with

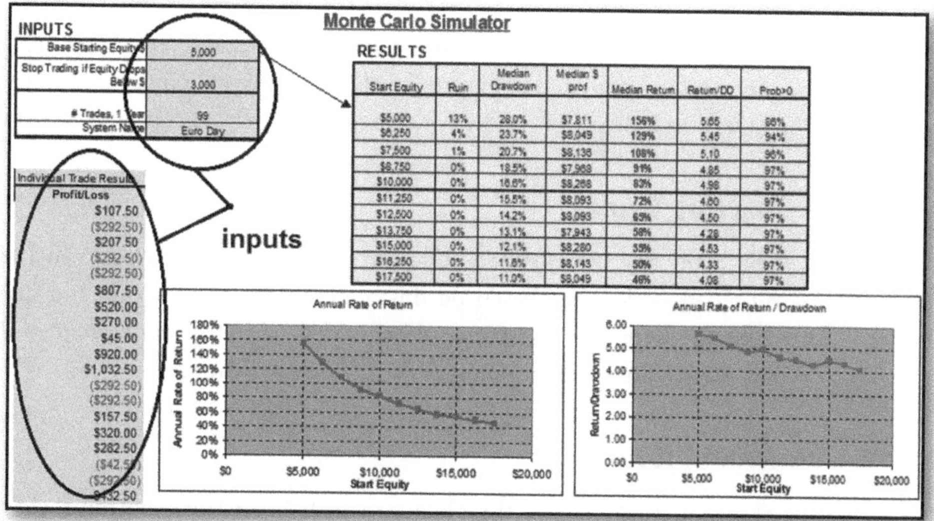

Start Equity	Ruin	Median Drawdown	Median $ prof	Median Return	Return/DD	Prob>0
$5,000	13%	28.0%	$7,811	156%	5.65	96%
$6,250	4%	23.7%	$8,049	129%	5.45	94%
$7,500	1%	20.7%	$8,136	108%	5.10	96%
$8,750	0%	18.5%	$7,968	91%	4.85	97%
$10,000	0%	16.6%	$8,288	83%	4.98	97%
$11,250	0%	15.5%	$8,093	72%	4.60	97%
$12,500	0%	14.2%	$8,093	65%	4.50	97%
$13,750	0%	13.1%	$7,943	58%	4.28	97%
$15,000	0%	12.1%	$8,280	55%	4.53	97%
$16,250	0%	11.6%	$8,143	50%	4.33	97%
$17,500	0%	11.0%	$8,049	46%	4.08	97%

FIGURE 7.1 Monte Carlo Simulator Inputs

only enough capital to just meet the margin requirement, but for this simulation, the assumption is acceptable.

 # Trades, 1 Year. This is simply the number of trades that your system takes in a one-year period. My simulator is designed to trade for only one year, so each equity curve generated will consist of this number of trades. That is, of course, assuming the ruin point is not hit first.

Individual Trade Results. This column of data contains all the trade data, one trade per row. All trades should be based on the same reference point, that is, per contract, per day, and so on. You cannot mix some trades that were based on one contract with trades that had multiple contracts.

Limitations of the Simulator

To keep things simple, the simulator makes a few assumptions. First, it is assumed that one contract is traded for each trade. There is no position sizing built into the simulator. Second, the simulator assumes one year of trading. Both of these assumptions can be changed in the Excel macro code by anyone who understands macro programming language.

In the discussion that follows, a "run" or iteration is defined as the generation of one single equity curve. In a "simulation," there will be a number of runs—in the simulator discussed, this is 2,500 runs. To generate statistics, such as risk of ruin or median return, the results of a simulation (2,500 individual runs) are used.

Simulator Output

Once the simulator runs, a table of output values and corresponding curves will be generated, as depicted in Figure 7.2. Following is an explanation of each output value, how to interpret it, and what values I consider appropriate for a tradable system.

Starting Equity

This is the size of your account at the start of the Monte Carlo analysis. All rates of return are calculated based on this number, and risk of ruin and maximum drawdown are both heavily influenced by it. The simulator uses a range of different starting equities in order to generate the table and the output curves.

Risk of Ruin

This statistic tells you the chances (probability) that within a year's time, your account will be wiped out (i.e., fall below the "Stop Trading if Equity Drops

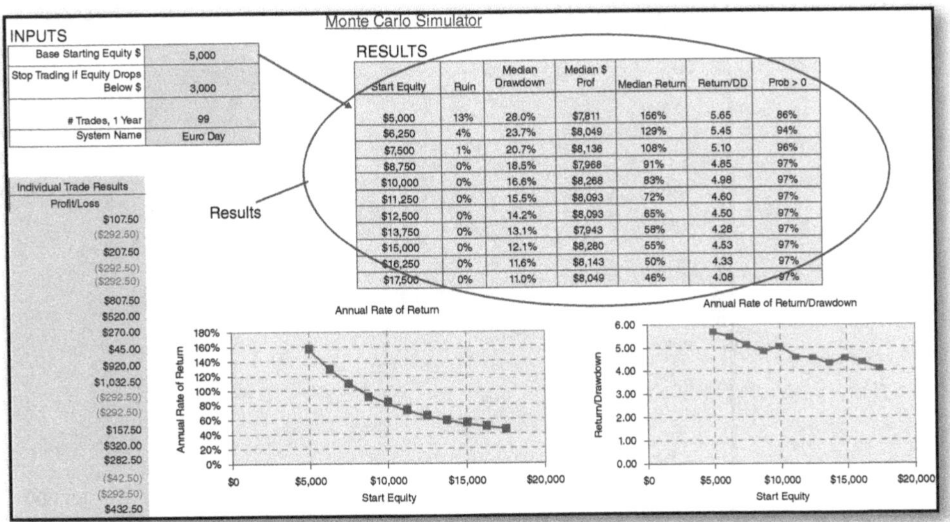

INPUTS	
Base Starting Equity $	5,000
Stop Trading If Equity Drops Below $	3,000
# Trades, 1 Year	99
System Name	Euro Day

Individual Trade Results
Profit/Loss
$107.50
($292.50)
$207.50
($292.50)
($292.50)
$807.50
$520.00
$270.00
$45.00
$920.00
$1,032.50
($292.50)
($292.50)
$157.50
$320.00
$282.50
($42.50)
($292.50)
$432.50

Start Equity	Ruin	Median Drawdown	Median $ Prof	Median Return	Return/DD	Prob > 0
$5,000	13%	28.0%	$7,811	156%	5.65	86%
$6,250	4%	23.7%	$8,049	129%	5.45	94%
$7,500	1%	20.7%	$8,136	108%	5.10	96%
$8,750	0%	18.5%	$7,968	91%	4.85	97%
$10,000	0%	16.6%	$8,268	83%	4.98	97%
$11,250	0%	15.5%	$8,093	72%	4.60	97%
$12,500	0%	14.2%	$8,093	65%	4.50	97%
$13,750	0%	13.1%	$7,943	58%	4.28	97%
$15,000	0%	12.1%	$8,280	55%	4.53	97%
$16,250	0%	11.6%	$8,143	50%	4.33	97%
$17,500	0%	11.0%	$8,049	46%	4.08	97%

FIGURE 7.2 Monte Carlo Simulator Outputs

Below $"). For example, if the risk of ruin is 12 percent, that means within the first year of trading the system, you have a 12 percent chance of having to cease trading.

Risk of ruin is an extremely important statistic, especially for traders with small accounts. The risk of ruin can be significant for small accounts, even if the system is a winning system! Here is an example that should make that clear:

Let's say you have a very good day trading system. It trades two times a day. Winning trades are $200 after all costs, 50 percent of the time. When it loses the other 50 percent of the time, it loses $175 net.

Per day, on average, you'd make $25 a day. In a year, you'd make $6,300 per contract. If you traded this with a $10,000 account, always with one contract, you'd make a 63 percent annual return, with somewhere around 15 percent maximum drawdown. By most measures that is really good.

Now, let's say you take this positive expectancy system and trade it with a small account, $5,000 and under. Let's say your broker allows $500 day trading margin, so that is your "ruin" point—if your account drops below $500, you are ruined and you quit trading.

In one year of trading, how likely are you to be ruined (drop below $500 and cease trading)? The results, depicted in Figure 7.3, might surprise you.

The question is: where do you feel most comfortable being on this curve? The person with $1,500 is probably panicking after each loss, since he doesn't have much wiggle room. But the trader with $5,000—still a small account, only 3.3 times the first trader's account—is 20 times less likely to be ruined.

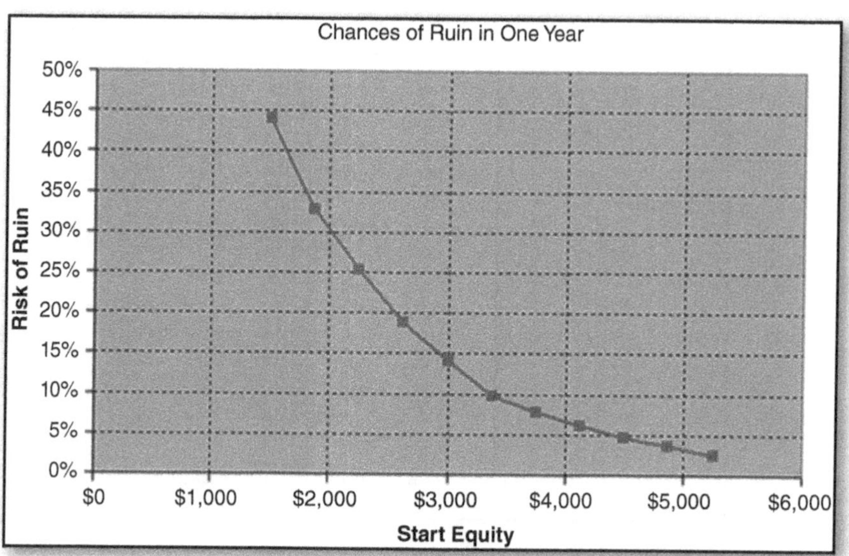

FIGURE 7.3 Account Size and Risk of Ruin

The conclusion is that being underfunded can be disastrous, *even with a winning system*. So I pay a lot of attention to the risk-of-ruin number that the simulator outputs. Any value above 10 percent means, for me, that I am trying to trade the system with too little capital, and that I should increase the amount of capital to get below 10 percent. Obviously, systems with 0 to 1 percent probability of ruin are the best, but as with anything in trading, it is a trade-off with rate of return. In my experience, I have found that simulation results with less than 10 percent risk of ruin are fairly safe, while still providing an acceptable rate of return.

Median Drawdown

This statistic can be a bit confusing at first. It is actually the median value of the maximum drawdown. Are you confused yet? Perhaps breaking it into pieces will help.

First, the maximum drawdown is the maximum percentage drop in account size from an equity peak. It should always be measured from the previous equity peak. Figure 7.4 gives an example of three different drawdowns:

Drawdown 1: $5,000 drawdown, after peak equity of $20,000 = $5,000/$20,000 = 25 percent drawdown

Drawdown 2: $10,000 drawdown, after peak equity of $30,000 = $10,000/$30,000 = 33 percent drawdown

Drawdown 3: $15,000 drawdown, after peak equity of $60,000 = $15,000/$60,000 = 25 percent drawdown

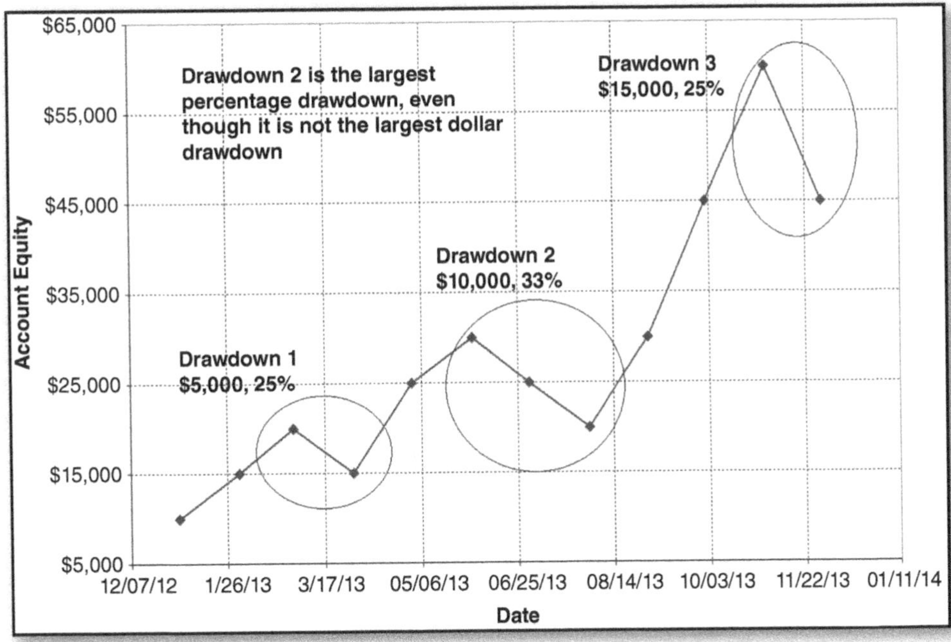

FIGURE 7.4 Maximum Drawdown Explained

In this example, the maximum percentage drawdown occurs during drawdown 2 and is 33 percent. It is interesting to note that it is the maximum percentage drawdown, not the absolute dollar maximum drawdown (drawdown 3, in dollar amounts, is higher than drawdown 2).

For every simulation run, there will be a corresponding maximum percentage drawdown. Over a great number of simulation runs, there will be a distribution of maximum drawdowns, varying from 0 percent (no drawdown at all, a hopelessly pie-in-the-sky case), to 100 percent (a complete ruin from the peak equity point, down to $0 equity). This distribution will have a median value, which means that 50 percent of the drawdown values exceed the median, and 50 percent are below it. Therefore, in the term "median maximum drawdown," the word *maximum* refers to the largest drawdown in a particular simulation run, and *median* refers to the midpoint of maximum drawdowns over a large number of simulation runs.

There is no magic in selecting the median maximum drawdown to be the output value for the simulation. It could easily be the 30 percent, 60 percent, 90 percent, and so on, percentile value, too. I chose the median value just to use for comparison purposes to other systems. If I instead wanted a worst-case value, I could have used the 95th percentile value of drawdown, meaning only 5 percent of maximum drawdowns are worse than this value.

Based on my own personal preference, I generally accept up to a 40 percent median maximum drawdown. That is, within 1 year I have a 50 percent chance of reaching a 40 percent maximum drawdown. This may be too extreme for most people, but it suits my objectives and my personality.

One thing to keep in mind with maximum drawdown is that traders, especially new traders, have a tendency to greatly overestimate their ability to withstand a drawdown. Based on my conversations with various traders, I have found that traders can generally handle half the maximum drawdown they think they can handle. For instance, if a trader decides before trading a system that he can handle a 30 percent maximum drawdown, when real money is on the line, he will start to panic, and likely quit or change the system, at the 15 percent drawdown point. I have coined a phrase for this phenomenon: "half of what you think it is." Just remember to keep this in mind when you establish your personal maximum allowable drawdown.

Median $ Profit, Median Return

As with the drawdown, over a full simulation of 2,500 runs, there will be a distribution of results. This distribution is used to calculate the median profit and median return. Median $ profit is simply the final equity minus the initial equity, after one year's worth of trades. Over the course of 2,500 runs, a median level can be calculated. This is the median $ profit. The median return is calculated in a similar fashion, although it is the final equity divided by the initial equity, in order to get it into percentage terms.

For my personal trading, I have no set goal for median $ profit. I do like to see median returns above 50 percent, especially since I stated earlier that I would allow up to 40 percent median drawdown values. It would not be wise of me to set the return threshold at 20 percent with a 40 percent drawdown. To keep me aware of this relationship between risk and reward, I also calculate the return/drawdown ratio.

Return/Drawdown

Of all the statistics produced by the Monte Carlo analysis, I feel this number is the most important. It is referred to in financial literature as the Calmar ratio when it is calculated over a three-year period. Since I am only simulating one year of performance, the simulator result is not exactly a Calmar ratio. The spreadsheet-produced number is simply the median annual percentage return divided by the median maximum percentage drawdown.

One way to think about this ratio is "it takes Y risk to make X." In this case, Y is the drawdown, and X is the profit return. Obviously, high values of this ratio are better. I generally look for return/drawdown ratios above 2.0, although I will accept lower values in special circumstances. In my experience, I find that ratios above 2.0 will usually produce acceptable results in the real world of trading live.

Prob > 0

This gives you the probability, expressed as a percentage, that the system will make money in the first year of trading. For example, if Prob > 0 equals 89 percent, that means you will have an 89 percent chance of showing profit in the first year. Of course, this is all based on your historical test results, so if they are not accurate, this result will not be either.

Summary

Now that we have discussed the performance report, equity curve, and Monte Carlo simulator, we can summarize the uses of all the values and threshold values for acceptability (Table 7.1).

TABLE 7.1 Important Performance Parameters

Parameter	Source	Utilized During	Threshold
Total net profit	Performance report	Initial review	~$10K per year per contract
Profit factor	Performance report	Initial review	>1.0 OK, >1.5 ideal
Average trade net profit	Performance report	Initial review	>$50 per contract
Tharp Expectancy	Performance report	Initial review	>0.10
Slippage and commission	Performance report	Initial review	Discard if $0, otherwise $5 commission 1–2 ticks slippage per round turn
Maximum drawdown	Performance report	Initial review	Should be much smaller than total net profit
Equity curve slope	Equity curve	Initial review	Ideally rises at 45-degree angle
Equity curve flat periods	Equity curve	Initial review	Short in duration
Equity curve drawdown, depth and duration	Equity curve	Initial review	Proportional to overall curve
Equity curve fuzziness	Equity curve	Initial review	Small is ideal
Risk of ruin	Monte Carlo simulation	Detailed review	<10%
Median maximum drawdown	Monte Carlo simulation	Detailed review	<40%
Median % return	Monte Carlo simulation	Detailed review	>40%
Return/drawdown ratio	Monte Carlo simulation	Detailed review	>2.0

CHAPTER 8

Designing and Developing Systems

With the vast multitude of trading system software packages now available, designing your own trading system has never been easier. Of course, the popularity of packages such as TradeStation, NinjaTrader, and MultiCharts is both a blessing and a curse. These simple-to-use software programs make turning ideas into strategies easier than ever before. What used to take weeks to accomplish in Microsoft Excel or in a hardcore programming language (such as C, C++, Visual Basic, or, for those older programmers out there, Fortran) now takes minutes or even seconds. Life is certainly easier in that respect.

The downside to this modern software—besides the fact that many people are testing millions of trading ideas every day and will likely discover any "edge" you find, eventually rendering it useless—is that trading software makes it too easy. Simply look a chart, insert a strategy—possibly one of the many standard strategies that come with the software—and you can quickly analyze and optimize to your heart's content.

Unfortunately, it is this simplicity that is also the Achilles' heel of the software. It is nearly impossible to create a viable strategy in the simplistic manner that trading software products describe. Taking the easy way may indeed give you a strategy with a terrific-looking back test, but when the strategy starts running live, all statistics turn bad. Perhaps this has happened to you, as it did to me in my earlier development days. I was adept at producing back tests that looked like the left side of Figure 5.3, only to turn them loose on the live market and experience the right side of the equity curve, which inevitably lost money.

Another drawback to the simplicity of ease of use of these "retail" trading software packages is that many professional traders can't or won't use them. That should give pause to every retail trader who thinks the well-known, commercially available package is the best. The fact is that many professionals are typically using far more sophisticated programming and analysis tools, such as R, Python, Matlab, and so on. Or they are developing their own platforms, from the ground up, using open source code available on the Internet. I'm not trying to imply that only professional software tools are good; rather, I am trying to alert traders to the fact that there are limitations and shortcomings to all trading software. If something does not provide the capability you need, either from an analysis, strategy development, or automation point of view, chances are very good that another, likely more expensive, software tool out there does provide it.

Over the years, I've progressed from evaluating systems by hand to analyzing them via spreadsheet, to creating strategy evaluators in Fortran (the engineer in me) and Visual Basic, to primarily using TradeStation and NinjaTrader today. Along the way, I made many mistakes developing trading systems and had to pay the market "tuition" in the form of trading losses. Eventually, I finally got smart in how I developed trading systems. Now, I follow a multistep approach, as shown in Figure 8.1. At each point of the process, there is a "gate"—criteria that a strategy must satisfy in order to advance to the next step. For strategies that fail along the way, small adjustments can be made to the strategy when appropriate. In most cases, however, it is better to place the strategy on the scrap heap and just move on to the next idea. Why? Many times, when a strategy doesn't work the first time through the process, changes to it may inadvertently introduce curve fitting, hindsight bias, or one of a million other strategy no-nos. The deceiving part is that the back test will look better—possibly a great deal better. But remember that the goal is not to create a superb back test; rather, the goal is to create a back test that will reflect the future performance of

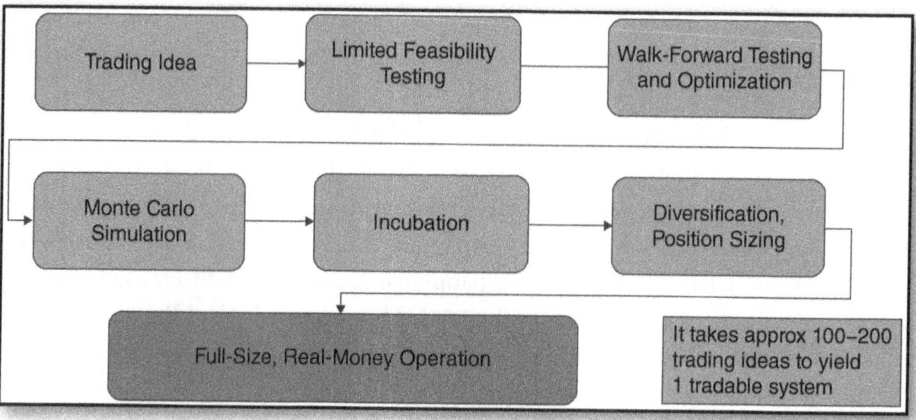

FIGURE 8.1 My Strategy Development Process

the strategy. Waterboarding or otherwise torturing your strategy until it gives great results is not a successful approach.

Back in the old days, before I developed the process I now use, I did what most other people do: I picked a market, selected a bar interval and time period, put a few rules in a strategy, and then optimized. Whatever turned out to be best is what I started to trade with live. The magic of the computer, with its ability to quickly do millions of iterations, uncovered what I was sure would be riches. Boy, was I ever disappointed!

Those early failures led me to a more involved, robust, and ideally trouble-free development process. I can't take credit for any of the individual concepts—certainly, many traders before me long ago developed most of the steps of my process. One great classic reference on system development is the "bible" of system design: *The Evaluation and Optimization of Trading Strategies*, by Robert Pardo (John Wiley and Sons, 1992). I have simply tailored all I have learned and read to create something that feels right to me, and by and large it has yielded good results in real time.

That is not to say it is an easy process for strategies to pass. When I first started using the basic process I use today (I have enhanced and refined it over the years, and if anything it is more stringent today than it was a few years ago), it probably took me about 100 to 200 trading ideas for entries and exits before I found something worth trading. With time and experience, that number has dropped significantly, but coming up with tradable strategies is not an easy task.

Traders that are new to using walk-forward analysis, Monte Carlo analysis, and the like frequently are frustrated by the difficulty of discovering a strategy. My answer to that dilemma usually is: "But that is how it is supposed to be!" Think about it for a second—if it were easy to find a strategy, don't you think others would have already found it and exploited it? There are thousands of traders and researchers out there every day looking for edges, mining data, and running tests. I guarantee you that all the easy strategies either no longer work or have been long ago discovered.

My good trader friend, who is a Commodity Trading Advisor (CTA), once told me that if he finds one new strategy a year to trade, he is a happy camper. He should be, since even one strategy, with proper money management, can make you rich. But to get that one strategy per year takes a lot of work. I frequently think of the strategy development process as a factory. At the receiving door of the factory are your trading ideas and strategies, the raw material you constantly need to run the factory. Your analysis tools, back-test software, and walk-forward algorithms are the machines in the factory. You, of course, are the skilled labor running the machines, monitoring the quality of the product. The output usually fills a big garbage bin right outside your factory, unfortunately. But what isn't thrown away as garbage is pure gold: your tradable strategy.

The factory metaphor is appropriate because strategy development is tough work. Factory workers are among the toughest people I know of, and that is how you need to be to develop strategies. I am always amazed by educators out there who gloss over strategy development. Instead, they focus on such nonsense as getting in touch with your feelings or writing everything down in a journal. Don't get me wrong—those items have their time and place in trading, but they are no substitute for having a strategy with an edge. If you don't have a good strategy, all the journaling in the world will not save you. As an aside, it is ironic, though, that many times "soft" skills such as psychology or journaling will be indispensable to a trader with an edge. You really do need both to succeed.

Since strategy development is a factory, you need to keep the factory running at all times. Here are some tips that I use or have used to keep things humming along:

- Any time you see a trading idea that intrigues you, write it down. Keep a list of ideas you want to test.
- Look for ideas anywhere. Trading books, magazines, and Internet forums are all good sources of raw ideas. I would not recommend taking an idea as presented and trading it exactly as is, though. I'd look to modify it first, and put your own unique spin on it.
- No idea is too silly, too stupid, or too dumb. The only dumb ideas are the ones you never test.
- If you make a big mistake in your coding, test it anyway. I'm a big proponent of "accidental" mistakes. Maybe they are really serendipitous creations of your subconscious. It sounds crazy, I realize, but I have successfully traded, with real money, more than one of my programming mistakes.
- If things are going bad, try the opposite. Buy when you think you should sell, and vice versa. Maybe something interesting will develop from your opposite idea.
- If you are a goal setter, try to test one to five strategies per week, at a minimum. It may take six months to a year of rigorous testing, but eventually you'll find something.
- If you run out of ideas, pull up random charts and just stare at them. You can even add an indicator or two. After staring a while, but not thinking, walk away from those charts and revisit them a few days or a week later. Then start to think: do you see anything in the relationship of the indicator to the chart or in the chart itself? Write down what you see, program it, and test it.
- Find other traders at roughly the same skill level as you. Offer to swap ideas or strategies. Take what these traders have, and then build strategies around their idea. I do this frequently with some of my fellow World Cup Championship of Futures Trading winners.

- Change your criteria. Maybe you are being too restrictive in what you consider acceptable. Open the door a bit to strategies that meet most, but not all, of your criteria. You can always tighten the criteria once your factory starts producing. If you loosen your criteria, don't necessarily trade the first strategy that passes. The point of that really is to give you more experience and confidence in developing "passing" systems. Then, tighten the criteria slowly, and ideally by then you'll be able to improve your systems to meet the tighter challenge. Keep repeating this, and eventually you'll have a strategy that meets your original criteria.

Isn't It All Just Optimizing?

After reading the next few chapters about my process, you might wonder to yourself, "Isn't strategy development just all about optimizing?" That is a fair question, and in a way, all strategy development is. If you start out with 10 million strategies to test, chances are good that at least a few will make it through whatever performance hurdles you put in place, and emerge after incubation as a potential winning strategy. At that point, a few possibilities emerge regarding the strategy:

- You have a true edge, and you will be profitable trading it for at least a little while, until the edge disappears.
- You have overoptimized and overfit the strategy to pass all the tests, but you have nothing that will really work in real time (this happens a lot to inexperienced developers).
- You have tested so many strategies that sooner or later one was bound to pass all your tests. You think this strategy has an edge, but it really doesn't. It is just random chance that you tried this particular strategy. Like a blind squirrel finding a nut once in a while, you simply got lucky!

Obviously, you are looking for strategies that fit into scenario 1. My process will help you avoid strategies in scenario 2 (although you can stretch the guidelines I give and end up overoptimizing). Scenario 3 is, in my mind, the scary alternative. With this scenario, you think you have an edge, but you really just got incredibly lucky. You'll never know for sure if this scenario applies. You could trade successfully for years with a lucky strategy, or you could lose money from day 1. You just never know what will happen.

My advice to avoid scenario 3—finding a "lucky" strategy:

- Have a logical basis for your strategy. Think about your entries and exits and how they can give you an edge. Use your brain to exploit what you see in the market.

- Keep things as simple as possible. Typically, more rules and conditions lead to a greater chance that the strategy will not work in the future.
- Don't just stick random indicators together until you find something that actually works. If you do enough of these tests, you will eventually find something, but it is probably just a lucky catch. There are products out there that use this technique, and they can be very useful if used correctly. Just don't expect the computer to do all your strategy thinking for you.
- Gently optimize whatever you do.

Sometimes I liken the strategy development process to fishing. If you want to catch a catfish, one way would be to get a huge net, capture thousands of fish, and then just pick your catfish out of the pile of fish stuck in the net. That would be comparable to randomly testing a million strategies, and finding a few seemingly great ones. A better way might be to think about what catfish like, and tailor your bait and fishing method to what you think might catch one. This is akin to developing an edge and then creating rules to exploit that edge. All things being equal, your chances of long-term success are probably better with the latter method.

In the chapters that follow, I detail the process I currently use to design and develop trading systems. Feel free to follow this exact process yourself, or just extract bits and pieces that apply to your situation. In either case, your development skills will improve by following what works for me.

PART III

DEVELOPING A STRATEGY

CHAPTER 9

Strategy Development—Goals and Objectives

When you go on a long trip in your car, do you have a map or global positioning system to guide you? Or do you just "wing it" and hope to find your destination by reading signs and going on instinct? Most people, of course, would have a map. It makes the journey so much easier. And it is the same with developing a trading system. You should know where you want to end up before you even start. It all starts with goals.

You've probably heard it a million times during your life: if you want to accomplish something, you must have goals. Unfortunately, after hearing it so many times, many people just list goals to say they did it, or list vague goals that have no way of being measured or realized.

To develop a good trading system, you absolutely need goals. To do that, I employ the SMART technique (Figure 9.1). SMART is a little mnemonic trick to assist in remembering all the important parts of a goal. Here is how I apply it to trading:

Specific. The goal must be specific, not vague. For example, it is not enough to say, "I want a trading system that makes me a lot of money" or "I want a trading system that has no risk." Such vague goals, besides being unrealistic, are just too general. How will you even know when you reach such a nebulous goal? The simple fact is that you won't know if you ever reach it.

Measurable. How will you know you've created a trading system that meets your goals unless the goal can be measured? That is the second key to a solid goal.

FIGURE 9.1 SMART Goals

At the end of the development process, you want to have a trading system with certain performance metrics, and compare them to the goals you set at the outset. It is a very simple concept, but you'd be amazed how many people develop goals that aren't measurable, such as "I want to create a trading system that makes my family proud." An admirable quality in a trading system, to be sure, but how do you measure this? Maybe if your teenage kids walk alongside you in a public place, rather than 10 feet in front or behind you, you'll know they are proud of you. But what if you don't have teenagers?

Attainable. The "A" in SMART stands for attainable. There is absolutely no sense in saying, "I need to develop a trading system that will provide 500 percent annual return with less than 2 percent maximum drawdown." That is not reality. You need to strive for a goal that is attainable. Otherwise, you will just become disappointed over and over, since you will be unable to create a trading system that meets such lofty goals. In the end, most people with unrealistic goals end up cutting corners by cheating in order to reach their goal. They'll produce an ultra-optimized back test, curve fit to the extreme, that shows them reaching their unrealistic goals. But as I've said before, "If it seems too good to be true, it probably is."

Relevant. If you set goals for developing a trading system that aren't relevant to the topic at hand, the whole goal exercise will be a waste of time. For example, let's say you hate creating trading systems and hate the whole development process. Is it even worthwhile for you to pursue creating trading systems? Meaning, is the whole process even worthwhile to you? If not, you should probably just quit right now. To be successful in this field, your heart and mind must be fully committed. Trust me, there are thousands of professional traders committed to the cause. In a fight between committed traders and noncommitted traders, who do you think will win?

Time bound. Creating a trading system takes time and consumes your free and working time, so having a time-based aspect to the goal is a great idea. It might be a certain amount of time you give yourself to create a strategy or a time limit for how long you'll spend evaluating a single idea. The idea will be to keep the process moving at all times. As you'll find out, it gets really difficult to find time and motivation to test new strategy ideas, especially when the last 100 ideas all failed.

Now that we have the framework for a goal, let's look at some examples:

"I will create a trading system that meets my performance objectives."

Specific? No. Measurable? Not as written. Attainable? Possibly. Relevant? Yes. Time bound? No. This kind of goal needs a lot of work.

"I will create a trading system in six months that meets my performance objectives."

Is this a SMART goal? Yes and no. The first part is specific and measurable ("create a trading system in six months"), but the phrase "meets performance objectives" is too vague. It can't be measured either. The beginning of the goal is very attainable—six months of hard work should yield a decent trading system, with subsequent systems developed even more quickly. It is also relevant and time bound. All in all it is a good goal, except for the last few words. Let's try to improve it.

"I will create a trading system in six months, one that trades the euro currency, returns an average of 50 percent per year, with a maximum drawdown of 30 percent, a winning percentage of 45 percent or higher, and follows all the steps in a well-defined development process."

Bingo! That goal meets all the requirements of a SMART goal. You can easily compare any system you create to those goals.

Once you have a SMART goal, and after you attempt to develop a few trading systems, you might find that what you felt were attainable goals are not that attainable. This usually hits people when they have annual returns and maximum drawdown listed in the goal. Sure, 100 percent annual returns is indeed possible (I am living proof!), but such returns are unrealistic if you also want a 10 percent maximum drawdown. Sometimes it is easy to see in advance that a goal is not attainable, but other times you'll learn this only by running through the development process.

In such cases, you'll want to turn your SMART goals into SMARTER goals. All that means is that after you try to reach the goal, if need be, you EVALUATE and REEVALUATE your goals. You adapt them to the situation at hand. This might seem to some like giving up—if your goal can't be reached, just lower the goal—but it can also improve your chances of succeeding and finding a good trading system. If you find yourself in a situation where your goals can never be met, you can either walk away from the process and find a new hobby or career, or you can evaluate and adjust your goals to something more relevant and attainable.

Like/Dislike	Does System Meet This?
LIKES:	
Trades e-minis only	
X% annual return, Y% max drawdown	
Calmar > Z, Sharpe > W	
No overnight exposure	
2 or fewer indicators	
100% mechanical (no discretionary trading)	
DISLIKES:	
More than 2 trades per day	
Adds to losing positions	

FIGURE 9.2 Sample Trading System "Wish List"

Your goal in developing a trading system should be only one or two sentences, enough to be SMART. But what about some of your wants and desires for a trading system? How do you handle them? They might not easily fit into your goal, but they are important nonetheless. Examples of this could be the market you trade, the time of day you trade, or any other feature you deem important.

To accommodate characteristics and traits I want in a trading system, but that are not important enough to include in the SMART goal, I create what I call a "wish list." It is as simple as it sounds; it is a checklist of features I want in my trading system.

What kinds of items can be in a wish list? Figure 9.2 gives an example of a checklist I once created. This was for a mini S&P futures (symbol ES) strategy I was trying to develop. They say that the strategy must fit your personality, and that is what I was attempting to do here. By detailing my likes and dislikes, and having them written down, it was easy for me to sketch out what my trading system should look like.

Of course, the longer the list of wishes, the tougher it will be to create a trading system. It will be very likely that you will not be able to satisfy all your wishes. That's okay, though—just like everything in life is a compromise, so it is in trading development. Compromising on your wish list forces you to determine what is really important, and then just keep those items. Things you thought were important maybe are not all that important. In the end, though, the more wishes you can meet with your strategy, the more likely you will trade it with confidence and resolution. This confidence and resolve, sooner or later, will really be of value to you.

CHAPTER 10

Trading Idea

Once you have firmly established goals, you are ready to start developing a trading system. At the end of the process, you'll have a trading system ready to test. To get to that point, however, you first have to address the following topics:

- Entry rules
- Exit rules
- Market selection
- Time frame/bar size
- Programming
- Data considerations

The important points in each of these areas are discussed in the next two chapters.

How Will You Enter a Market?

Entry rules are the easiest part of designing a trading system for most people. Think of all the trading articles, advertisements, and information you have seen recently. What is usually the focus? "80 percent winning signals!" "Unique neural network entry techniques!" "Never-fail indicators!" "A former rocket scientist develops a foolproof technique for finding winning stocks!" The list goes on and on. Most traders are obsessed with getting the proper entry. Solve that problem, and everything else is a piece of cake, or so they think. The entry lovers love to point to the stock market and say, "Look what would have happened if you had bought Microsoft way back when." These folks tend to ignore the drawdowns during the trade, as long as the entry was correct.

There is an even more fundamental reason, I believe, for entries being the focus of most traders. The time before entry is really the only time you feel in complete control. You tell the market, "Mr. Market, you must do this, that, and the other before I place a trade to enter. If you do not follow my rules, Mr. Market, I will not enter a trade. I am in charge here."That feels nice, as opposed to the time spent in a trade, where many times you hope and pray the market roller coaster will go your way!

Entries, of course, are just one piece of the trading strategy puzzle. For ages, people have argued that entries were the most important aspect of a system, or that entries were the least important part. Dr. Van Tharp did a study years ago with random entries, and created successful trading systems by carefully designing the exits. However, I'm sure some people have also created good systems with random exits.

In my experience, the importance of the entry is directly related to the time you spend in a trade. If you are a long-term swing trader, with trades lasting weeks to months, you don't need pinpoint accuracy on the entry. An entry a few days early or a few days late will probably not ruin the profitability of your strategy. If you are scalping, however, then entry becomes very important. An entry off by a tick or two could turn a winning system into a piece of garbage. Keep that in mind when you design your system. Know how exact your entry needs to be before you develop it.

Many people have trouble developing entry ideas, and that is a shame because entry ideas are all around us. I have a very good trader friend who uses magazine covers as part of his decision process. When he sees a few magazine covers talking about the upcoming drought or the shortage of physical gold, for example, he knows this might be a great time to enter the impacted markets—in the opposite direction, of course!

I provided some sources for entries in an earlier chapter, and I suggest you keep the list handy when you run out of inspiration. The key, once you have this list of ideas, is to turn them into solid entries that can be back tested. This is where discretion has no place. An algorithmic strategy, by definition, consists of an algorithm, a set of rules that define behavior. If your entry rules cannot be defined rigidly, then creating an algorithmic system is not appropriate.

Once you have your entry idea, you need to convert it to computer language. If you do not know how to program in your trading back-test software, you will likely have to hire someone to do the work for you. Before you do that, it is best to put the rule into what is called *pseudo code*. This is simply the entry instruction, given in plain English. Here is an example:

If close this bar is the highest close of last X bars, then buy next bar at market.

Converting to a language such as TradeStation's Easy Language would yield the following:

If close = highest (close, X) then buy next bar at market.

Creating pseudo code is a really important step, since it will help you clarify your entry rule, and help you identify any important variables that you want to optimize ("X" in the preceding example).

A few pointers on creating a good entry:

- *Keep it simple.* If you cannot explain the rule in plain English, you will have a tough time converting it to computer code, and chances are that what you program may not be what you really want.
- *Limit the number of input parameters.* If you have two or three conditions to your entry, it is easy to have 5, 10, or even more parameters you feel should be optimized. Remember, though, that for every parameter you optimize, the more you run the risk of overfitting your model. Keep it simple. I personally like to use only 1 or 2 optimizable parameters for my entries.
- *Try to think differently.* Moving average crossovers have been tested ad nauseum by professionals and amateurs alike. Try to develop an entry unlike any you've ever seen—one that very few others might have tried.
- *Use a single rule at first.* If you want an entry with multiple conditions, first start out with just one condition. Then, slowly add new conditions only if they significantly improve performance. You will likely find that many entry conditions you thought were important really were not.

How Will You Exit a Market?

Compared to entries, exits are the red-headed stepchildren of trading strategies. Most people, myself included from time to time, pay very little attention to exits. I suppose it has to do with the lack of control mentioned earlier, since during a trade Mr. Market is in control. It can also be uneasy for many people to think of different ways to escape a losing trade, since the whole point of trading is to have money making trades, right?

Exits, simply put, have a huge impact on overall profitability, and a trader really needs to spend a great deal of time preparing proper exits. Just as with entries, there are many different ways to exit. The most common ways are listed below:

- *Stop and reverse.* Your entry signal for a new position also becomes your exit signal for your existing position. Many people like to be in the market at all times, and this method accomplishes just that.
- *Technical-based exits.* Support/resistance lines, moving averages, candlestick patterns, and the like can all be formed into viable exit rules. The key with using such rules is to make sure they coordinate with the entry rules. Otherwise, exits could trigger immediately after entries triggered.

- *Breakeven stops.* Many people swear by a breakeven stop, where as soon as practical, you move the stop-loss to a breakeven level. This may indeed be useful for the psyche of discretionary traders or for those obsessed with "winning," who don't want to see a winning trade turn into a loser. In my experience, though, breakeven stops always seem to limit profit potential, since they typically exit on a retracement, with the market then resuming its earlier trend.
- *Stop-losses.* Some people swear *by* stop-losses, and some people swear *at* stop-losses. I look at it this way: if a stop-loss, even one far away from your entry, significantly reduces your strategy's performance, perhaps your entry signal is the real problem. Stop-losses, when coupled with good entries, can help prevent catastrophe. Can you imagine trading the mini S&P, without a stop, right before a terrorist attack? True, you can get excessive slippage with stop-losses, but barring a market shutdown, at least you can get out, and live to trade another day. Stop-losses can be dollar based, chart based (i.e., exit near support/resistance), or based on parameters such as average true range. A simple stop-loss can become very complicated, indeed.
- *Profit targets.* The old adage "let your profits run" is a tried-and-true trading malapropism. But letting profits run is not always the optimum way to trade. Sometimes it is better to hit a target, profit based or chart based, and then set up for the next entry signal. I tend to test with profit targets, but I also allow for a huge profit on the upper end. Many times, this becomes the best alternative.
- *Trailing stops.* As the market rises in your favor, you keep a certain percentage of the profit. This really is a moving stop-loss, but instead of the stop leading to a loss, it leads to a smaller profit. The one problem with trailing stops is that they can have many parameters that need optimization. The extra parameters may not be worth the effort in live trading, although they will certainly make a back test look better.

What Markets Will You Trade?

One of the toughest decisions you will make when designing your system is which market or markets to trade. There are really two schools of thought in this area, and I'll describe the advantages and disadvantages of each.

The first method is to design a system for all markets. This would be a "one size fits all" approach, where the rules for the system never change as you move from market to market. The parameters, though, could be tuned (or not) for each market. The advantage to this approach is that if one single strategy works well on all markets, then it likely has a high degree of robustness. This may make the system less vulnerable to market changes, since the system has likely seen many types of different markets across the tested history. The big disadvantage to such an approach is that development becomes infinitely more difficult. Designing a system for one market is tough enough. If you now demand that the system work for many markets, you will struggle to find an acceptable strategy. In such situations, developers typically do one of two things: (1) they relax their acceptance criteria, or (2) they test on all markets, and then select the best 5 to 10 performers to trade.

Realize that both of these compromises, while likely necessary to create a multi-market system, are very bad. Relaxing acceptance criteria will lead you to abandon the system early, as you realize with real money that the strategy does not meet your initial objectives. Testing on multiple markets, and then "cherry picking" the best performers to trade, is just another, albeit sneaky, way of optimizing.

Creating a strategy for one particular market is the other popular approach. One advantage to this method is that it can be customized to the characteristics of the market. For example, it is known that currencies tend to trend well, so maybe a breakout-type system is appropriate. Or, for the equity markets, a mean-reverting strategy with a long bias might be best. Another advantage is that, as mentioned earlier, it is always easier to create a system for one market than for multiple markets. That doesn't mean it is a better system, though; it just means it is easier to create. The disadvantage to creating a single-market system is that when you create a system knowing the characteristics of the market, you are assuming those characteristics will remain the same forever. While that may be true, what if it isn't? How will your trend-following currency system perform when currencies, for whatever reason, become mean-reverting markets?

As you can see, there are valid points for and against each approach to market selection. I personally have used both over the years. When I finished first or second in the World Cup Championship of Futures Trading three straight years, I used a "one size fits all" system, traded on roughly a half-dozen to a dozen markets. That worked well. Currently, about half of the systems I trade are of this variety. I also like single-market systems, not only because they are easier to create, but also because I can mix and match them for diversification. In any given year, some of these systems will underperform, some will be around breakeven, and some will outperform. Having a multitude of single-market approaches makes this more manageable, especially when strategies have to be retired.

What Type of System Do You Want?

Whenever I begin looking at a new strategy, I almost always see if it can be made into a day-trading strategy. I define "day trading" as in and out of a trade, or multiple trades, in a single session. There are some nice benefits to such a strategy:

- No overnight risk from unexpected events, since you are flat.
- Reduced margin requirements, making it easier to trade with large size (although most people should not be doing this, as the higher leverage can lead to a greater chance of disaster).

- A "working job"–type feeling. You fire up the computer in the morning, trade a while, make your daily nut, turn off the computer, and go home and play with your kids the rest of the day—a very satisfying way to live.

Usually, when I start development, I select short time frame bars (one- to five-minute), throw in the "set exit on close" statement to exit at the end of the day, and jump into development. Nine times out of 10, though, the strategy fails. Regardless of the entry idea (trend, countertrend, whatever) and exit scheme (fixed stops, moving stops, breakeven stops, profit targets, etc.), nothing ever seems to work consistently.

Inevitably, if I like the strategy idea, I'll then open up the time frame to 60-minute bars, 240-minute bars, daily bars. I want to see if my idea has any validity at all. What almost always happens? Performance gets better! Maybe the performance still doesn't meet my goals, but the performance on a daily chart is almost always better than on a 1-minute chart. I've seen it enough times to realize it is more than a coincidence. The question then becomes: why do I see this behavior? Here's what I have come up with:

- Number of trades and trading costs. Let's say I have a daily bar strategy that trades 1 time per month, or once every 20 bars. That will cost me roughly $25 in trading costs. If I go down to 1-minute bars, the same strategy might trade 10 times per day (once every 120 bars), leading to $250 in trading costs. That is a huge difference in costs that must be overcome. Add in the fact that 1-minute moves are smaller than daily moves, and it gets even harder.

- There seems to be more randomness in the data as you go to smaller time frame bars. Look at a 1-minute chart of the mini S&P futures (symbol ES) and most days it is just narrow range noise. It is harder to find the true price path when the random noise level is high. Daily bars, as an alternative, seem to have more trends. Of course, where I see random noise in data could just be due to other biases I have floating around in my brain.

- Entry and exits become a much more important part of the system when you have small stops and targets, as most day-trading systems are set up to be. So I must have really great entries and exits, ones with very good edges. But the better the entry, the harder it is to find during development. Plus, miss the entry by a tick, and you may lose a good percentage of your profit. If you are swing trading with daily bars, a tick or two at entry probably won't mean as much, relative to overall size of an average trade.

- With tick charts or 1- to 5-minute charts, think about who you are trading against. Many times, it is high-frequency trading firms, which probably have better entries than you and have a speed advantage over you. I feel that the impact of the pros is less noticeable at higher time frames, although I realize many pros trade daily bars, too.

- With most strategies, as I mentioned before, I find the fewer trades there are, the better. This could be due to trading costs, but it also could be due to a very bad reason: maybe you think you have an edge, but with fewer trades, the statistical confidence that you have an edge is a lot lower. Put another way, if I had 2 strategies that averaged a $50 profit per trade, and one had 100 trades over the past 10 years, and another had 1,000, I'd always pick the 1,000-trade strategy (so would every rational person). But the reality is that the 100-trade strategies are a lot easier to find—maybe because they aren't really edges at all, but just temporarily lucky strategies?

I really wish that all my strategies were day-trading-type strategies. In actuality, probably 9 out of 10 are the exact opposite. My best strategy over the past four or five years holds a position for weeks to months—definitely not a day-trading approach.

What Time Frame/Bar Size Will You Trade?

Almost as important as the market you will trade is the time frame(s) you select. For most people who look at bar charts, this is simply the length of time for each bar. Of course, strategies will perform radically differently on different time frames, so it is best to select a time frame that meets your objectives. Do you want to be in and out quickly? Maybe a 1-minute or a tick-based chart is best. Do you prefer long-term swing trading? If so, maybe a daily or even weekly time frame is what you need. The point is to select a time frame that matches your interest.

One important factor to realize with time frame is that typically shorter time frames lead to more trades. If you have small transaction costs, with many quick trades, this is terrific—just witness the success of all the high-frequency trading firms. Even a small edge can yield big profits when repeated enough times. But, for most of us retail traders, higher transactions costs are just part of the game, making quick strategies that much tougher to succeed with.

When settling on a time size for a bar, an approach that many developers use is what I call *time frame contraction and dilation*. The concept is to test a strategy with a 10-minute time frame. If it is successful, the thinking goes, then testing on a 9-minute bar and an 11-minute bar should also be profitable. One minute either way should not destroy the strategy, and good performance in these contraction and dilated periods suggests robustness.

I personally have had little success with this approach, and I believe there are two reasons for it. First, by changing the time length of a bar, over the course of a day there are now a different number of bars to evaluate. In the preceding example, changing a 10-minute bar by 1 minute leads to 9 percent more bars or fewer bars. This can heavily influence the performance of indicators you may employ. The other issue I have with this approach is that many traders make their decisions on the close of a standard period bar. Think of all the people trading off charts, most of them using standard time periods of 5, 10, 15, or more minutes. If your system is trading at a different time, your results can vary widely from the results with a standard (i.e., 10-minute) bar.

Putting my personal objections aside, if you have success with 9-, 10-, and 11-minute charts, then I'd agree that your system has robustness in it. It would give me extra confidence. At the same time, though, if 10-minute performance was good, but 9- and 11-minute performances were awful, I would not necessarily throw out the baby with the bathwater.

If you decide to test with tick charts, one important consideration with bar size and time frame is the amount of historical data available. I discuss the question "how much data to use" in a later section, but for now realize that many data vendors provide only six months of data. This can also be an issue with short time frame bars (1- to 5-minute), where orders are triggered intrabar. Tick data are also important for specialty bars, such as point-and-figure charts, Kase bars, Renko bars, and so on. The important point is that if you rely on tick charts or tick data, think carefully about the implications of limited historical data before you test.

One final important consideration involves the daily settlement price and the daily last price traded, which is important if you are using daily bars. "What is the problem," you ask, "aren't closing/settlement prices and the last price traded the same thing?" In some markets, yes, and in some markets no. Plus, the meaning of these terms has changed with the advent of 24-hour trading. The gold market is a good example. Back in the days when gold was only pit traded (which may easily be part of your historical testing period), the market closed at 1:30 P.M. Eastern time, and the last trade of the day was usually very close, but not necessarily identical to, the exchange published settlement price. Now, however, the gold market trades electronically, and it trades until 5:00 P.M. Eastern time. Unfortunately, the exchange settlement price is derived from the trading that occurs from 1:28 to 1:30 P.M. You can imagine how the price at 1:29 P.M., the settlement time, can vary widely from the last price traded at 5:00 P.M. The price action on Wednesday, September 18, 2013, is a great example, as shown in Figure 10.1. A Federal Reserve announcement at 2:00 P.M., after the settlement price had been established, roiled the markets. The settlement price and the last traded price were dramatically different!

Data vendors differ on how they treat settlement prices and last traded prices. As of the time of this writing, TradeStation, for example, uses the exchange settlement as the closing price for daily and weekly bars. For X minute bars, the close of the last bar of the day is also the last traded price. Kinetick, a provider for NinjaTrader, follows the same approach. Another popular data vendor, CQG, however, uses the last price traded as its daily bar close.

How can this be a problem in your testing? Well, say, for example, you are testing with daily bars, and your strategy uses the instruction "sell the bar at close." Your strategy

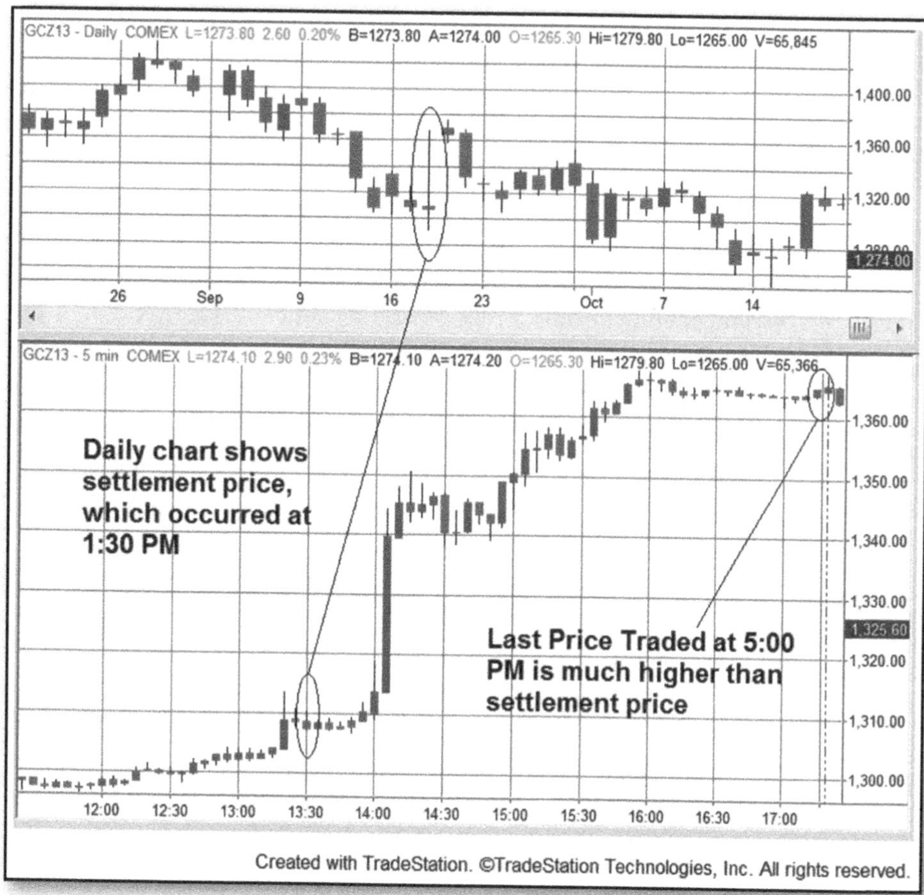

FIGURE 10.1 Don't Assume that Settlement Price = Last Price Traded

dutifully executes the command at 4:59 P.M., and you are filled. But later, when the exchange settlement price is applied to the data, the strategy will think you were filled at the settlement price (which is now the daily bar closing price), but you were actually filled near the last traded price. This is just one of the ways back-test results can fool you.

How Will You Program the Strategy?

Once you have your basic entry and exit rules thought out; you have selected a market, time frame, and bar size to test; and you have obtained the desired amount of historical data, it is time to put together your strategy for testing. The question for most people at this point is "can I program the strategy myself?" The answer for a true do-it-yourselfer is undoubtedly "yes." But if you have never programmed before in the language of your strategy-testing software, you might find this to be a daunting task. Here are a few tips that might help you out.

If you are completely clueless about computer programming, and you have no desire to learn how to do it, your programming tasks are best left in the hands of professionals. You can hire an expert at an hourly rate or even a team of experts so that no one developer knows all your trading secrets. The drawback here is that every time you need a code change, even a small one, you will have to wait for the developer to do it, and you'll likely be charged extra for the privilege. The extra time and cost associated with changes, updates, enhancements, and the like can add up quickly. If you still feel that a programmer is the right choice, you can find them at various trading forums, or by contacting your software vendor.

An alternative is to partner with a programming expert, ideally someone who will be interested in trading the finished project. You won't have to worry about your partner's stealing your idea, and the collaboration can lead to far more profitable systems. I have done this before, usually as the programming expert, and it is really satisfying when it works. The problem is in finding people you can trust enough to help you.

My preferred and recommended approach is that you should program everything by yourself. All the trading software packages out there have classes, books, online tutorials, and sample strategies to help you develop your skills. By going this route, you will not have to worry about people stealing your "secret sauce." Plus, as you learn the programming aspect, you will get more familiar with the idiosyncrasies of the back-test engine. This is really important when results look too good to be true. Once you know the software and programming well enough, you'll never have to wonder if you have only fooled the back-test engine but not the real world.

CHAPTER 11

Let's Talk about Data

With the entry, exit, market, and time frame/bar length decided, now comes one of the most important, most underappreciated, yet least understood aspects of testing: market data. People take data for granted, and that can be a big mistake. I've seen huge differences in strategy performance just due to different data sources. I'll make the grand assumption that your data are clean, without bad data points, missing data, and so on. Of course, that is not the case at all, practically regardless of vendor. But most people understand that data may have errors; what most do not understand is the impact behind the answers to these data-related questions:

- How much data should you use?
- Should you use pit data or electronic data?
- Should you use continuous contract data?
- Did the advent of electronic trading impact market data?
- How do you test with foreign exchange (forex) data?

Now, before you start testing, is the time to look at all these issues, and make some decisions. To go back and retest with different a data structure typically means you will be using tainted data, and that is not good.

How Much?

If you are like me, you've probably done the "eyeball" test more than a few times. You look at a chart and, knowing your entry and exit criteria, perform a quick test of the past few days or weeks of data. After a few trades, if you see a lot of profit, you get excited and venture into more in-depth testing. If you have losses, you either abandon the strategy or tweak it a bit and try again.

Hopefully, you realize the futility of such a simple test. Not enough trades, not enough market conditions, just not enough of anything to make an informed decision—period. To attain long-term success, you must look at more data than this.

So what is an acceptable amount of data? When I am asked this question, I almost always reply, "As much as possible." More data provides more market conditions—more bull markets, more bear markets, more flat markets. It also provides more quiet periods and more volatile periods. As you make more trades, and your system remains profitable, it becomes less and less likely that the results were due to just chance. Think of a coin flip. If you flip it once, chances are 50/50 that it will be heads. If you flip a coin 10 times, the chances of heads' coming up at least once is quite good. Flip the coin 100 times, and you are practically guaranteed that heads will appear at least once. More flips leads to more certainty, just as more trades leads to more confidence.

For daily bar systems, which tend to be swing systems (trades lasting days to weeks), I find that 10 years of data is a good compromise. It allows your strategy to see many different market conditions and works well with walk-forward testing (which requires some initialization time).

For intraday or short-term systems, I also like using 10 years of data. Practical considerations, though, such as the introduction of electronic data, may make this a difficult task. So, in many cases I will use only 5 years of data, realizing that my results may not be as robust as a 10-year tested system.

For some people, 5 to 10 years of data is too long a time period to test, or the data are not available. In such cases, I recommend the following rules of thumb: for each rule and parameter you have in your strategy, have at least 30 to 100 trades. As an example, consider a strategy with two entry conditions, and two exit conditions. For such a system, I'd like to see 120 to 400 trades. Anything less than this might be acceptable but also runs the risk of the strategy's being "matched" or fitted to the data.

The drawback to using as much data as possible is that it makes development much tougher. Let's face it—at best, most trading systems out there are probably breakeven before commissions and slippage. This means the longer you test it, the more likely it is that gross profits will revert back to zero. I'm sure you witnessed this before, when a strategy has fantastic performance in a one-, three-, or six-month period, only to give it all back in the next period. So, in the end, ask yourself if you want a long-running positive system, or do you want a great performer over a short period of time? The former is much tougher to find, and the latter is much more likely to lead to real-time losses.

Pit or Electronic Data?

Back in the old days of pit trading, knowing what data to use was easy—just use the pit data because that was all there was! Today, with electronic data taking over, there are multiple options:

- Pit data only
- Electronic data only
- Pit and electronic data together
- Data during traditional pit times only
- Data during all hours
- Data during day session/evening session

The choice for data going forward might be easy—electronic data are the best because that is where the volume currently is, but what do you do when you are historically testing a strategy?

I'll give you a simple example to highlight the dilemma. Let's say you are trading gold, and you want to use 20 years (excellent choice!) of data, with 60-minute bars. Twenty years ago, the pit was the only data source, so you have to use that. In a daily pit session, there were probably six to eight bars roughly (since pit trading hours over the years changed, the number of 60-minute bars per day will change, too). For your strategy, let's say you use a 14-period moving average. This will typically represent two trading days.

Now, fast-forward to today's electronic markets. Today's markets trade for roughly 23 hours per day. If you still use a 14-period moving average, that will only equate to a half trading day, instead of the previous two trading days. Do you think that can radically influence your historical tests? It sure can!

How do you handle this? Typically, I rely heavily on daily data, especially the daily settlement prices. Pit and electronic settlements are identical. I do not like using daily highs and lows, since the average range between pit high and low will usually be less than electronic day high and low. If this sounds confusing, just think of an overnight price shock that lasts for an hour before reverting to the previous price level. In the old pit days, such a shock would never have shown up in the data, since it happened overnight. For electronic data, though, the daily high would include this price shock. Therefore, your strategy may perform quite a bit differently in the old days versus today's market.

One trick that helps make all the data the same is to select a standard daily session time, and apply it to your complete historical database. For currencies, for example, the pit used to be open from 8:20 A.M. to 3:00 P.M. Eastern time. To keep this time intact in the electronic era, I simply create a special "currency pit" session from 8:20 A.M. to 3:00 P.M. for all the historical data. Then all my data are consistent.

With all the available options with data, I highly recommend you take time and think about the data you are using. Making sure it is consistent throughout your test history is definitely the best way to test. It may not be that easy to create those data, though.

Continuous Contracts

One concept that stymies most junior system developers is the use of continuous contracts in futures market testing. Continuous contracts are needed because each futures contract has a limited life, and continuous contracts create a never-ending data stream. The concept is simple—just artificially stitch together expiring futures contracts to create one continuous data stream—but the implementation path is peppered with pitfalls, just waiting to catch the unwary. I'll discuss these pitfalls for the three major techniques of futures data selection.

The purest way to test with futures data is just to use the raw contract data. Then you don't have to worry about continuous contracts at all. The problem is that most trading software is not set up to easily accomplish this. Let's say, for example, that you want to test a strategy on the euro currency. If you were testing in 2013, from January 1 to approximately March 15, you would use the March contract, 6EH13. From March 15 to June 15, you'd use the June contract, 6EM13. In this way, you'd progress through all the years of your data. But you'd have some problems in testing this way. First, you'd have to put in logic to (1) determine the proper end date for each contract (i.e., before first notice day or last trading day, whichever comes first) and (2) "roll over" the current position from the current contract to the new contract. Certainly, this could be accomplished, but it would require some detailed programming. The bigger issue is if you wanted to optimize the strategy over all these contracts. Most trading software requires an optimization on one chart of data. With multiple contracts of data, you cannot optimize without doing it manually, a tedious and painstaking process.

To get around these limitations of testing with the individual contracts, many people splice the contract data together in a continuous contract. There are two primary (and numerous less popular) ways to create a continuous contract, and, of course, both have some serious pitfalls. The first type of continuous contract is a nonadjusted continuous contract. Using the preceding example, on March 15 the contract data would switch from March to June. The nice thing about this method is that the original data are preserved—no adjustments have been made to the data. The pitfall with these data is that, at rollover, rarely if ever will the two contracts be the exact same price. Frequently, the front month will have a significant discount or premium to the next month. An example of this is shown in Figure 11.1. Using these data as is will create false signals and false profits and losses. Assume you are long November soybeans, and then you roll over to the May soybeans. With a spread of 38 points, with an unadjusted continuous contract, a trading strategy will think that gap is real and that you profited from it. The reality, though, is that you would not actually benefit from the gap. The gap exists only because the contract month has changed.

Many people get around this artificial gap by using what is called a *back-adjusted contract*. With this type of contract, the gaps are subtracted out, and all previous data

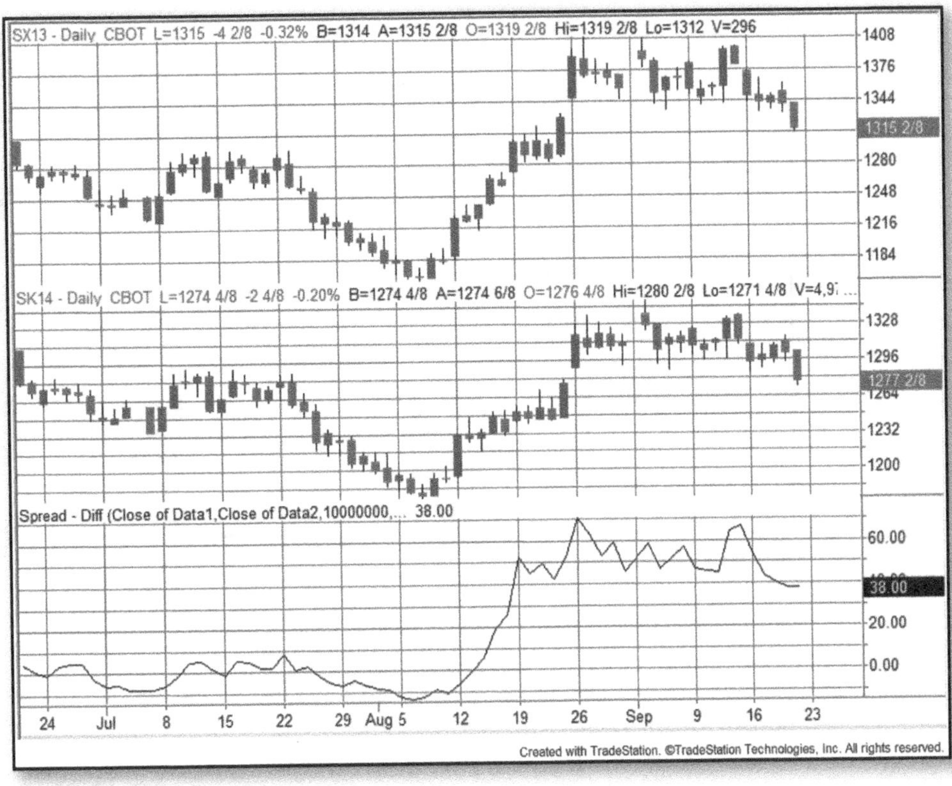

FIGURE 11.1 Contract Prices Will Be Different for Different Months

are adjusted appropriately. An example would be as follows: Suppose on March 15, June euro closes at 1.3512, and March euro closes at 1.3516, a difference of .0004. To remove this gap of .0004, all data from March and before must have .0004 added to it. This will remove the gap from all data, and provide a nice continuous data stream. It seems like the ideal solution.

Of course, no method is perfect, and this technique has a couple of problems, one of which practically no one talks about, at least that I've ever seen. The first problem is that constantly accounting for gaps at every rollover leads to a situation where the historical data actually become negative. An example of this is shown in Figure 11.2. Clearly, crude oil never had a negative price, but that is what the continuous contract shows and what your strategy will test with. Although the continuous data may seem strange (don't show your friends your "Holy Grail" trading system with these market data, since they'll think you are crazy for testing with negative prices!), the results are accurate, provided you do not fall victim to the second pitfall.

The second pitfall with continuous back-adjusted contracts is also the issue most likely to lead to invalid trading results. In a nutshell, you cannot have any indicators

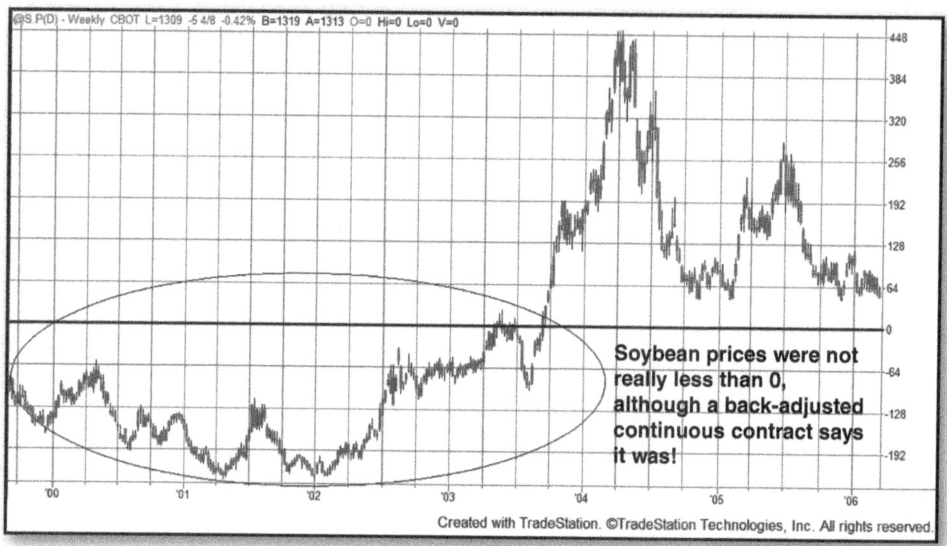

FIGURE 11.2 Back-Adjusted Continuous Contracts Can Have Negative Prices

that divide or multiply prices when you use back-adjusted contracts. An example best shows the point:

Suppose you have a strategy that uses the percentage change in day-to-day close, $close_i/close_{i-1}$. On March 10, you are using the March contract, and the close is 1.3500. The previous day close is 1.3420. The percentage change calculation is then 1.3500/1.3420 = 1.00596.

Fast-forward to March 20, when the June contract is the front contract. When you performed the continuous contract back adjusting, .0030 was added to it. This is an extreme amount for rollover adjustment, just to prove my point. Thus, now the March 10 close is 1.353, the previous day close is 1.345, and the ratio is now 1.353/1.345 = 1.00595. The ratio for the same date has changed! Plus, it will change again at every rollover in the future. This means that when you back test a strategy with ratios, your back-test signals will be different than real-time signals. The difference may not be much, but it will certainly be there. The question will then be "can you rely on performance histories that you know will change in the future?"

If this seems like a subtle distinction, just imagine what happens when the price data approach zero, the other known pitfall on back-adjusted data. Dividing by zero or a number close to zero will lead to a huge result! Clearly, that would never happen in real time—unless, of course, the actual price of the instrument in question went to zero. Just do not count on that ever happening!

The only way around this pitfall is to take special care that division or multiplication is not used with price data in back-adjusted continuous contracts. Both ratios of prices and percentage changes in prices are no-nos. If you choose not to follow this rule, do not be surprised when (1) your historical performance results change over time and (2) that your historical results and future results do not match.

The Impact of Electronic Markets

Many trading system developers test strategies only on electronic data. They ignore any pit data, so their strategies typically only test for the past few years. Their reasoning is that the markets fundamentally changed when electronic markets came on the scene, so strategies that work now don't necessarily have to work in the long-forgotten pit era. To that argument, I both agree and disagree.

Electronic markets have undoubtedly changed the futures markets. Without a pit full of traders, the whole dynamic of pricing has been altered. In fact, many former pit traders, who made a very good living while on the floor, struggled mightily when they moved to electronic trading. Most were trying to trade as they did on the floor, and the market had changed enough that those techniques were no longer profitable. Add in today's high-frequency trading firms, and the short-term market is certainly different than the old pit trading days.

On a longer-term scale, though, almost all commodities are dictated by the law of supply and demand. The venue for trading—electronic, pit, or a combination of the two—doesn't have a long-term impact. It doesn't make sense to think that high-frequency traders, who are in a trade for only a few seconds, have an impact on the price two or three months from now.

With those contrasting views in mind, I still use pit-traded data, and the history they provide, for my longer-term swing-trading development. That way, my strategy is able to experience more market conditions. If a strategy I develop for soybeans works well in the 1990s, 2000s, and 2010s, I am more confident and impressed with the system. Some people would even go back to the 1970s and 1980s! For shorter-term systems, especially intraday ones, using only the electronic data may make sense. If it also works on pit data, that is great, but I probably would not make it a requirement.

Testing with Forex Data

If you are testing a forex system, there are two major concerns you need to be aware of. The first issue is that not all forex data are the same. In fact, since the forex is decentralized, there is no official price stream like there is for futures markets. That means that each broker will have its own unique price data set. Of course, if you back test with the same data source that you will use going forward, then there is no issue.

But if you test with data from broker A, and then want to trade it live with broker B, the system will now have different data to deal with. In that case, you can basically toss all your back tests out the window, as they are no longer valid. Depending on the data differences, your results might be better, and they might be worse. The point is, though, that you have invalidated all your testing by changing data sources.

The second issue with testing forex data is in the types of orders you use. If you are testing your system with forex data, you really need to be careful with how your strategy places orders. Because of the issue I show later, I only use market orders for entry and exits. My forex strategies never have limit or stop orders in them. Of course, I always add the spread cost into the final profit/loss on each trade, but by using market orders, I never have to worry about "phantom" fills.

What is the pitfall to using limit and/or stop orders with forex data? In futures markets, there is one price data stream, which always represents the traded price. With forex, however, there is both a bid data stream and an ask data stream. The difference between these two data streams is the current spread, which is typically a few pips. By definition, you can only buy at the ask and sell at the bid.

The problem with testing a trading strategy with forex data is that the data stream shown on the chart is typically the bid data stream. Although you could alternatively show the ask data stream (if available), most trading software back-test engines can use only one to calculate trade results. If your trading software can calculate fills using bid and ask data simultaneously, you may not encounter this issue. For example, non-object-oriented TradeStation can only test with bid *or* ask data. MultiCharts, on the other hand, can test with both bid *and* ask data. It is a good idea to check your software first, though, before assuming this is not a potential issue for you. If it is a potential issue for you, here is an example of how it could be a problem:

Suppose you are trading the EURUSD forex pair. The current price is 1.3502/1.3505 (I am using an unrealistically high three-pip spread for this example, but the principle holds for even smaller spreads). That means the bid is at 1.3502, and the ask is at 1.3505. Remember, you can buy at the ask but not below, and you can sell at the bid but not above. Let's also assume your trading software shows you the bid data, so currently it shows 1.3502.

For this example, your strategy places an order to buy at 1.3500. Shortly after your order, the price drops to 1.3499/1.3502. Since the price on the chart is now 1.3499, and your buy price is 1.3500, the software strategy engine thinks you were filled at 1.3500. It thinks you are currently long, but the ask price only hit 1.3502, so in real life you would never be filled.

"Big deal!" you might say. "How often can this possibly happen?" Well, it will never happen for losing trades, since for losers the price will keep falling and you will get filled in real life, just as your back-test engine got filled. But for winning trades that turn profitable before the ask price hits 1.3500, you will never get filled. Depending on your trading methodology, it could lead to a huge discrepancy between back-test engine results and real-world results. At the very least, your back-test report will *always* be on the optimistic side. Since you use that information to develop your strategy, you could be basing your trading decisions on some very suspect results. Although the example I presented is for limit orders, the same type of situation occurs with stop orders. You will have stops filled at prices that never show up on the bid data chart.

To get around this issue, you cannot just add slippage to each trade like you can with futures. This is because the bid/ask problem is not a situation of slightly worse fills—it is a case of fills or no fills. Or your software platform may offer advanced order techniques and methods (TradeStation refers to the method as "price series providers"). The key is to be able to back test the same way you trade live. That is precisely why I use market orders for all my forex strategies. Since I use orders such as "sell next bar at market," I can have some losses that are much bigger than a stop-loss would be, and that is the big disadvantage of market orders. Just imagine, for example, how much the price could change in a five-minute bar around a Federal Reserve announcement. In the long run, though, I know market orders will always be filled, and they back test the same, after accounting for the spread, as they trade in live accounts. Therefore, I have found this situation to be acceptable, since it provides back-test results that match real market fills fairly well.

Summary

As you can see, the issues behind market data are much more complex than the trading software leads you to believe. It is critical that you put in the time and effort up front to examine and understand the market data you are using. Utilizing the wrong data, or using the right data incorrectly, can lead to completely bogus test results. In most cases, unfortunately, you will not even realize there is an issue at all. I recommend that you spend as much time in the beginning reviewing your market data as you do in formulating your entry and exit criteria.

CHAPTER 12

Limited Testing

At this point, I'll assume you have the strategy coded, debugged, and ready to test. Unfortunately, when they get to this step, many traders will just test the strategy over the whole market history that they are interested in and see how profitable the strategy is. Some will go a step beyond this and actually run thousands or even millions of optimization iterations as part of this. What better way to see how good strategy can be than by running it to its extreme?

As you may have guessed, I am firmly against running these kinds of comprehensive tests. These tests may lead to a few great-looking optimized back tests but will almost always fail in real-time trading. Since successful real-time trading is the goal, shouldn't that be our success criteria, rather than a nice-looking back test?

The other major problem with testing on all the data is that once you test the data, you "burn" it. This means that any subsequent retests will be just a bit more curve fit, a bit more optimized. Think about it: You run strategy A over all your data. It looks good, but not great. You make a few minor tweaks and rule changes to your strategy and then test the new strategy B. Now, it yields much better results. You are ecstatic. But do you realize you just optimized? No, you did not optimize in the sense of running strategy A with optimized parameters, which is how most trading software describes optimization. But you certainly did optimize, as you tested both strategy A and strategy B, and picked the best one. Even though in this case strategy B has a better back test than strategy A, I'd believe the results of strategy A more (unless strategy B is much, much better than A), since A was run with untouched data.

Theoretically, you should run a strategy on a set of data one time, and one time only. If it works, great, but if it doesn't work, you should just move on to the next data set or instrument. That original data are tainted by your testing, to a degree. This is the point where theory and practice deviate. In actual practice, you will eventually test multiple strategies over the same data, maybe not right away, but eventually it is inevitable. That is why you need to be careful. In my testing, I like to follow the teachings of Don Juan described in the book *Journey to Itxlan: The Lessons of Don Juan* (Simon & Schuster, 1972): "He taps it lightly, stays for as long as he needs to, and then swiftly moves away leaving hardly a mark."

If you treat the data as fragile, you are more likely to avoid this issue. Treat your data with utmost care!

Since testing with all the data is a no-no, what is a reasonable and acceptable way to test a strategy? On one hand, you want to see if the core idea you developed has any merit to it; but on the other hand, you want the ability to add or change rules to the strategy, without falling victim to curve fitting or hindsight bias. Also, you want to leave as much data in your dataset untouched as possible, since this will create a better and more realistic walk-forward test (walk-forward testing will be discussed in the next chapter).

Given all these competing forces, I have found it best to do preliminary testing on a chunk of historical data, but not the whole data set. For example, if I have 10 years of data for my full test, I will do the preliminary limited testing described below on one or two years' worth of data. I try to use as little as possible, while still getting enough trades to be statistically meaningful. I will try to take the two years of data at random, not using the same data all the time or favoring any particular years.

Some traders advocate testing first on the "most interesting" data. For most commodities and futures, that would be the 2007–2009 time frame, when the world markets nearly collapsed. Their point is that if a system performs badly at this time, it will likely perform poorly at the next market shock. While I understand their approach, I respectfully disagree. I would try to avoid preliminary testing during the financial crisis, since it may lead me to a system that performs well only during severe shocks and panics. While a system such as this might be nice at those times, I'd fear that the system would lose a lot more during the more prevalent "normal" times.

If I take my two-year chunk of data and adhere to the following process, I'll end up fairly certain whether my idea has any merit. The objective at the limited testing phase isn't to determine if a system is tradable; rather, it is used as a hurdle to see if the trading system has any potential. Frequently, I have trading strategies that survive the limited two-year test but later fail the more rigorous tests. Only infrequently does the reverse occur, where I dismiss a strategy because of the limited results, and it turns out later to be a fantastic strategy.

Entry Testing

The first thing I usually want to know when testing a trading system is whether the entry has any usefulness. Many times, what looks like a good entry appears that way only because of the exits. Frequently it is difficult to know the true impact of entries when tested as a whole system.

When I evaluate entries by themselves, I typically perform the analysis three ways:

- Fixed-stop and target exit
- Fixed-bar exit
- Random exit

Fixed-Stop and Target Exit

For the fixed-stop and target exit test, I simply choose a set stop-loss and profit target that is appropriate for the instrument and time frame I am trading. For a swing-type system lasting a few days, $500 to $1,500 is a reasonable amount for a stop-loss. Similarly, I set an appropriate profit target. All things being equal, if you set the stop and target to the same dollar amount, before commissions and slippage you should prevail on 50 percent of your trades, assuming that your entry is no better than random. Using set dollar amounts for stop and profit, I simply create a strategy with my entry signal, set stop-loss, and set profit target.

Fixed-Bar Exit

For the fixed-bar exit test, I create an exit condition that closes the trade after X number of bars pass. The idea behind this is that most good trades show profit right away and could be exited with a profit almost immediately. If your entries don't show profit until 10 or more bars, for example, perhaps your entry is too early and should be delayed. This test really helps to check if the entry signal gets you going in the correct direction.

Random Exit

For the random exit test, I typically use this as part of the "monkey test" process, described later. However, sometimes I use it right at the beginning of testing. The concept is based on eliminating the impact of any exit and just seeing the ability of the entry to generate winning trades. If an entry is always profitable with a randomly generated exit, then chances are much better that there is an edge there.

Entry Evaluation Criteria

For each of the three test techniques just described, there are a few ways to look at and analyze the results. Winning percentage, for example, is a very valid way to compare entries. If you test without slippage and commissions, your entry should be able to win more than 50 percent of the time, since that is what a random entry would give you. In my experience, I have found that 52 to 60 percent is achievable, and values that high suggest a worthwhile entry technique is present.

The counterargument to using winning percentage is that, while it is nice to be right, it is even better to make money. A 60 percent winning percentage might make less money than a 40 percent winning percentage, especially if the entry is a trend-following entry. Trend-following entries, such as breakouts and moving average crossovers, are generally much lower winning percentage systems. They get their revenge on high-win-percentage systems by yielding few big winners and many small losers, with the win amount easily outpacing the loss amount. In these situations, therefore, the average profit per trade becomes useful.

Since both winning percentage and average profit give meaningful information, I use them both. Since this is preliminary testing, I do not worry about drawdown or any other metric. All I want to know at this point is if my entry seems to have any edge. These two metrics can help tell me that.

You may be wondering about optimization at this point. Should you use it? I will, but when I look at the results, I will not just look at the best iterations. Instead, I look at all of them. For example, let's say I run 100 iterations, with various values for my entry input parameters. If only a handful of iterations are profitable or have a winning percentage above 50 percent, I will likely discard that system. But, if 70 percent or more of the iterations are favorable, then I will consider the entry as having successfully passed the test.

Exit Testing

In a similar fashion to entry testing, there are a few different ways to test an exit. Where it gets complicated is when the exit is tied to the entry is some fashion. An example of this might be using support lines for entries, and resistance lines for exits. It is hard to separate the two. In these cases, I might choose not to even test exits by themselves, and rather proceed to a complete system test, discussed later.

When I do evaluate exits by themselves, I typically perform the analysis two ways:

- Similar-approach entry
- Random entry

Similar-Approach Entry

The core idea behind testing exits by themselves is to see if they can help give you an edge. Most people see edges as being applicable only when you enter, but really, exits have just as much, if not more, impact on the bottom line. A carefully designed exit, it has been shown, can make even bad entry systems profitable!

Since I will be testing the actual entry with the actual exit a bit later, at this point I want to see how the exit performs. To do this, I create an entry similar to the entry I want to use. This usually falls in one of two primary categories: trend following and countertrend following. Since I know what type of entry I have, I just create a generic one similar to it. For a trend-following approach, for example, I may just employ an X-bar breakout strategy. For a countertrend strategy, maybe I will use a relative strength index (RSI)-based entry. In either case, I create an entry that is comparable to my actual entry. Then I test it with my exit strategy. A robust exit strategy that is profitable to my similar-approach entries will likely also be profitable with my actual entry. This is a way to test an exit without involving the entry.

Random Entry

Discussed in a later section, if you have an exit strategy that works well with a random entry, you might have a really good system when you combine it with a solid entry technique. I do not use this approach as much as I used to, but occasionally I do like to see how a new exit technique works with random, no-edge entries.

Exit Evaluation Criteria

When I test exits by themselves, I generally do not look at winning percentages at all, and just focus on overall profitability. In addition, I will use maximum favorable excursion (MFE) and maximum adverse excursion (MAE) as measurement criteria. With these metrics, the idea is that you do not want the exit to get you into too much trouble (adverse excursion), and you do not want it to give back too much of the potential profit (found by comparing actual profit to the favorable excursion). The trouble with these metrics, I have found, is that it becomes too easy to design just to these values, and in my experience that doesn't necessarily lead to better systems. They are good, though, to see the potential of your system.

Core System Testing

Although there are benefits to testing the entry and exit signals by themselves (one being that you can always file away good entries and exits for use with another system), the interaction of entries and exits, as previously mentioned, is usually quite important. Regardless of whether I test entries and exits by themselves, I always test the complete core system during the preliminary phase.

My objective in testing the whole system is to see whether, on a limited history of data, the strategy performs well. The main criteria I use at this point is net profit, and I like to see profitable results over a wide range of variables and over most of the iterations. For example, if I have a simple breakout with 10 possible values of the breakout amount, and 10 stop-loss/profit values, that creates $10 \times 10 = 100$ iterations. I would expect a good strategy to be profitable over 70 or more of these iterations on the small data set. If I do see this type of behavior, I generally will run the monkey test shown later, and then go on to more in-depth testing.

Most of the time, the number of profitable iterations is on the order of 30 to 70 percent of total cases. This puts me in a "no man's land"—obviously, the strategy is not good enough as is, but there may be something there to work with. In situations like this, I may decide to add a rule, a filter, or otherwise change the entry and exit. Unfortunately, there is no set protocol for doing this. Many times, I'll use extra rules or conditions that I have had previous success with. Once I make some minor changes, I reevaluate my sample results.

The downside to this iterative process of modifying the rules is that you run the risk of fitting the system to the historical data. One or two modifications may be okay, but if you spend a lot of time modifying your strategy to get better results, you may very well fall into the "create a great-looking back test, but the real world performance suffers"–type scenario. Most times, if the first or second modification doesn't dramatically improve things, then the strategy is best left for the scrap heap.

As I have stated, when I do the preliminary testing with limited optimization, I like to see 70 percent or higher of cases with net profit, and I will work with the 30 to 70 percent cases a bit to see if I can improve them. But, what about strategies that are just awful, with less than 30 percent of iterations generating any profit? In these cases I use the George Costanza approach: if everything I built is bad, then the opposite must be good! I will reverse the signals and buy when I was selling, and vice versa. Depending on the strategy logic, this doesn't always produce the exact opposite result, but in many cases it is close. Without a doubt, though, this opposite effect is really apparent only before commissions and slippage are added in. Why is that? Well, take a trading system that has −\$50 average profit per trade, after \$30 commissions and slippage. That might be a decent candidate for an opposite approach, since many people will assume that it would average \$50 − \$30 = \$20 per trade. But in reality, the opposite trade would be a −\$10 loser. When reversing systems, you must add in double the commissions and slippage. Here is the math:

−\$50 average trade, after slippage and commissions
+\$30 commission and slippage
−\$20 average trade, no slippage or commissions

Now flip the system to produce the opposite result, and then add commissions and slippage back in

+\$20 average trade, no slippage or commissions
−\$30 commission and slippage
−\$10 average trade, opposite system, with slippage and commissions

I believe when people ponder trading the opposite system, they neglect to add in the commissions and slippage correctly. This is why most "opposite" systems, while appealing on the surface, rarely if ever work in the real world.

At this point in the process, if my strategy has performed successfully, I will have tested the entry, the exit, and the core system, with all results suggesting that a tradable system *might* be achievable (remember, we have many more steps to go through before deciding a system is indeed tradable). This is just preliminary testing, the first hurdle, but when I even make it this far, I am somewhat encouraged. At this point, it is on to the last step in the preliminary process. This step involves animals, at least on a figurative level.

Monkey See, Monkey Do

One of the last tests I like to run is what I call "Monkey See, Monkey Do." The essence of the test is to see if my strategy does better than a dart-throwing monkey. In 1973, a book by Burton Malkiel claimed that "throwing darts at a newspaper's financial pages could select a portfolio that would do just as well as one carefully selected by experts." The book, "*A Random Walk Down Wall Street*" (W. W. Norton, 1973), is a classic for investors and traders, and the monkey idea resonated with many people. After all, no one wants to perform worse than a monkey! I personally don't subscribe to all the talk about markets being random—if I did, I would really have no business searching for a trading edge. Since prolonged edges would not exist in random markets, I find the monkey test a very useful one.

With any strategy I create, the strategy's performance better be significantly improved over what any monkey could do by just throwing darts. If it is not, then I have no desire to trade such a strategy. I use three different monkey tests and two different time frames for testing. Passing all of the tests gives me confidence I have something better than random.

Test 1: "Monkey Entry"

The first test I run is to see if the entry I developed is better than random. I simply replace the entry in my strategy with an entry than creates a randomly generated entry. I run the random entry, with the rest of my strategy intact, 8,000 times. This generates 8,000 unique performance reports, since each run will have different randomly generated entries. By adjusting the frequency of the entry signals, I ensure that I get close to the same number of trades as my walk-forward history. Also, I try to match the percentage of long and short trades. These two conditions mean that the "monkey" trades as often as my system does, and in roughly the same proportion of long and short trades.

Typically, a good strategy will beat the monkey 9 times out of 10 in net profit and in maximum drawdown. For my 8,000 monkey trials, that means approximately 7,200 must have net profit worse than my results, and the same number of runs with higher maximum drawdown than my walk-forward results. If I don't reach these goals, I really have to wonder if my entry is truly better than random.

Test 2: "Monkey Exit"

The second test I run is to see if the exit I developed is better than random. It is much like the entry test, obviously, except in this case the monkey randomly exits the position. I control the random exit primarily by keeping the number of bars in a trade the same as my walk-forward history. For example, if my walk-forward history has an average of four bars per trade and always exits at the end of the day, I will tune the random exit to be on average the same. Also, it will always exit at the end of the day, if that is my criterion.

As with the monkey entry, I look for my walk-forward results to be better than 90 percent of the monkey exits.

Test 3: "Monkey Entry, Monkey Exit"

After determining that my strategy is better than both a monkey entry and a monkey exit, I like to see that my strategy is better than a monkey entry *and* exit. I do this because sometimes my edge is in the interaction of the entry and exit. For example, it might be that my entry is valid only because I set the exit near a support or resistance zone. It might be that the entry, taken alone, or the exit, taken alone, isn't enough without the other.

In this test, I replace all entry and exit code with random monkey code. I adjust the parameters of the random entry and exit to match my strategy in the following ways:

- Number of trades
- Ratio of long trades to short trades
- Average bars spent in a trade

Note that these conditions are the same I apply to the other monkey tests. Then I run the monkey entry, monkey exit strategy 8,000 times, just like the other tests, and compare results the same way.

Time Frames

The first time I run the monkey tests is in the development stage, as one more hurdle for a strategy to overcome. Most of the time, though, running these tests over the walk-forward time frame will almost always yield good results. This is because bad strategies will likely never get this far in the development process. Still, though, I like to see my strategy pass this test. It gives me confidence that I may indeed have an edge.

The other time frame I use to run the monkey tests is when running the strategy live. I take the results of the past 6 to 12 months (3 months may also be a good number, although the validity may be questionable if the number of trades is low). If, in that 6- to 12-month time period, the monkeys became a lot better, I know that my assumed edge has either degraded or disappeared completely. It might then be time for me to quit trading that system.

Monkey Testing—Example

To give you an idea of how the monkey test works, in both the walk-forward history and the real-time history, I will provide an example in this section.

Figure 12.1 shows the walk-forward performance of the as-developed system, along with the performance after initial development. The system did quite well for a while, but eventually endured some significant drawdowns. The question is: could the 6-month monkey test have shown that the edge in this system was gone, and that trading should have ceased? To answer that question, I will perform monkey tests at the points shown on the graph.

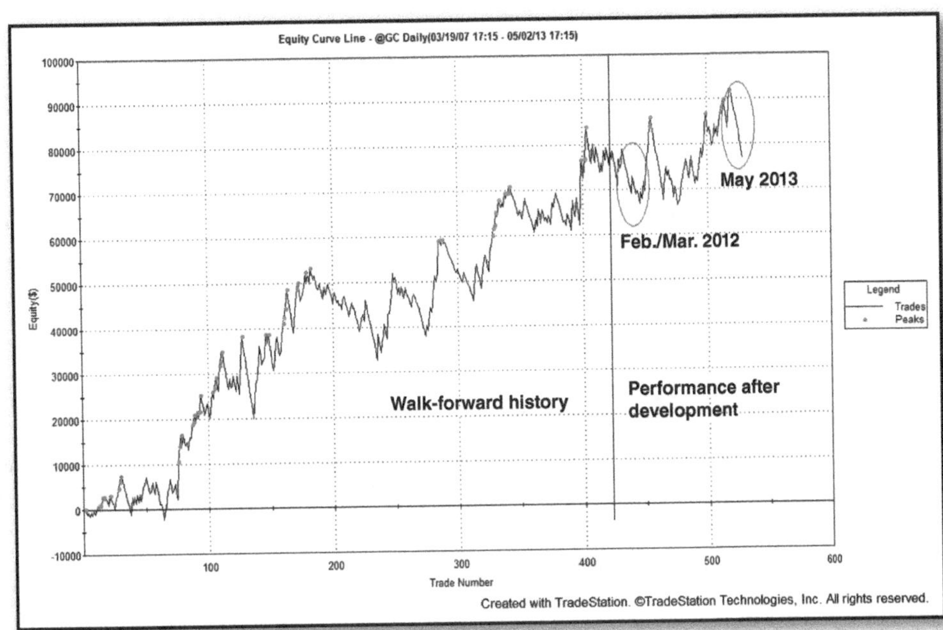

FIGURE 12.1 Sample System Walk-Forward Performance

TABLE 12.1 Baseline Performance

Parameter	Value
Time period	3/19/2007–11/1/2011
Net profit	$72,650
Maximum intraday drawdown	−$22,270
Number of trades	430
Percentage of long trades	40 percent
Average bars in trade	2.5
Number of trading days	1,165
Number of trades/Number of trading days	0.37

The code, in TradeStation Easy Language, for the baseline strategy, and the three monkey strategies, are shown in Appendix A.

The first step in creating random strategies that are comparable to the baseline strategy is to gather the pertinent statistics of the baseline strategy. These are shown in Table 12.1.

All of the information in Table 12.1 can be obtained from the performance report. The two parameters I will use to compare to random strategies are the net profit and the maximum intraday drawdown. All other parameters listed will be used to "tune" the random strategy. The goal with tuning is to have roughly the same numbers of trades, the same percentage of long and short trades, and the same average time in trades for the random strategy as for the baseline strategy. Doing this will allow a fair comparison of the two strategies.

Once the random strategies all yield roughly the same number of trades as the baseline strategy, I can run each random strategy 8,000 times. Then I can compare the results. These results are shown in Table 12.2.

The results are pretty clear—the baseline strategy is much, much better than any random strategy. Score one for the humans over the monkeys! Based on this information, the baseline strategy clearly passes the random test.

TABLE 12.2 Random "Monkey" Test 1

Test Period: 3/19/2007 to 11/1/2011	Percentage of Cases with Net Profit Worse than Baseline Case	Percentage of Cases with Maximum Intraday Drawdown Worse than Baseline Case
Random entry, baseline exit	100%	99%
Baseline entry, random exit	99%	94%
Random entry, random exit	99%	99%

TABLE 12.3 Random "Monkey" Test 2

Test Period: 3/1/2011 to 3/1/2012	Percentage of Random Cases with Net Profit Worse than Baseline Case ($780)	Percentage of Random Cases with Maximum Intraday Drawdown Worse than Baseline Case (–$15,680)
Random entry, baseline exit	49%	73%
Baseline entry, random exit	99%	100%
Random entry, random exit	60%	95%

But how does the baseline strategy compare to the random strategies a few months later? Referring to Figure 12.1, the baseline strategy ran into some difficulty around February–March 2012. Assuming an end date of March 1, 2012, over the previous 12 months, the strategy had a net profit of $780, and a maximum intraday drawdown of −$15,680. How does that compare with the random strategies? After 8,000 runs, here are the results (see Table 12.3).

The results should present some cause for concern. Clearly, the baseline strategy has performed only slightly better than a random strategy, depending on the number you focus on. Personally, I look at all the numbers as a group, and if I see most of them at or below 60 to 70 percent, I become concerned. If most of the numbers are below 50 percent, I become very concerned, since by all measures, my strategy is not performing better than the monkeys.

In this particular case, with only one value below 50 percent, and two values below 70 percent, I'd probably let the strategy continue trading. More conservative traders might decide to stop trading at this point, and that is a reasonable decision, too.

The next time the baseline strategy caused concern was in May 2013. Over the year ending May 1, 2013, the baseline strategy lost −$1,105, with a maximum intraday drawdown of −$15,100. How does that compare to the random monkey systems? See Table 12.4.

TABLE 12.4 Random "Monkey" Test 3

Test Period: 5/1/2012 to 5/1/2012	Percentage of Random Cases with Net Profit Worse than Baseline Case (–$1,105)	Percentage of Random Cases with Maximum Intraday Drawdown Worse than Baseline Case (–$15,100)
Random entry, baseline exit	50%	64%
Baseline entry, random exit	1%	1%
Random entry, random exit	49%	72%

The results here are much clearer now. On average, the monkey systems are equal to or better than the baseline strategy. This indicates that any edge the strategy originally had is gone or is certainly on hiatus. Wise traders would stop trading this system near the beginning of May 2013. In this case, judging from the performance of the baseline strategy after May 1, 2013, that was a good decision.

Comparison of your strategy to randomly generated strategies can be useful, too. In the preceding example system, the analysis was able to show that the strategy as developed was significantly better than a random, monkey-throwing-darts system. That is nice to know, as it gives you confidence as you begin to trade.

Unfortunately, running this analysis when you develop the strategy tells you nothing about how well the strategy will work going forward. The strategy itself could be defective, leading to real-time losses. Or the characteristics of the market may have changed, and your strategy cannot adapt to it. In either case, periodically comparing the baseline strategy results to the random monkey results can help you decide whether the strategy is broken. As the earlier analysis shows, the random test can be an early warning detection method of sorts, and can suggest that you stop trading the strategy until performance becomes better than random. Thus, it can be a useful tool in deciding when to stop trading a strategy.

CHAPTER 13

In-Depth Testing/ Walk-Forward Analysis

Once I have a trading system that I believe has some sort of edge to it, and it passes all the preliminary tests I throw at it, then I feel comfortable going on to more in-depth testing. As stated earlier, there are four primary ways of testing:

- Historical back testing—all in-sample
- Out-of-sample testing
- Walk-forward testing
- Real-time testing

Over the years I have successfully and unsuccessfully used each one of these approaches. Currently, I believe that walk-forward analysis offers the best combination of amount of history that can be tested, degree of match between historical and real-time results, and sensitivity to changing market conditions. During the in-depth testing phase described in this chapter, I will use only walk-forward testing. But before we get into a discussion about walk-forward testing, what if you don't have any parameters to optimize?

No Parameters

Occasionally, you may develop a system that has no parameters to optimize at all. For example, your entry may be based on a specific candlestick chart pattern, and your exit might be a set-dollar-amount stop-loss, with a set profit target. For whatever reason, you may decide that you never want to change these values for stop-loss and target, and you do not want to change the entry. Your philosophy may be "no optimization, ever," which is certainly one way to avoid curve fitting or overfitting of the system to the data.

In situations such as this, your in-depth analysis will simply consist of one historical test through the data. If the results meet your goals, you can simply move on to the next step. If not, you should discard the strategy and move on to the next idea.

One important point is that if your optimizationless strategy does not work, you should not go back and tweak the strategy, followed by rerunning it. For example, if you run it the first time and are displeased with the results, you should not change the entry to a different candlestick pattern and try again. That is just an optimization of the entry, done a different way. But it is still optimization.

If you think this technique might apply to you, you can turn these two unique strategies into one optimizable strategy, following the pseudo code technique shown below:

Strategy 1
Enter long with candlestick pattern A
Stop-loss $X, profit target $Y

Strategy 2
Enter long with candlestick pattern B
Stop-loss $X, profit target $Y

Strategy 3—strategies 1 and 2 combined
For i = 1 to 2
If i = 1, enter long with candlestick pattern A
If i = 2, enter long with candlestick pattern B
Stop-loss $X, profit target $Y

The benefit of such an approach is that you know up front that you are optimizing (no hidden or forgotten optimizations to taint your results), and it may very well be that a combination of strategies (e.g., strategy 1 might be better in year 1, but strategy 2 might be better in year 2) might be better than either by itself.

If you truly decide that you have no parameters to optimize, simply substitute the walk-forward analysis shown later for a single-run historical analysis. If the results are favorable, you can then proceed to the next step. In most situations, though, you will have at least one parameter to optimize, and for those cases walk-forward analysis is the best way to go.

A Walk-Forward Primer

Many people are confused by walk-forward testing and how it really is different from traditional optimization. I think understanding the walk-forward concept has been made even more difficult to understand by the introduction of it in most trading software packages. In the "old" days, without specialized software or a spreadsheet, walk-forward testing had to be performed by hand or custom computer programming. In fact, when I had my successful run in the World Cup trading contest, I relied on strategies developed with walk-forward testing conducted by hand. It was difficult and tedious, but it gave me a clear understanding of how the process works.

To bring the concept down to earth, I will first demonstrate the process on a simple breakout trading system. In this way, you can see step by step how the walk-forward analysis is done.

First, some simple definitions regarding the walk-forward analysis are in order:

In period. This is the chunk of historical data that will be optimized.

Out period. This is the chunk of historical data that will be evaluated using optimized results from the adjacent in period.

Fitness factor. This is the criterion used to determine the "best" result, allowing us to select the optimized parameters.

Anchored/Unanchored test. This tells us whether or not the in period start date shifts with time, or if the start date is always the same.

Although I will discuss the details of how to select these parameters a bit later, for our test case we will use a 5-year in period, a 1-year out period, fitness factor of net profit, and an unanchored test.

Our strategy will be a very simple one: a countertrend breakout-type system:

Enter short if the close is an "X"-day high close
Enter long if the close is a "Y"-day low close
Stop-loss of "Z"

In TradeStation Easy Language, the system code becomes:

```
input: X(5), Y(5), Z(200);

if close=highest(close,X) then buy next bar at market;

if close=lowest(close,Y) then sellshort next bar at market;

SetStopLoss(Z);
```

For this example, we will use the continuous contract for the mini S&P (ES), and use 10 years of data, from January 1, 2000, to January 1, 2010. We will use daily bars and include $25 slippage and commission per round trip trade.

For comparison purposes, first we will optimize over all the data from 2000 to 2010. Using net profit as our fitness function criteria, we get the optimum values:

X = 9
Y = 5
Z = $600

This complete optimization produces a net profit of $55,162 over the 10-year period.

Now, we will run the walk-forward analysis. Since we are running a 5-year optimization period, we will first optimize from January 1, 2000, to January 1, 2005. When we do this, we get the following parameters for the highest net profit case:

X = 7
Y = 17
Z = $600

That completes out first in-sample evaluation. Now we apply the preceding parameters to our first out-of-sample period, January 1, 2005, to January 1, 2006. Note that it is considered out-of-sample because it was not in the first optimization period. The results of this first out-of-sample yields a loss of $3,138.

In a similar fashion, we then run the in-sample optimizations, and the out-of-sample performance runs for each of the rows shown in Table 13.1.

Once we are complete, we have our walk-forward analysis. To create a complete performance report of the walk-forward data, we can create a strategy where the values change every time the walk-forward period changes. Such a strategy looks like this:

```
var: X(5), Y(5), Z(200);

If date>1050101 and date<1060101 then begin
  x=7; y=17; z=600;
end;
```

TABLE 13.1 Sample Walk-Forward Test Results

In-Sample Test Period	Best Parameters X, Y, Z	Out-of-Sample Period	Out-of-Sample Result
1/1/2000–1/1/2005	7,17,600	1/1/2005–1/1/2006	−$3,138
1/1/2001–1/1/2006	7,45,100	1/1/2006–1/1/2007	−$2,325
1/1/2002–1/1/2007	49,7,600	1/1/2007–1/1/2008	+$5,963
1/1/2003–1/1/2008	21,11,1000	1/1/2008–1/1/2009	−$19,113
1/1/2004–1/1/2009	9,5,600	1/1/2009–1/1/2010	+$8,675

```
If date>1060101 and date<1070101 then begin
  x=7; y=45; z=100;
end;
If date>1070101 and date<1080101 then begin
  x=49; y=7; z=600;
end;
If date>1080101 and date<1090101 then begin
  x=21; y=11; z=1000;
end;
If date>1090101 and date<1100101 then begin
  x=9; y=5; z=600;
end;
If date>1100101 and date<1110101 then begin
  x=9; y=5; z=600;
end;
If date>1110101 and date<1120101 then begin
  x=9; y=5; z=700;
end;
If date>1120101 and date<1130101 then begin
  x=9; y=5; z=700;
end;

If date>1130101 and date<1140101 then begin
  x=9; y=5; z=700;
end;

if close=highest(close,X) then sellshort next bar at market;
if close=lowest(close,Y) then buy next bar at market;
SetStopLoss(Z);
```

This will allow us to compare the walk-forward results to the optimized results. This is shown in Figure 13.1. The interesting points of this comparison are:

- The optimized equity curve is much, much better than the walk-forward curve. This is to be expected, since the optimized curve is a result of optimization. This should tell you that practically any strategy can be made to look good, if you optimize the parameters over the time period you are interested in.
- The walk-forward results are not very good. Walk-forward analysis is a tough test for a strategy to "pass." Most strategies fail at this analysis. But since this simulates real life more than fully optimized results do, it is a more accurate method of analysis.

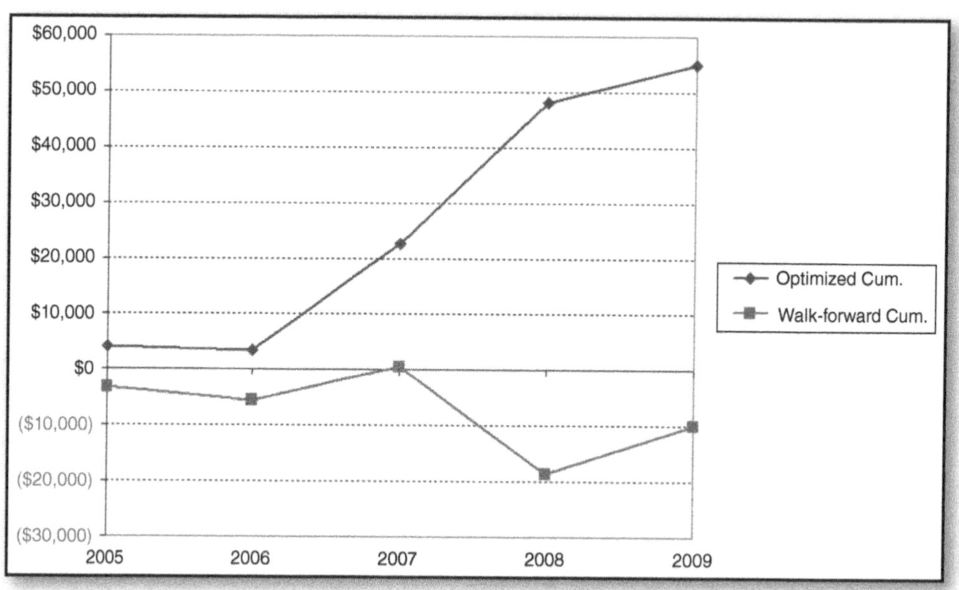

FIGURE 13.1 Walk-Forward Results vs. Optimized Results, as Developed

I have mentioned it a few times, but you still might be wondering, "How do you know walk-forward analysis is more representative of future performance that the fully optimized test?" I claim this based on my experience. The current system is a good example of this performance difference. For the analysis just completed, here is how the optimized and walk-forward analysis performed from January 1, 2010, to November 14, 2013. As you can see in Figure 13.2, for the optimized case, the performance during the out-of-sample period 2010–2013 was flat. It looks nothing at all like the optimized portion of the curve from 2005 to 2009, where the average annual gain was approximately $10,000. It is a different story for the walk-forward analysis, as depicted in Figure 13.2. The years 2010–2013 were flat for the walk-forward equity curve also, but it mimics the 2005–2009 walk-forward results. In other words, the performance of the walk-forward system did not change through the years—it was consistently flat to down most of the years.

While one example does not make it a rule, in general this is the kind of performance you can expect from optimized back tests and walk-forward back tests. Optimized results, when applied to out of sample data, generally degrade. This is why so many people get frustrated with systems sold by unscrupulous vendors. These vendors show optimized results, and the performance in the future is almost never as good as the back test. Walk-forward results, however, should perform about the same throughout the whole test period. This is why many traders prefer

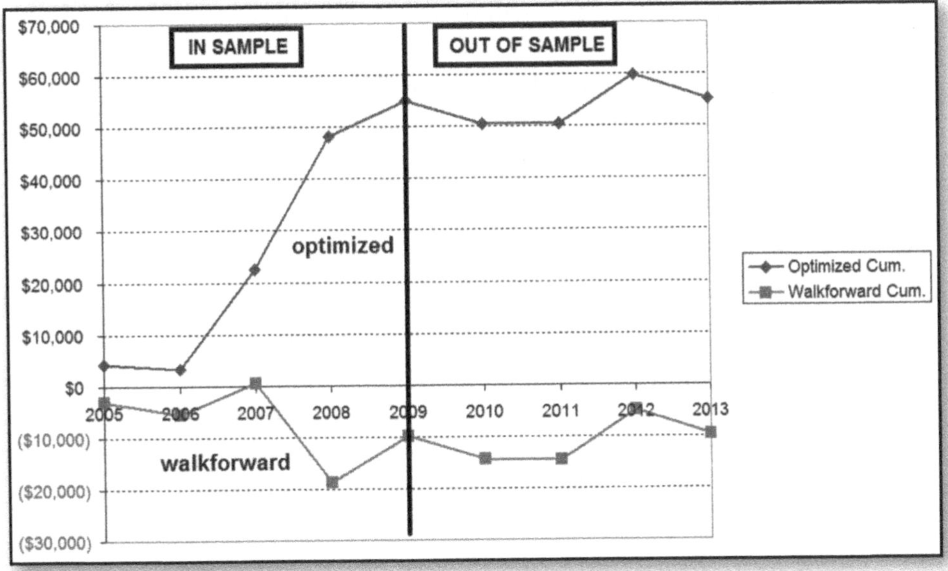

FIGURE 13.2 Walk-Forward Results vs. Optimized Results, Before and After Development

walk-forward results. Walk-forward analysis tends to produce equity curves that are more stable going forward. Again, that is not a rule, but it is my experience that this is generally true.

Walk-Forward Inputs

If we are performing the analysis by hand, as described above, we must know the following parameters *before* we start the analysis:

In period
Out period
Fitness function
Method: anchored or unanchored

In you are using software to perform the analysis (as I currently do), you do not necessarily have to know these values in advance. That is both a blessing and a curse. It is good because you only have to run the optimization once and not keep repeating the walk-forward analysis over and over. It is bad because these parameters can be optimized, just like any traditional input parameter in your strategy. It may not seem like an optimization, at least in the traditional sense, but if you, for example, look at two values of in period, and choose the one with better results, that is still optimizing. You want to make the decision before you do the analysis.

Assuming you will be choosing the walk-forward inputs beforehand (we will examine an alternative method to this later), how do we choose values for each of them? A method for determining each value is described below.

In Period

For the in period, the goal is to get enough trades to make a meaningful conclusion as to the best parameters to use for each period. It makes sense, then, to get a certain amount of trades per input variable in your in period. For example, if you have four inputs to optimize, then you might want 100 to 200 trades in your in period, which would be equivalent to 25 to 50 trades per input. Unfortunately, there is no set number of trades per input that is "best," although many people say that 30 is a good number for statistical significance.

Out Period

As crazy as it sounds, I know people who do walk-forward analysis every day, which means their out period is one day. Personally, I think this is extreme, but who am I to argue if they are having success? There are a couple of factors at play in the selection of an out period. First, if you set the out period too big, you might only have one or two out periods for your walk-forward analysis, which means the test becomes similar to a single-period out-of-sample test. Second, if you set the out period too small, you will be conducting reoptimizations on a daily or weekly basis. This might not be sustainable given the limited time you likely have to develop and trade, if you have many systems to reoptimize. Knowing that there are boundaries to the out period, I generally set my out period to between 10 to 50 percent of the in period. So, if my in period is 1,000 days, my out period might be in the range of 100 to 500 days. This is a very wide range, but with robust systems you will generally see that the final results are not extremely sensitive to out period. A 100-day out period may very well perform about the same as a 500-day out period.

Fitness Function

Of all the parameters in walk-forward analysis, the fitness function is the most contentious. I'm sure that raucous debate by two developers over the fitness function has at some time resulted in physical violence (such dedication to the cause!). I don't want to stir the pot by going into the pros and cons of various fitness functions, but I will tell you the ones I have had the most success with.

Net Profit

For many people, this is the default choice, and it is a pretty good one. After all, without profit at the end of the test, all other parameters are meaningless. I personally use this fitness factor the most, since it is easy to understand and implement. But it does not take into account another important results: drawdown. My experience, however, has been that in general high net profit runs hand in hand with low maximum drawdown. If you decide drawdown is a must have, then one of the fitness function below should suit you.

Linearity of Equity Curve

Think for a minute of your ideal equity curve. The equity would go up every day, and it would be consistent. A real-world example is interest on a banking or money market account. Interest earned might be very small, but with a bank account, you make money every day, and there is never a day where you lose money. If only you could design a futures system that made money every day, with never a drawdown! A linear, upward-sloping equity curve is the ideal, and is a great parameter to optimize for. The problem is that, unless your software includes this fitness function as a set choice, it may be difficult in actual practice to actually optimize for it. Also, it may be difficult to implement in a nonanchored walk-forward test. Finally, this method of optimization may select very low net profit iterations as the optimum, since they may exhibit the most linearity. There are two potential problems with the low-profit cases: first, since there is not much profit, if you underestimate your slippage and commissions, you might actually be selecting a real-time losing strategy. Second, if the end result is very small average profit per trade, minor changes in the market may render your effective ineffective.

One big plus to using a linear equity curve as your optimization criteria is that it is very good for position sizing. Think about a strategy where your drawdowns are minimal and your profits are slow and steady. Such an approach would be ideal for aggressive position sizing.

Return on Account

If you explicitly use maximum drawdown in your fitness function, then return on account is a good option. Although some software packages vary in their definition, return on account is generally defined as:

$$\text{Return on Account} = \text{Net Profit}/(\text{Maximum Drawdown} + \text{Required Margin})$$

Since required margin varies over time, many people just eliminate this from the calculation by assuming it is equal to zero or some other arbitrary value. As a fitness function, return on account is nice to use, since it takes into account both the profit, and the risk it took to get that profit. The biggest drawback to using it is that it can give wildly different results from period to period using unanchored walk-forward analysis.

Anchored/Unanchored

One subtle aspect of walk-forward analysis is the optimization window. You can go one of two ways with this window: you can move it with time, or you can keep the start point anchored. Figure 13.3 shows the difference between these two approaches.

In general, the two methods will give similar results, especially at the beginning of the analysis. But as time goes on, the results will tend to diverge. This is because the anchored walk-forward is always taking into account results over the whole data set, while the unanchored results include results for only the most recent window. There may be times where one is more appropriate than the other, but I tend to use the unanchored method much more. I like that approach, since it ensures that only the most recent data is included in the optimization. I don't necessarily want results from 10 years ago still impacting my optimization results today.

One point of caution with using unanchored data, with certain fitness functions, is that the results you get might be faulty, depending on your walk-forward analysis software. If you are using a manual method, this should not be a problem, but if you use software, make sure that the calculations are based on the start and end dates in question, not on difference in fitness functions during the period.

	2007	2008	2009	2010	2011	2012	2013
Anchored Test							
Anchored in sample 1							
Walk-forward 1							
Anchored in sample 2							
Walk-forward 2							
Anchored in sample 3							
Walk-forward 3							
Unanchored Test							
In sample 1							
Walk-forward 1							
In sample 2							
Walk-forward 2							
In sample 3							
Walk-forward 3							

FIGURE 13.3 Anchored vs. Unanchored Walk-Forward Analysis

TABLE 13.2 Many Performance Metrics Are Not Additive			
Optimization Period	**Net Profit**	**Max Drawdown**	**Return on Account = Net Profit/ Max Drawdown**
Year 1	$12,000	$6,000	2.0
Year 2	$6,000	$4,000	1.5
Year 1–Year 2	$18,000	$6,000	3.0

A simple example explains it well. Suppose you have the optimized results shown in Table 13.2.

Note in this example that while net profit is additive (the net profit in year 1 plus the net profit in year 2 equals the combined net profit for year 1 + year 2), the maximum drawdown and return on account are not. Some walk-forward software packages may assume your fitness function is additive (like net profit), so make sure you understand how the software works when using unanchored results. Your analysis could be completely flawed depending on the fitness function you choose.

Running the Analysis

Once you have all your walk-forward inputs defined, you simply run the analysis manually as I have shown in the earlier example, or automatically with the software. Either way, in the end, you will have the completed walk-forward analysis and equity curve for your strategy. At this point, you have to compare the results to your goals and objectives. If the system passes, you of course go on to the next step. If it fails, theoretically you should discard the strategy and start with something different. In reality, of course, that is extremely difficult to do. You have already invested a great deal of time in preliminary testing and in-depth testing, and it seems a shame that you should just discard your work. This is especially true if the results are close to your goal. Maybe lowering the goal or making a small change to the strategy and rerunning walk-forward might be the path to success. Or does that just lead to more bad habits and decisions?

In general, I normally would discard a strategy at this point, rather than compromise my goals or change my strategy. But sometimes I do one or both of these things. Occasionally, that turned out to be a good decision, but likely more often than not it did not work out well. Remember, the more you touch (test) historical data, the more likely you are to fit your system to the data. Plus, when you relax your standards, you end up with something you really did not want. When real money is on the line, this may become a major point of contention for your psyche—why continue to trade a currently losing system that you had doubts about in the first place?

One common mistake during walk-forward analysis is to surreptitiously optimize the *in* and *out* periods. Say, for example, that you run the walk-forward analysis with four-year in period, and one-year out period. Walk-forward results for that case are good, but not great, so you think "maybe I should use four years in, with two years out." That case is 200 percent better and meets all your goals, so you decide "that's the combination to use. Let's go!"

Stop.

Do you realize what just happened? As soon as you selected a second set of in/out parameters, reran the results, and selected the best case, you just optimized. Sure, it is not a full optimization, since you only compared two cases, but it was optimization nevertheless. Remembering the rule that optimized results can't be trusted, you have a dilemma here: accept the first run (4 year/1 year), and then discard the strategy because it did not meet your goals, or accept the second run, and pretend you never optimized.

Once again, I'll admit to doing the above on occasion, although I can't recall it ever ending well. The big question in all this is "is there a way to test multiple in/out periods, and select the best one, while still maintaining walk-forward integrity?" The answer, thankfully, is yes. The way to do it is to create, in essence, a second walk-forward analysis inside of the first. The way to do this is to run the walk-forward analysis, as usual, but leave the last few years of data untouched. I typically will leave three years untouched. Then, with the walk-forward data I have, I select the best in/out pair I have, and then run it on the last three years of data. If it passes, then I go on to the next step. If it doesn't, I discard the strategy. But, in either case, at least I have made some effort to select the best in/out combination. The downside to this approach is that you have optimized, and the more optimization you do, the worse off you generally are.

This process would look like this:

1. Years 2000–2008 >> run walk-foward analysis for different combinations of in/out periods, select the best in/out.
2. Years 2009–present >> run walk-forward analysis, using best in/out determined from Step 1.

3a. If walk-forward results from 2009–present look good, continue with development.

3b. If results do not look good, it is probably best to abandon strategy, rather than try again with another in/out pair.

Figure 13.4 depicts the approach of optimizing in/out periods, compared to a traditional walk-forward analysis.

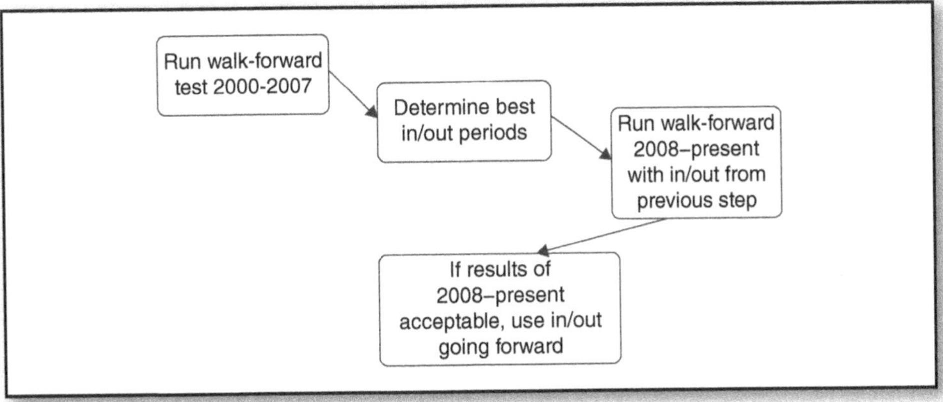

FIGURE 13.4 Walk-Forward Test, Inside Another Walk-Forward Test

Put the Walk-Forward Strategy Together

Once you have completed the walk-forward analysis, analyzed the results, and found that your results compare favorably to your objectives, you are almost ready for the next step. There is just one more check to run, and that is with the completed walk-forward history strategy. The difference between the walk-forward history strategy and the optimizable strategy is shown next:

Optimizable Strategy

```
input: avg(10);
// strategy code
```

Walk-Foward History Strategy

```
var: avg(10);
If date is between Jan 1, 2010 and Jan 1, 2011 then
avg=8
If date is between Jan 1, 2011 and Jan 1, 2012 then
avg=12
If date is between Jan 1, 2012 and Jan 1, 2013 then
avg=6
// strategy code
```

The strategy with the walk-forward history changes the variables based on the date. In this way, you will have a seamless history for your strategy to run; you will not have to cut and paste results together to create the walk-forward history.

Note that the results you get from this strategy might be different from the results of a piece-by-piece analysis method. This is especially true for swing strategies that last for days or weeks. The reason this is so is that, based on the walk-forward parameters, variables might change in the middle of a trade, causing trades to be exited or reversed. To see if this is important for your strategy, then, it becomes critical to create a stand-alone walk-forward history strategy.

CHAPTER 14

Monte Carlo Analysis and Incubation

Once you have the walk-forward strategy set up, and you are satisfied with the results, it is time to evaluate the strategy in a Monte Carlo simulation. This is an important step because random simulations may show dramatically different profits and drawdown. It may be that the way the historical trades lined up, the maximum drawdown was very small. But since history isn't likely to repeat itself, it is important to see what type of maximum drawdown you could possibly incur trading this strategy.

As stated earlier in Chapter 7, I use an Excel spreadsheet to do the Monte Carlo analysis. You can download this tool for yourself at the book resource web site (www.wiley.com/go/algotradingsystems). There are also numerous free and paid Monte Carlo simulators available on the Internet, should you choose to go that route. One good free simulator is Equity Monaco by NeoTick (equitymonaco.software.informer.com/). A good pay tool is @Risk (www.palisade.com/). All of these choices will give you the same basic results, and you might prefer the presentation of results and capabilities of one over the other. The key is to get simulation results that you can base your decision on.

If you use the simulator spreadsheet I created, you simply copy trade results from your strategy performance report, paste them in the spreadsheet, enter your initial capital, quitting-point capital, and number of trades in a year, and then press calculate. The spreadsheet will calculate the simulated equity curves for 2,500 iterations, and present you with summary results. These results will be based on one year of trading. Sample output of the spreadsheet was shown earlier in Figure 7.2. I typically focus on the return to max drawdown ratio (ret/DD), and I like to see values above 2.0 for an acceptable strategy. Anything below 2.0 suggests that the strategy is taking on too much risk for the reward attained and might not be worth trading.

If you are proficient in writing macros in Excel, you can easily take the Monte Carlo spreadsheet I have created and modify it to suit your own needs. You could add position sizing, for example, or you could change which results are presented. In the end, the point of the simulation is to give you results that you can understand and interpret. I have told you what works for me; maybe that will work for you, but maybe you'll think of something better.

Incubation

One of the most crucial steps in strategy development, in my opinion, is also the toughest psychologically to implement. Before I discuss this last step, let's review where we have been in the strategy development process:

1. We have established goals and objectives for our completed strategy and also goals for the steps along the way. In this manner, we can quickly eliminate strategies before spending too much time on them.
2. We have developed a trading idea for our strategy that we feel has an edge. We have also defined the market, time frame, and other important factors for our testing.
3. We have performed limited testing with the strategy, and we are happy with the results. We believe we might have an edge.
4. We have conducted in-depth testing, using walk-forward testing if possible. Again, we are happy with the performance results obtained.
5. We have performed Monte Carlo testing, to help us establish probabilities for the strategy performance and also to give us realistic future scenarios of performance.

These completed five steps represent a lot of work and likely caused us to discard tens or hundreds of strategies before finding success. To get through the last step, Monte Carlo testing, is certainly an accomplishment. When this happens, you likely will be so excited you will want to trade immediately! That, of course, would be the wrong thing to do. Incubation is the right thing to do.

What exactly is incubation? Simply put, it is watching and waiting. With incubation, you wait three to six months before you start live trading. During this time, you occasionally monitor the performance of the strategy, as if it is another out-of-sample test period. I like to check on my incubated strategies once per month.

Why is it important to incubate a strategy? Here are a few reasons:

- When you finish Monte Carlo testing, you are at an emotional high. Your "baby" has survived and has a lot of promise. You have a lot of emotional capital invested in this strategy, as well as your time and effort. You want it to succeed. You may even *need* it to succeed. Of course, this leads to a fragile emotional state. If you immediately start trading it with real money, you might not think clearly if things start out bad for the strategy, as so often seems to happen. This could lead you to quit the strategy early, or worse yet, haphazardly increase size when performance starts out bad ("doubling down").

- By waiting for a while before live trading, you will forget about the blood, sweat, and tears you expended to create the strategy, and you will look at it more objectively. If it passes incubation, great—but if it doesn't, you won't be distraught. Remember, short-term hardship is sometimes the price for long-term success, and that definitely holds true with trading systems.

- As I have shown, the system development process is difficult and complicated. There are probably a thousand different mistakes you can make along the way. Some can be blatant, like overoptimizing, while others may be subtle, such as using hindsight bias to develop your strategy rules. The point is that, because of development mistakes, there can be no way to know for sure if you have done something wrong until you test your strategy on live, unseen data. Major mistakes will show up in live results almost immediately, and by keeping your cash on the sidelines during this period, you will save a great deal of money.

- Incubating gives you a chance to see how a strategy performs in real time. You may find out that you do not like the strategy, even if it makes money. For example, maybe your strategy sells every pivot high. In historical back testing, that may not bother you. But in real time, watching your strategy fight every market high might not be your cup of tea. It is far better to realize that now, rather than after you commit money to trading it.

I generally perform incubation without real money. This is because, over time, I have concluded that the way I place orders, the bar types I use, and so on all can be fairly well replicated by the strategy back-test engine. There are times, however, where you may want to commit real money on a small scale. For example, if your strategy relies on limit orders for entries, you may want to test with real money to ensure that your fills match strategy engine fills. With some software packages, this might not be the case. Also, if you use exotic bar types, back-test results and real-money results can be totally different. You might need a live real-money test to check this, but once you confirm an issue, you will be able to avoid those bar types in later strategies. Sometimes the only way to see if a back test is accurate is by testing the strategy with real money.

As I mentioned, I normally do not need to perform real-money testing during incubation. One reason is that I avoid back tests that show or contain the following:

- Any buy fills at the low of a bar or sell fills at the high of a bar. Rare will be the day this occurs in real life, but many unscrupulous system vendors and naive developers develop strategies that frequently show this phenomenon.
- Limit orders that fill when price is touched. On occasion, maybe 0 to 30 percent of the time, you will get filled at your limit price, when it is just touched. Most of the time, though, the price has to penetrate your price to guarantee a fill.
- Any exotic bars, such as Renko, Kase, and even point-and-figure. Due to the way the bars are built from history, your strategy fills many times cannot be believed. Better to just avoid these bars, except for real-time discretionary trading.
- Strategies that exit on same bar as entry or that have stops and targets so tight that a profit and loss exit could occur on the same bar. My experience is that it is easy to trick a strategy engine, even with tick data, when exits or entry and exits occur on the same bar. This is due to the assumptions the strategy engine must make regarding price travel. Usually, the results will be overly optimistic when compared to real live trading.

Evaluating Incubation

My goals with incubation are to give me reasonable assurance that I made no major mistakes during development, to remove my emotions from the process, and also to see if real-time performance is appealing enough to trade. Later in this book, I'll share some techniques I use to see if these goals are indeed met.

CHAPTER 15

Diversification

As you progress through the trading system development process numerous times, you'll start to realize that you have an algorithmic strategy factory on your hands. Raw material comes in the door as strategy ideas for entry and exit. Machines, such as limited testing, walk-forward testing, and Monte Carlo simulation, work on your ideas and either shape it into a better product, or tear it to shreds. At the end of your factory, you end up with trading systems you can trade or garbage destined for the scrap heap. If you do this over and over, you'll create a lot of garbage, but you'll also have a stack of strategies to trade. That's where diversification can be a big contributor.

I'm sure you've heard the old saw, "Put your eggs in one basket, then watch that basket!" In trading, this would be analogous to finding one trading system (the basket) and then putting all your money (eggs) into it. That is great if it works. I'm sure there are traders out there who concentrate on trading one system. I'm not one of them, though, and I do not recommend that you try to be one either. Why not? Well, the simple fact is that trading systems fail, and very few, if any, trading systems last forever. In addition, all trading systems go through drawdowns, and sometimes they recover and sometimes they don't. Do you really want your money tied to the fortunes (or misfortunes) of one trading strategy? I sure don't!

To get around this issue, I take the opposite approach and use diversification. Instead of one basket (trading system), I spread my capital among numerous, uncorrelated trading systems. In effect, I have many baskets, and although it takes more effort to watch and track each basket, the benefits are clear:

- *Less worry about a system's failing.* When you trade one system, you are at the mercy of that system or the approach behind the system. If you have a trend-following approach and the market goes flat for a few years, you will be in drawdown until the market starts to trend. When you trade multiple systems with different styles, it is very likely that your countertrend systems will do good when your trend systems do bad, and vice versa.

- *Fewer fill issues.* In trading one system, as your capital grows, so will your trading size. Eventually, your size will become large enough to affect your fills. Even trading 10 contracts in gold, for example, is enough that any stop-loss orders you have will likely experience a few extra ticks of slippage as your 10 lot gets filled. However, if you trade numerous systems, your size on any one trade will be smaller, making fills less of an issue.
- *Smoother equity curve.* When you diversify correctly, you will have different styles, different markets, and different time frames with your trading systems. These differences come together to produce a smoother equity curve, many times reducing drawdown, and almost always reducing overall volatility.

Diversification, done properly, is probably the closest thing I've ever seen to the so-called trading "Holy Grail." The tricks behind diversification are then (1) how to design systems with diversification in mind and (2) how to measure that you actually have diversification. I'll discuss each of these topics in this chapter.

Designing with Diversification in Mind

In the next section, I describe simple ways to measure diversification, but I use these measures after the fact, not during the design process. This is because it is difficult to look at a trading system, identify its weak points, and then design a second complementary system to smooth the first one. It can be done, but I think that is the tough way. I take a much simpler approach, and it seems to work quite well.

If you look back at the initial stages of strategy development, you'll recall that we identify certain characteristics of the system we are trading:

- Market
- Bar type/size
- Any custom time sessions
- Entry
- Exit

As it turns out, taking an initial strategy and varying a couple of these strategy characteristics will likely produce an uncorrelated system. It becomes as simple as doing something different with your trading idea!

A good example of this is with the two euro futures strategies I design in Part IV of this book. Although the market traded is exactly the same, I altered the bar size (105-minute bars versus 60-minute bars), the time session (one strategy trades at night, the other during the day), the entries (completely different entries for each strategy) and exits (different exits, where one system strives for small profits, and the other goes for outsized gains). These change cause completely different system behavior, leading to different results, and consequently diversification.

Measuring Diversification

Once we have two or more systems, how do we check that trading these two systems actually increase diversification? I generally use four methods to check.

Daily Return Correlation

With this method, you simply run a correlation analysis in Excel on the daily returns of each system. For intraday systems, you could run the analysis on shorter time period bars, such as hourly. When I use daily results, I generally check the correlation over the entire history, and then over six-month to one-year periods. This analysis can easily be performed in Excel. I take the daily strategy results for each strategy, plot one as X and one as Y, and calculate the R^2 correlation coefficient. The lower the correlation coefficient, the better the diversification. If in all cases the correlation is much less than 1.0, I can safely assume the correlation is low, and therefore the diversification is high. One caveat, though: because of the fact that the longer term correlation is low does not mean that the systems will never be correlated. There could be weeks or months where the results are highly correlated. If you are aggressive with position sizing, you need to be extra careful—strategies that you assume are not correlated can suddenly become correlated and, instead of reducing your risk, may actually amplify it. A good example of this occurred during the financial crisis of 2008, where heretofore uncorrelated markets and approaches suddenly all moved in lockstep. Diversification might not help you much in periods of crisis.

TABLE 15.1 Using Correlation Measures for Diversification Check

Strategy	R^2 Correlation Coefficient
Euro night	0.9370
Euro day	0.9745
Euro day + night	0.9817

Linearity of Equity Curve

As I have stated previously, a perfectly linear equity curve is the ideal curve for a trading system. It is also a terrific way to measure the diversification effect. All you have to do is take the strategy's equity curve, run a linear regression on it (which can be done in Excel), and report the correlation coefficient R^2 value. An R^2 value of 1 is ideal, as it represents a perfectly linear equity curve. An example of this measurement is shown in Table 15.1 for the euro systems, which are discussed in later chapters. As you can see, the R^2 value for the combined equity is better than the R^2 for each of the pieces. Thus, combining these strategies into one system provides diversification, resulting in a smoother equity curve.

Maximum Drawdown

Another way to measure the impact of diversification is through the maximum drawdown. Although trading multiple systems might not always lead to a reduced maximum drawdown, especially on an absolute basis, many times it does. This is easy to check if you have the equity curve for each system and the combined system. This is shown in Table 15.2 for the euro systems.

In this case, the drawdown for the combined system is in between that of the euro day and euro night systems. This makes it a bit unclear as to whether diversification is occurring. But once we look at reward relative to risk, the answer is clear.

Monte Carlo, Return/Drawdown

Since measuring the drawdown by itself doesn't always give a clear answer, I use Monte Carlo analysis to see whether the combined system is better on a risk-adjusted basis. I measure this by looking at the annual percentage return divided by the max percentage drawdown. Higher values mean that I am getting more reward for my risk. I also look at the probability of making money in a year for confirmation. When I run this analysis, the results are clear (see Table 15.3).

When looking at all the analysis results, note that the conclusion is pretty obvious: combining the two systems produces a smoother equity curve, smaller drawdown

TABLE 15.2 Utilizing Drawdown for Diversification Check

Strategy	Maximum Drawdown
Euro night	\$3,008
Euro day	\$3,523
Euro day + night	\$3,265

TABLE 15.3 Using Return/Drawdown and Probability of Profit for Diversification Check

Strategy	Return/Drawdown	Probability of Profit in One Year
Euro night	2.2	89%
Euro day	5.2	97%
Euro day + night	6.7	98%

than the worst system by itself, a better return-to-risk ratio, and increased probability of profit. Clearly, diversification made the combined system better than each of its parts.

The really nice thing about this diversification technique is that it did not take any real mathematical effort to ensure that the systems were diversified. By simply taking care to make the strategies different, by some combination of different entries, exits, and other general parameters, diversification was practically ensured. This might not always be the case, but this is true enough of the time to make it a useful and simple technique.

One final benefit of diversification will help you increase the output of your strategy development factory. As I have shown, two good systems became a lot better by trading them together. Thus, it might mean that your individual system performance goals can be relaxed a bit, since diversification will later improve the performance. In this manner, you might be more successful creating many "decent" or "just good enough" strategies, rather than one "super-terrific" strategy. Since it is much, much easier to create good, but not great systems, you might get to your overall goal much more quickly by employing diversification.

CHAPTER 16

Position Sizing and Money Management

Up until this point I haven't discussed position sizing or money management in any detail. That isn't to say I don't value it; I agree in large part with position-sizing guru and author Ralph Vince, who states that position sizing is one of the most important things in trading. The problem is some people take that view to the extreme, and believe that position sizing is the only thing that matters. That is simply not true. Use superb position sizing with a losing strategy, and you'll still lose in the long run.

Many people have written books about position sizing and money management, and just like with general trading books, some are good and some are bad. The best ones I have found include Van Tharp's *The Definitive Guide to Position Sizing* (Van Tharp Institute, 2013 [2nd ed.]) and the numerous books by Ralph Vince. Vince's books are more mathematically based, and tough for inexperienced traders to understand and follow, but the underlying messages he puts forth are usually good ones. So in this chapter I won't try to recreate the wheel; I'll instead refer you to those authors for more in-depth information. In this chapter, I'll discuss how I employ position sizing, both for a single system and on a portfolio level. But first, I'll share with you my thoughts on general position-sizing issues.

No Optimum Position Sizing

In all my studies on position sizing, I have determined there is no optimum or one and only one correct way to position size, regardless of trading system. Some trading books out there claim that their unique method is the best, and then prove it to you through an example or two. This, of course, is bogus. For any given equity curve, you can try different position-sizing models and find one that is the best for that particular curve. But, you can't then say that is the best way to position size for any system. A good case in point was a book written a while back (I will not mention the title) that developed a new position-sizing method. This method basically took more risk at the start of trading and, as the account grew, scaled back the position sizing. This works great when the equity curve does well at the beginning, which is what most of the book's examples showed. What most people don't know is that same author applied his "superb" method in real time and quickly blew out numerous accounts. This was likely because his account started out going down instead of up. So, don't assume that a position-sizing method that works well with one trading system will work well with all trading systems.

Risk and Reward Are a Team

Many people look for a magic position-sizing technique that provides extra reward, without any extra risk. In general, though, reward and risk go hand in hand—if you want more reward, you have to be willing to risk more. Where this gets a bit murky is in reviewing results. Based on the return and drawdown shown in an equity curve, it may look like you received a lot of extra reward (return) for no extra risk (drawdown). But you must remember that the risk taken at the start of the trade won't show up in an equity curve. The risk is there; it was just never realized. No matter what the final results say, in the long run you'll be better off assuming that when you want more reward, you have to be willing to risk more.

Position Sizing Can Be Optimized

Many traders will develop a strategy, run it through all the development steps, and afterwards, test out 5 or 10 different position-sizing techniques, picking the best one. Many of these same people don't realize that they have just optimized—not on a particular entry or exit parameter, but instead on the position-sizing method itself. Just as with optimizing trading strategies, just because one method was optimum on past data, it does not mean it will be optimum going forward. In fact, chances are it will not be the best. If you are dead set on testing different position-sizing techniques on a trading strategy, make sure you use Monte Carlo analysis. This will give you a much better indication as to which position-sizing method, if any, is better.

Losing Systems Cannot Become Winners

No matter what type of position-sizing approach you use, if your core trading strategy is a loser, no position-sizing method will save you. That is where it gets confusing, when certain trading gurus state that position sizing is all that matters. While they are espousing the importance of position sizing, they are not saying you can win with a losing system. If this idea was true, you would have more rich casino gamblers out there. No one, to my knowledge, has ever used position sizing to succeed long term in any casino game where they don't have an edge. This doesn't include cheating, or card counting, or any other method that gives you an advantage or edge. In those cases position sizing can help you immensely. If you have a terrible strategy, in the long run the choice of position-sizing technique is irrelevant; you will lose no matter how you size. Start with a strategy that gives you an edge, then apply position sizing.

Winning Systems Can Become Losers

You would think that since loser trading systems cannot become winning systems through position sizing, the opposite is also true: winning trading systems can never become losers when employing position sizing. Nothing, and I mean nothing, could be further from the truth. It is exceedingly easy to take a winning system, apply an overly aggressive or inappropriate position-sizing method, and still lose all your money. Over the years, I have seen many people do this. Most think that when they have a winning system, they must push "the pedal to the metal" and trade as aggressively as they can. Most of these same people crash in spectacular fashion during an inevitable future drawdown.

The Fantasy of Size

Almost every two-bit huckster out there selling a trading system will have some sort of sales pitch that goes like this: "If you use my method, you can get $5,000 profit per contract per year. So if you trade 100 contracts—all it takes is adding a few zeros to your order quantity—you'll soon be making a very good living!" If you can't immediately see through the transparency of this claim, I'll explain the fallacy. First, the huckster assumes you'll have enough margin in your account to actually trade 100 contracts. If you have determined that a $10,000 account is appropriate to trade one contract (which, by the way, is already considered aggressive by many traders), then you would need a $1 million trading account. If you had that much money in your account, you'd probably be smart enough to never listen to the huckster's pitch in the first place! Remember, drawdown is always possible, and your account needs to consider that.

The second fallacy in the "trade 100 contracts" scenario is that most people could not handle it psychologically. Sure, if the equity curve is always increasing, trading 100 contracts and banking $500,000 a year is easy. But when you have 5 losing trades in a row, and you lose $100,000, psychologically that could be a killer. Your best bet, therefore, is to ignore the hucksters and position size so that you slowly add on contracts, and acclimate yourself to the dollar amounts involved before you increase size again.

Short Term—Go for Broke

If your edge is small, and you want to trade for only a very short time, just go crazy with position sizing. Chances are, over the short run, you probably will win. In the long run, you'll be toast, but in the short run you'll be profitable. A classic example of this is with a Martingale betting strategy. You begin by betting one coin. Every time you lose, you double your bet (two, four, eight, etc. coins). When you eventually win, you win back all your original bets, plus $1 profit. The interesting thing about this approach is that if you play it just once with no bet limit, you will almost always make $1 (i.e., winning one betting sequence). But if you play it over and over, your odds of overall success go to zero because eventually there will be a betting run of consecutive losses you cannot recover from. Of course, betting one sequence and then walking away is impossible for most people. Still, it is an option that is usually successful. When you add in bet limits for Martingale, the approach becomes even less attractive. I know quite a few former traders who tried Martingale over the years; note I described them as "former."

No Position Sizing = No Good!

Whether it is fear of loss, lack of confidence or some other issue, many people who have winning trading systems never position size. Instead, they continue to trade the same size for years. This to me is almost as bad as being too aggressive with sizing. When you have a winning system, you have the goose with the golden egg. Take care of that goose, learn what it can eat to maximize egg production, but don't overdo it. After all, you need to make full use of the goose while you have it.

Strategy, Then Position Size, or Strategy and Position Size Together?

For most of my development career, I have developed the strategy first, based on always trading a single contract. After development is completed, I then apply position sizing. This is a good way to go, especially when your final position sizing is for a portfolio of systems.

Fellow trader Andrea Unger, who also trades for a living, disagrees with my approach. Considering that he has won the World Cup Championship of Futures Trading four times, I think I am safe in listening to him. His argument is as follows:

when you develop a system trading a single contract, you'll get a good system, but maybe not one that takes advantage of position sizing. For example, if you include position sizing in your development process, you are likely to end up with smaller losing trades, since that will allow you to trade with more contracts, leading to a higher net profit. This definitely makes sense, based on my own experience. One of my favorite trading systems I developed was based on one contract being traded. Unfortunately, that system has relatively large losses ($2,000 to $3,000 per contract), making it tough to position size, unless the account is very large. Just think of the account size you need if you want to trade 10 contracts, where a $30,000 loss on one trade is possible. With a $300,000 account, one losing trade would lead to a 10 percent account loss. This is much too large a loss, even for the most reckless of traders. Therefore, in this case, maybe developing the system with position sizing would have suggested a parameter set where $500 maximum loss was optimum. This system would be much easier to apply position sizing for a smaller account.

So, even though I prefer not using position sizing during development, recognize that at least one (and probably many more) great traders do develop with position sizing. It might be worth trying both approaches on your development projects, to see which one you like the best.

Positioning Size—Single System

Whenever I begin trading a new strategy, I almost always start at the smallest size possible, typically only one contract. Many people think the exact opposite; if you have an edge, you need to exploit it with big size as soon as possible. After all, what if the edge disappears? That is a good point, but in my experience, starting small is better. First, even with all the development, testing, and incubation, the system still might not have an edge, even though I think it does. Trading small will limit my loss in such a case. Second, I always become emotionally invested in strategies when I start trading—after all, I want to see my creation succeed—so trading a small size takes any emotion out of the equation. This new strategy becomes just another strategy in my portfolio. My final reason for starting small is that I want to increase size based on the profits of the strategy. If the strategy makes money, it will ramp up in size. If it stays flat or loses money, my downside is limited.

Even though I start with one contract, I always know in advance what my sizing scheme will be as I build equity. Most of the time, I just use fixed fractional sizing:

$$N = int(x * \text{Equity}/\text{Largest Loss})$$

where

N = Integer number of contracts (always round down)
int = Integer function

x = Fraction of equity to bet on each trade
Equity = Current account equity
Largest loss = Largest historical loss from walk-forward back testing

The only variable that is at my discretion is the fixed fraction x. Many traders will say that x can be no more than .02, or some other value. While I can't argue with keeping the value of x low, I prefer to use Monte Carlo simulation to show me the best value of x, which for me is one that maximizes my return/drawdown ratio. This is, of course, subject to other constraints such as risk of ruin and maximum allowable drawdown. An example will make this clearer.

To look at the impact of fixed fractional sizing, I use the Monte Carlo simulation analysis of the euro system I will present later. I run the analysis with various values of the fixed fraction x, and look at the following charts:

Median rate of return—I want as high as possible.
Return/DD ratio—I want as high as possible.
Median max drawdown—I want this as low as possible.
Risk of ruin—I want this as low as possible.

Obviously, since I am trying to maximize return and minimize drawdown, there has to be a happy medium somewhere. This depends not only on the results but also my personal preferences. For instance, if I did not care what the drawdown or risk of ruin was, I'd select the peak point on the return or return/DD chart. This corresponds to $x = 0.32$, and also is Ralph Vince's optimal *f*. But, with $x = 0.32$, I'd have a 50 percent chance of having a max drawdown equal to or greater than 67.4 percent. Plus, my risk of ruin would be 21 percent. Wow! Those values are too high for me. But I will accept a 45 percent maximum drawdown and a 10 percent risk of ruin. Eliminating all chart points that do not meet these criteria result in a max value of $x = 0.175$, as shown in Figure 16.1. Therefore, I will use this value of x in my trading for this particular system.

Positioning Size—Multiple Systems

Since I am trading multiple systems at any one time, I have to respect any correlation between the results. That is, I can't independently determine the value of x for each system, and then just trade them together. Instead, I analyze all the systems together, and try all values of x for each of them. Just as with the single system, I want values of x for each system (each system will indeed have a different value of x) that maximizes my return/DD ratio, subject to maximum allowable drawdown and risk of ruin. An example of this process is shown in Figure 16.2, where five different systems are traded at the same time. The values for x for each system maximizes the return/DD, subject to the loss constraints I have chosen.

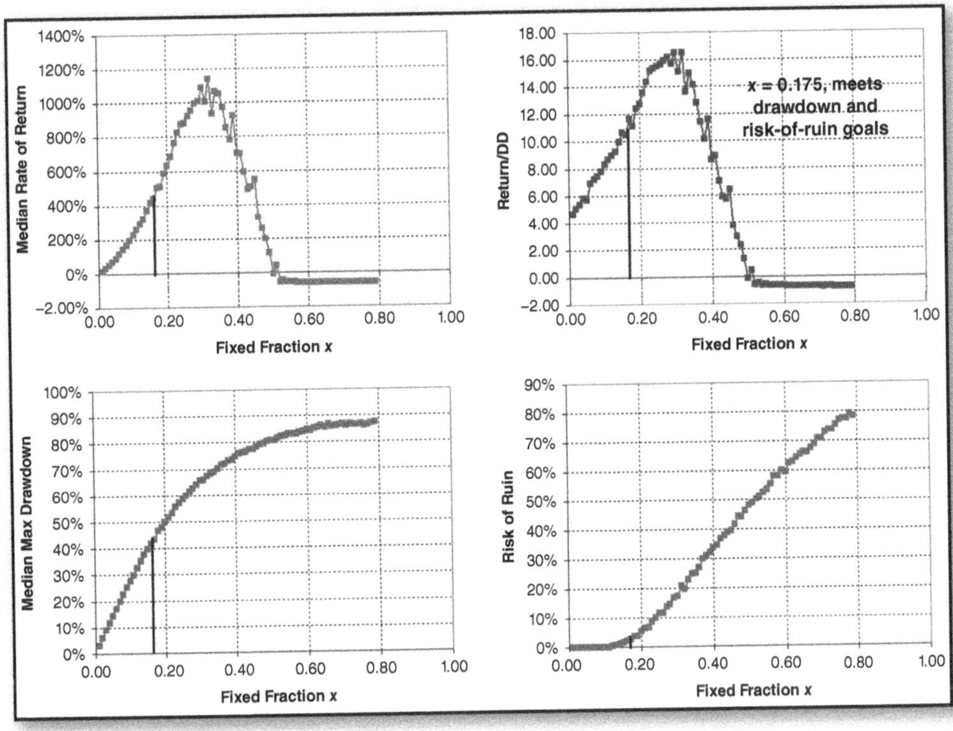

FIGURE 16.1 Single-System Position Sizing

Start Equity	System 1 "X"	System 2 "X"	System 3 "X"	System 4 "X"	System 5 "X"	Ruin	% Profitable Weeks	90 %ile Drawdown	Median $ prof	Median Return	Median Return/DD
$55,000	0.13	0.1	0.1	0.2	0.15	4%	78%	24.0%	$1,409,964	199%	63.59
$55,000	0.14	0.11	0.1	0.2	0.15	3%	79%	24.7%	$1,526,904	206%	68.71
$55,000	0.13	0.1	0.1	0.21	0.15	3%	78%	24.8%	$1,461,254	202%	64.88
$55,000	0.13	0.11	0.1	0.21	0.15	4%	78%	25.0%	$1,599,621	211%	70.42
$55,000	0.13	0.12	0.1	0.2	0.16	3%	79%	25.2%	$1,491,816	204%	66.33
$55,000	0.14	0.1	0.1	0.21	0.15	4%	78%	25.3%	$1,512,240	205%	66.83
$55,000	0.13	0.12	0.11	0.2	0.16	4%	79%	25.3%	$1,656,845	215%	71.10
$55,000	0.13	0.1	0.11	0.2	0.16	4%	78%	25.4%	$1,464,586	202%	64.13
$55,000	0.14	0.1	0.11	0.2	0.15	4%	77%	25.7%	$1,589,272	210%	69.66
$55,000	0.15	0.1	0.1	0.2	0.15	3%	79%	25.7%	$1,531,103	207%	66.45
$55,000	0.14	0.12	0.1	0.2	0.15	4%	79%	25.7%	$1,404,228	198%	61.12
$55,000	0.13	0.1	0.11	0.2	0.15	4%	78%	25.8%	$1,435,627	200%	65.17
$55,000	0.13	0.12	0.1	0.21	0.15	4%	78%	25.8%	$1,576,721	210%	67.71
$55,000	0.13	0.1	0.1	0.21	0.16	4%	79%	25.8%	$1,538,894	207%	66.67
$55,000	0.14	0.12	0.1	0.21	0.15	4%	78%	25.8%	$1,589,530	210%	66.89
$55,000	0.13	0.1	0.1	0.22	0.17	4%	79%	25.8%	$1,710,702	218%	74.38
$55,000	0.13	0.12	0.1	0.21	0.16	4%	79%	25.8%	$1,496,538	204%	66.32
$55,000	0.13	0.13	0.1	0.21	0.15	4%	78%	25.9%	$1,572,240	209%	67.86
$55,000	0.13	0.11	0.1	0.2	0.15	5%	78%	25.9%	$1,388,113	197%	62.79
$55,000	0.13	0.12	0.1	0.2	0.15	4%	78%	26.0%	$1,444,798	201%	63.21
$55,000	0.14	0.12	0.11	0.21	0.15	4%	78%	26.0%	$1,662,600	215%	69.06

FIGURE 16.2 Position Sizing, Multiple Systems

Obviously, I have just scratched the surface with position sizing, but I have given you an idea of how I approach it. As stated earlier, my philosophy is to go slow at first and let the system profits generate most of the extra capital needed for position sizing. This helps me keep the risk at a manageable level. Since I use fixed fractional sizing, you might wonder how you could employ a different sizing technique in your analysis. Simply take what I have shown here and modify it for your sizing approach, and conduct the same analysis. You'll then have a logical analysis for whatever position-sizing method you decide to employ.

CHAPTER 17

Documenting the Process

As you can imagine, keeping track of all the strategies you create and run through this development process can quickly become a nightmare. Proper documentation is the key to successfully managing this effort. Currently, I use an Excel spreadsheet to manage my strategies. This is available on the book resource web site (www.wiley.com/go/algotradingsystems) for you to download and use, and is also shown in Figures 17.1 and 17.2. I have set it up to identify the items I feel are the most important. Of course, as you progress in system development, you will likely have different items you want to track. In that case, simply edit the spreadsheet to fit your own needs.

The items I track with the spreadsheet will be discussed in this chapter.

Trading Goals

I list all my goals for profit, drawdown, rate of return, number of trades, and so on. I find it much more difficult to accept systems that do not meet my goals when the goals are clearly written at the start!

Trading Idea

Here I list all the particulars of the strategy I am testing.

Strategy name. Sounds simple, but having a unique name for every strategy helps you keep track of things. I use a standard naming convention, which allows me to easily find it in my trading software's list of strategies.

KJD2013-10 BrkOut A

System Development Process Checklist		
Trading Goals	**Criteria**	**Completion Date**
List All Goals		
Trading Idea		**Completion Date**
Strategy Name		
Strategy—Gen Description		
Edge		
Markets to Test		
Bar Size		
Historical Test Period Market Data Streams Market Data Customization		
Entry Rules		
Exit Rules		
Limited Testing	**Results**	**Completion Date**
Test Period		
Entry Testing		
Fixed Stop, Fixed Target		
Fixed Bar		
Exit Testing		
Similar Approach Entry		
Core System Test		
Monkey Testing		
Random Entry Random Exit Random Entry & Exit		
Limited Testing—Overall	Pass	Fail

FIGURE 17.1 Documenting the Development Process

System Development Process Checklist

Walk-forward Testing	Results	Completion Date
In Period		
Out Period		
Fitness Function		
Anchored/Unanchored		
Optimum In/Out (if applicable)		
Walk-forward Historical Strategy Created		
Walk-forward Testing—Overall	**Pass**	**Fail**

Monte Carlo Analysis	Results	Completion Date
Start Equity		
Quit Equity		
Number Trades, 1 Year		
Return/DD Ratio		
Monte Carlo—Overall	**Pass**	**Fail**

Incubation	Results	Completion Date
Meets Goals	**Pass**	**Fail**

Diversification		
Meets Goals	**Pass**	**Fail**

Position Sizing		
Meets Goals	**Pass**	**Fail**

Final Notes	Completion Date

FIGURE 17.2 Documenting the Development Process (cont'd)

where:

KJD = My initials—in a list of 1,000 strategies, you want to easily find the ones you wrote.

2013-10 = Year, followed by two-digit month. I created this strategy in October 2013.

BrkOut = A simple description of the strategy. This example would be a breakout strategy.

A = Version of strategy. If I later change or add rules, the next version would be "B." This serves a couple of purposes. First, it helps you keep track of how the strategy changed over time. Second, it reminds you how many changes you made to the strategy. If you consistently find yourself testing up to version "M," for example, you are probably spending too much time revising your strategy. Remember, the risk of overfitting goes up with each version.

As part of this naming, I will also add a "W" to the end if the walk-forward version has a different code than the baseline version, and I will use "H" at the end to signify a historical walk-forward version of the strategy.

Strategy—general description. In simple words, I will describe my strategy.

Edge. What do I think my edge is? Enter it here. This is a good warning sign—if you do not have a clue what your edge is, you probably do not have one!

Markets to test. List the market or markets you plan to examine.

Bar size. Enter the type of bar you are testing with.

Historical test period. List the start and end dates for your analysis.

Market data streams. List the data identifier you are using. For example, if I wanted to test the continuous gold contract, in TradeStation I would use "@GC."

Market data customization. If you use any special session times or anything else unique, enter it here.

Entry rules. Describe your entry rules. You can use plain English, pseudo code, or actual code. The idea is to archive the entry method for later reference.

Exit rules. Describe your exit rules in the same manner as your entry rules.

Limited Testing

Here I list all the particulars of the limited testing phase:

Test period. The one or two-year sample of historical data that I am using to perform the limited testing.

Entry testing. Here, I will record the general results (e.g., excellent, good, poor) for the entry testing (fixed stop, fixed target, and/or fixed bar).

Exit testing. Here, I will record the general results (e.g., excellent, good, poor) for the exit testing (similar-approach entry).

Core system testing. General results of the whole system.

Monkey testing. If I perform any random "monkey" testing, I will record the results here.

Limited testing—overall. Based on all the limited tests run, does the system pass or fail?

Walk-Forward Testing

Assuming the strategy passes the limited testing phase, I now move on to the walk-forward testing step.

In period. The number of trading days in the in-sample periods.

Out period. The number of trading days in the out-sample periods.

Fitness function. List the fitness function used.

Anchored/Unanchored. Identify whether you are using anchored testing or unanchored testing.

Optimum in/out. If you optimize the in/out periods, identify that here, and also provide information on the true out-of-sample date range.

Walk-forward historical strategy created. If you create a strategy version specifically with walk-forward history, identify it here. I signify this by putting the letter "H" on the end of the strategy.

Walk-forward testing—overall. Based on all the walk-forward testing, does the system pass or fail?

Monte Carlo Testing

Assuming the strategy passes the walk-forward testing phase, I now move on to the Monte Carlo testing step:

Start equity. Enter the starting equity you are using for the simulation.

Quit equity. Enter the equity level below which you will quit trading the strategy.

Number trades, 1 year. Number of trades in one year of trading.

Return/DD ratio. Enter this result from the Monte Carlo simulation.

Monte Carlo testing—overall. Based on all the Monte Carlo testing, does the system pass or fail?

Incubation Testing

Assuming the strategy passes the Monte Carlo phase, I now move on to the incubation testing step:

Meets goals. Did the strategy pass or fail incubation?

■ Diversification Check

Applicable only to strategies that you plan to trade with other strategies. Was the current strategy developed with diversification in mind?

Meets goals. Did the strategy pass or fail diversification?

■ Position-Sizing Check

Since I usually test a strategy with "one trade per contract" rules, this is an easy check. If, however, I used a particular position sizing during development, it should not be the outcome of optimization and should be identified here (especially if it will be traded with other systems).

Meets goals. Was the strategy developed using one contract per trade, or some other position-sizing technique that did *not* involve optimization?

■ Final Notes

After testing and development is completed, enter any information you feel is appropriate. For example, you could list the date you started trading. If the strategy does not pass but you like the entry or exit rules, you could always identify that fact here. I have had strategies that failed, but I still liked a particular aspect of it. With the notes at the end, you can always refer to it later and easily remember, "Oh yes, I wanted to test this entry with soybeans, due to its high volatility."

■ One Final List

The individual sheets provide an excellent way to manage each strategy. In addition, I also keep a list of entry and exit ideas. These might not be fully formed strategies, but they are ideas I can take and later use in a strategy. For example, if I see an intriguing entry idea in a book or trading magazine, and I cannot immediately test it, I'll just add it to my entry list. This list serves two purposes. First, it functions as an idea manager, saving any idea you have for future testing. Second, having this list means you will never run out of ideas to test. Trust me, the list will grow far faster than you can test!

PART IV

CREATING A SYSTEM

CHAPTER 18

Goals, Initial and Walk-Forward Testing

Now that I've walked you through the strategy development process I use, I think it will be instructive and informative for me to walk you through the development of two strategies I created in March 2013 and started real-money trading in August 2013. If you go to the web site (www.wiley.com/go/algotradingsystems) you will see updates for these strategies, assuming I am still trading them, or a post-mortem analysis if I decide to stop trading them.

The next chapters will walk you through the process, and after that Chapter 24 will give running commentary and updates as I trade it live.

Developing a New Strategy

As with all new trading strategies, first I start out with a SMART goal:

"I want to create a trading system for the euro currency that is an intraday strategy that can earn 50 percent annual return with a median maximum drawdown (determined by Monte Carlo simulation) of 25 percent or less, which is a return to drawdown ratio of 2.0 or better. The system (which may include more than one independent strategy) should make money on 55 percent or more of the days it trades. This trading system will take no more than two trades per day. I will give myself one month of development to complete this task (end of March 2013), and if I do not have a system at that time, I will move on to the next idea."

Is this goal sufficient for a SMART goal? Let's take a look:

Specific. Intraday euro strategy, with specific performance goals. Yes, it is specific. In fact, it may be too specific—it is a pretty long goal statement.

Measurable. 50 percent annual return, less than 25 percent drawdown, return/drawdown ratio greater than 2.0, 55 percent winning days. Yes, it will easy to measure performance against these benchmarks.

Attainable. 50 percent annual return, less than 25 percent drawdown, return/drawdown ratio greater than 2.0. When I first started developing systems, these goals were very ambitious. It turns out that developing a strategy the *correct* way is pretty difficult. Many people will scoff at these numbers, since they seem small compared to what a decent optimized strategy looks like. Remember, though, that a great-looking back test does not always mean too much. So, yes, the goals here are attainable. The toughest part will be making the system an intraday strategy.

Relevant. Everything in my goal statement relates to development of this system. Yes, it is relevant.

Time bound. Since I limit myself to one month of development time, this is a time-bound goal. This time limit will also prevent me from making too many changes to a decent strategy, which will prevent overfitting and other bad development habits.

Once I had the SMART goal identified, I could proceed to developing my trading idea.

From past development experience, I know that intraday systems are difficult to develop, much more so than a longer-term swing system. The best intraday systems, in my experience, are those that trade infrequently and tend to ride winners (trends) as long as possible. That leads me in the direction of a strategy that cuts losses relatively quickly, but keeps winners until the end of the day. To get the biggest bang for the buck, then, this system should trade during the U.S. day session, as many of the big moves occur during this very liquid time period. The problem with this approach is that a system with many small losses and a few big winners will inevitably have a low winning percentage. To counteract this, I will likely need another strategy, one that has small winners, larger losers, and a high winning percentage.

As you can see, just thinking about the kind of system I want really helped me figure out the best way to proceed. After some more thought, I ended up with the following:

Create two strategies for the euro currency, using continuous contract @EC:

Strategy 1: Nighttime strategy "euro night." Runs on 105-minute bars, from 6 P.M. ET to 7 A.M. ET. All trades are exited by 7 A.M., so they do not interfere with strategy 2. This strategy will focus on small wins, larger losses, and will initiate trades only until 1 A.M. ET (I have to sleep sometime, in case I do not automate this strategy).

Strategy 2: Daytime strategy "euro day." Runs on 60-minute bars from 7 A.M. to 3 P.M. ET, with all trades exited by 3 P.M. The end of the trading day is 5 P.M., but I am closing all trades at 3 P.M., since trading volume is a lot less from 3 P.M. to 5 P.M.

For the test period, since I am using small bars, I will test back only to January 1, 2009. Typically, for swing systems I use 5 to 10 years of historical data, which means this is a slightly different approach for me. This also avoids my having to test during the 2008 financial crisis, which would likely make development tougher. So note that, in a way, I am taking some shortcuts with this strategy development, since I am (1) using only about 4 years of historical data, and (2) avoiding a major market event. I realize that these shortcuts will lead to a system that is not as robust as it could be, but that is a sacrifice I am willing to accept. Strategy development is full of these trade-offs, and there is not always a correct way to resolve them. Sometimes you just have to try and see what happens, and that is what I am doing here.

Now that I have the preliminary information established, I can go ahead with the entry and exit rules. I'll start with the exit rules, since those will be relatively fixed, compared to the entries. For both strategies, I want to lose no more than $450 per trade, after slippage and commission of $17.50 per trade. This equates to a loss of 34 ticks. When I go to detailed development, I will allow this stop amount to be lower than 34 ticks, but never more.

For profit, with both strategies I will allow the profit target to be optimized for euro night strategy, and fixed at $5,000 for the euro day strategy. Since there has never been a $5,000 intraday move in euro, the $5,000 limit is effectively saying, "Go for as much profit as you can, and hold until the end of the trading session."

The final exit for both strategies will be to close all open trades at the end of the session. This will be a rigid exit, with no optimization needed.

With the simple exits firmly established, the trick to making these strategies successful will lie in the entries. After some cursory examination and testing, it became apparent that reversal-type entries would be the best thing for both strategies. With a reversal entry, an example of which is shown in Figure 18.1, the idea is to catch an excursion up or down, before it stops and reverses. This makes these strategies a type of mean reversion, since you are entering against a trend and banking on its reversing before turning into a trend in the opposing direction.

For strategy 1, the euro night strategy, the long entry is based on the average high of the previous X bars, reduced by a multiplier of the average true range. Of course, the exact opposite entry is true for a short entry. See Figure 18.1.

For strategy 2, the euro day strategy, when a highest high of the past Y bars is hit, and the X bar momentum is down, then a limit order to sell short will be placed Z ticks above the current high. The opposite logic holds for long trades. Thus, to get filled, the strategy is planning on one more price thrust before the price reverses. An example entry is shown in Figure 18.2.

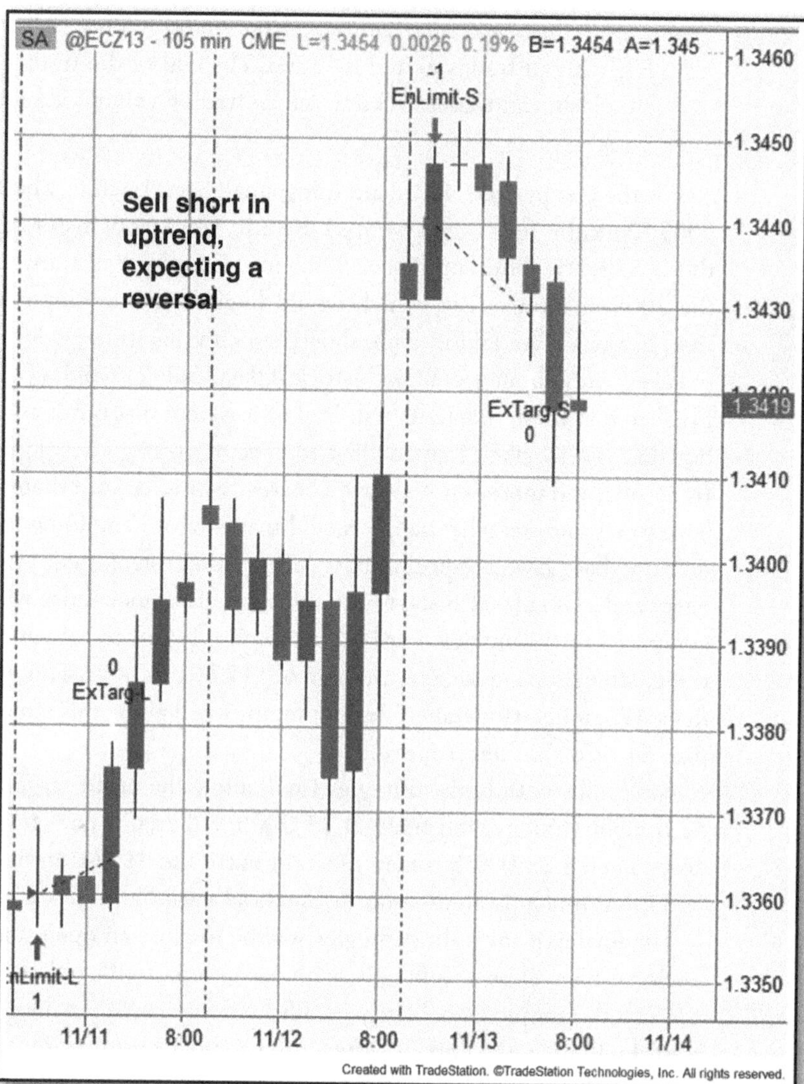

FIGURE 18.1 Reversal Entry Example

What do I think my edge actually is? Based on the reversal entries I am employing, I feel my edge is in identifying very-short-term (for night strategy 1) and medium-term (for day strategy 2) areas where the price is likely to reverse. By having limit orders away from the current market, I liken my edge to a rubber band. It keeps stretching and stretching until I get my limit fill, then it bounces back, giving me profit. Of course, if the rubber band keeps stretching after my order is filled, that means my premise was wrong, and I pay the price with a full stop-loss or a loss at the end of the trading session.

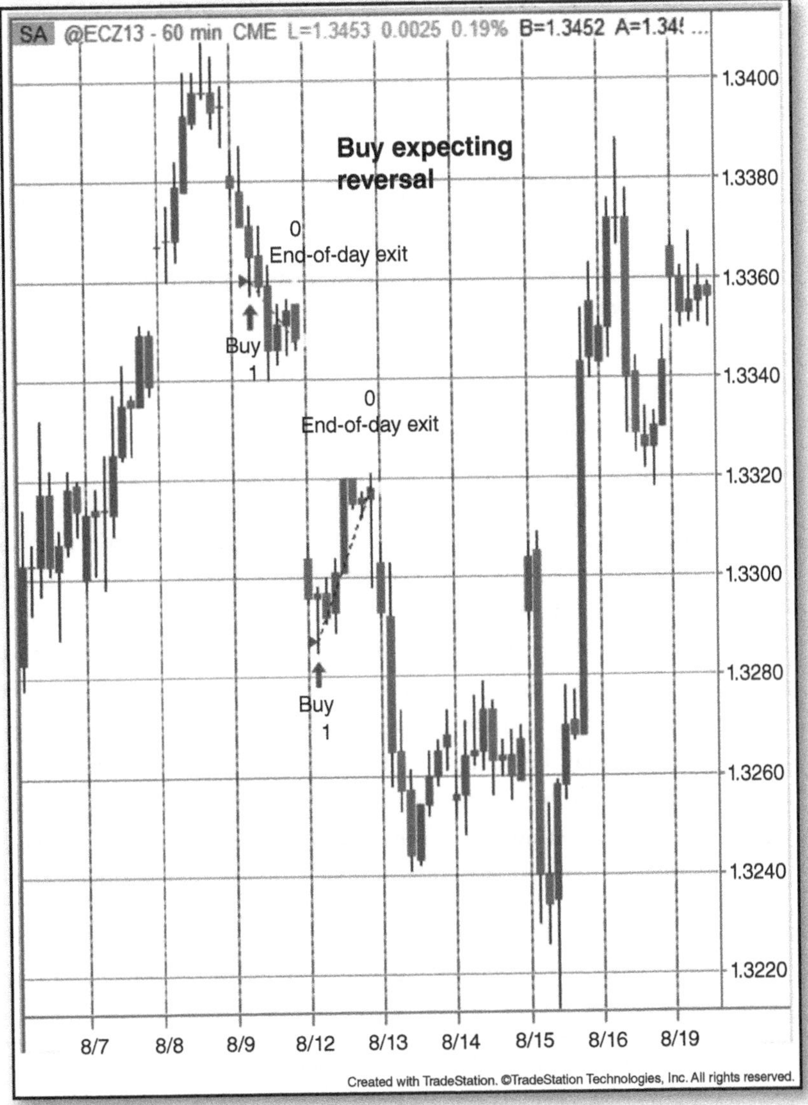

FIGURE 18.2 Euro Day Strategy Entry Example

With all the basic structure of the strategy, along with the entry and exit in place, I can now start the preliminary testing.

Limited Testing

For limited testing, I chose to look at the results for just 2009. Since my full-size test will be 2009–present, I am using about 25 percent of the data to do my initial tests. This will give me a good indication of whether my strategy is viable. Remember, with these tests I am looking for a general indication that my entries, exits, and entries and exits combined are working well.

Entry test—fixed-stop and target. The results of this test, and all other limited tests are shown in Table 18.1. All results are acceptable, which allows me to proceed to the in-depth testing phase.

Entry test—fixed-bar exit. The results look good and lead me to think I possibly have some sort of edge here with my entry.

Exit test—similar-approach entry. To test the exit, I created an entry condition similar in style (mean-reverting limit order) to the one I am using. If the results are good, it gives me just a bit more confidence in the exit I have chosen. Results do indeed look good.

Core system test. This test is a gentle optimization of the whole system, with entry and exit conditions working together. Results show that the system performs pretty well and is acceptable for further investigation.

Monkey testing. This random testing can be very useful it certain situations. Other times, it really doesn't provide any additional information. Such is the case here.

Limited testing summary. Both strategies passed all the tests I ran, so the strategies can proceed further through the process. Note that this is the exception, not the rule. Most times, the results will be so poor that no further testing is required, and you can simply move on to the next idea. In a minority of situations, the results will be so-so, and you may add a rule or filter to get better results. In very rare cases, strategies will be acceptable the first time through, which is what happened here. As you develop experience creating and testing ideas, you will find that more and more of your strategies fall into this third category. At the start of your development

TABLE 18.1 Limited Testing Summary, Euro Day and Night System

	Euro Night	Euro Day
Entry Test—Fixed-Stop and Target	82% of optimizations profitable	76% of optimizations profitable
Entry Test—Fixed-Bar Exit	Exit after one to five bars >> good	Exit after one to five bars >> good
Exit Test—Similar-Approach Entry	Generic mean reversion limit order entry >> acceptable	Generic mean reversion limit order entry >> acceptable
Core System Test	85% of optimizations profitable	81% of optimizations profitable
Monkey Testing	Entry better than random	Entry better than random
	Exit better than random	Exit better than random

journey, though, plan on discarding a lot of garbage strategies and adding rules and conditions to most of the rest.

Walk-Forward Testing

With the limited testing complete, I can now proceed to the detailed walk-forward testing. This consists of running a full optimization, and then running through the walk-forward analysis. Figure 18.3 shows the process.

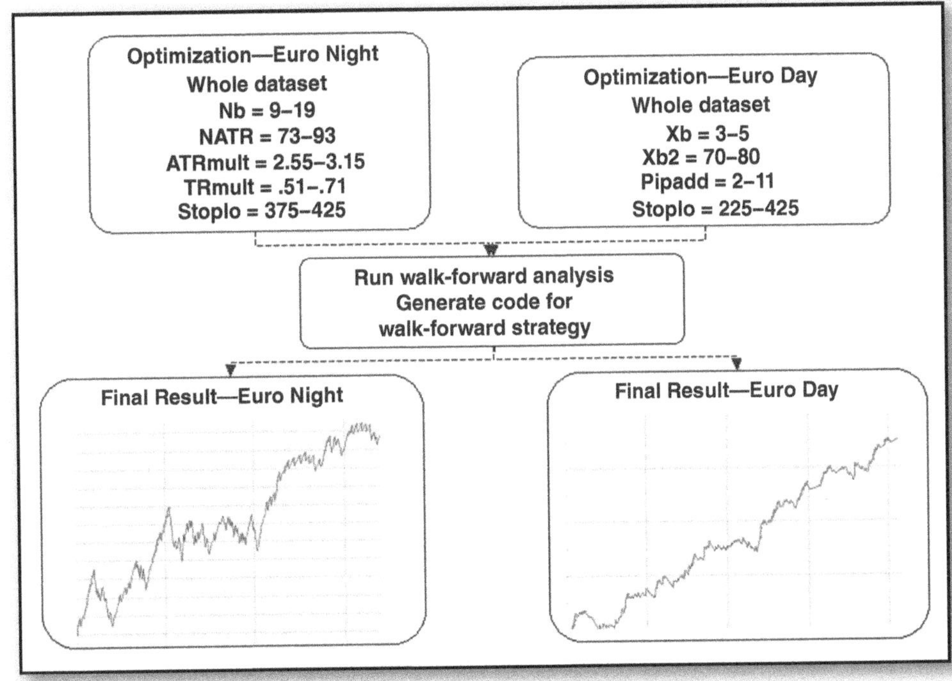

FIGURE 18.3 Walk-Forward Testing, Euro Day and Night Strategy

CHAPTER 19

Monte Carlo Testing and Incubation

With the walk-forward testing complete, based on the results I am confident I have a viable strategy. The equity curve for walk-forward testing looks nice, but at the same time I realize that there is no possible way the future equity curve will look exactly like the past equity curve. My hope, and the hope of all developers at this stage, is that the components of the equity curve (i.e., individual trades) are roughly the same as the walk-forward history. The easiest way to imagine this is to think about the average trade profit and its standard deviation (scatter). If either of these values significantly changes, the system might fail in the future. If, for example, the average trade turns negative, future performance will obviously be negative. Similarly, if the standard deviation increases, the drawdowns will likely be much more severe, the system will be harder to trade with position sizing, and the resulting equity curve will probably give you more ulcers.

Assuming, then, that the walk-forward trade performance will continue in the future, it becomes useful to see how the future performance might vary over time. For this analysis, I simulate one year's worth of trades with Monte Carlo analysis.

Euro Day Strategy

As previously discussed in Chapter 7, the only information required to do a simple Monte Carlo analysis is:

- Starting equity
- Quitting-point equity

- Number of trades in one year
- Individual trade results

For any simulations that you run, you might want to simulate more than one year's worth of trades, or you might want to include position sizing, or you may even want to eliminate the quitting-point equity—the point at which you stop trading. These particulars will be something you develop over time, as you determine what you like and don't like in the simulation. The exact method I use may not suit you, and that is fine.

Once I have all the inputs for the Monte Carlo simulation, I simply enter them in the spreadsheet and press the "Calculate" button. Results are as shown in Figure 19.1. For the day strategy, if I keep the risk of ruin below 10 percent (my personal threshold for ruin), I find I need $6,250 to begin trading this system, and in an "average" year I can expect:

23.7 percent maximum drawdown
129 percent return
5.45 return/drawdown ratio

Other points of interest are that I have a 4 percent chance of ruin in that first year, where my equity would drop below $3,000. I also have a 94 percent probability of making money in that first year (i.e., ending the year with more than $6,250).

Based on my goals and objectives, all of these parameters are acceptable, and I consider the Monte Carlo simulation results successful. Note that, based on your goals and objectives, this system—with the $6,250 starting equity—may not be good enough for you. For example, many people want a near 0 percent chance of risk of ruin. Others may feel that 25.5 percent maximum drawdown is too high. The point is that what is right for me might not be right for you. That is why I think it is so important that you come up with your own goals and objectives. In the end, you need to feel comfortable trading what you have developed, and trading something that does not fit you is a sure recipe for disaster.

Euro Night Strategy

Now, I will perform the exact same procedure on the euro night strategy. Results are as shown in Figure 19.2. For the night strategy, if I again keep the risk of ruin below 10 percent, I find I need $6,250 to begin trading this system, and in an "average" year I can expect:

25.0 percent maximum drawdown
52 percent return
2.0 return/drawdown ratio

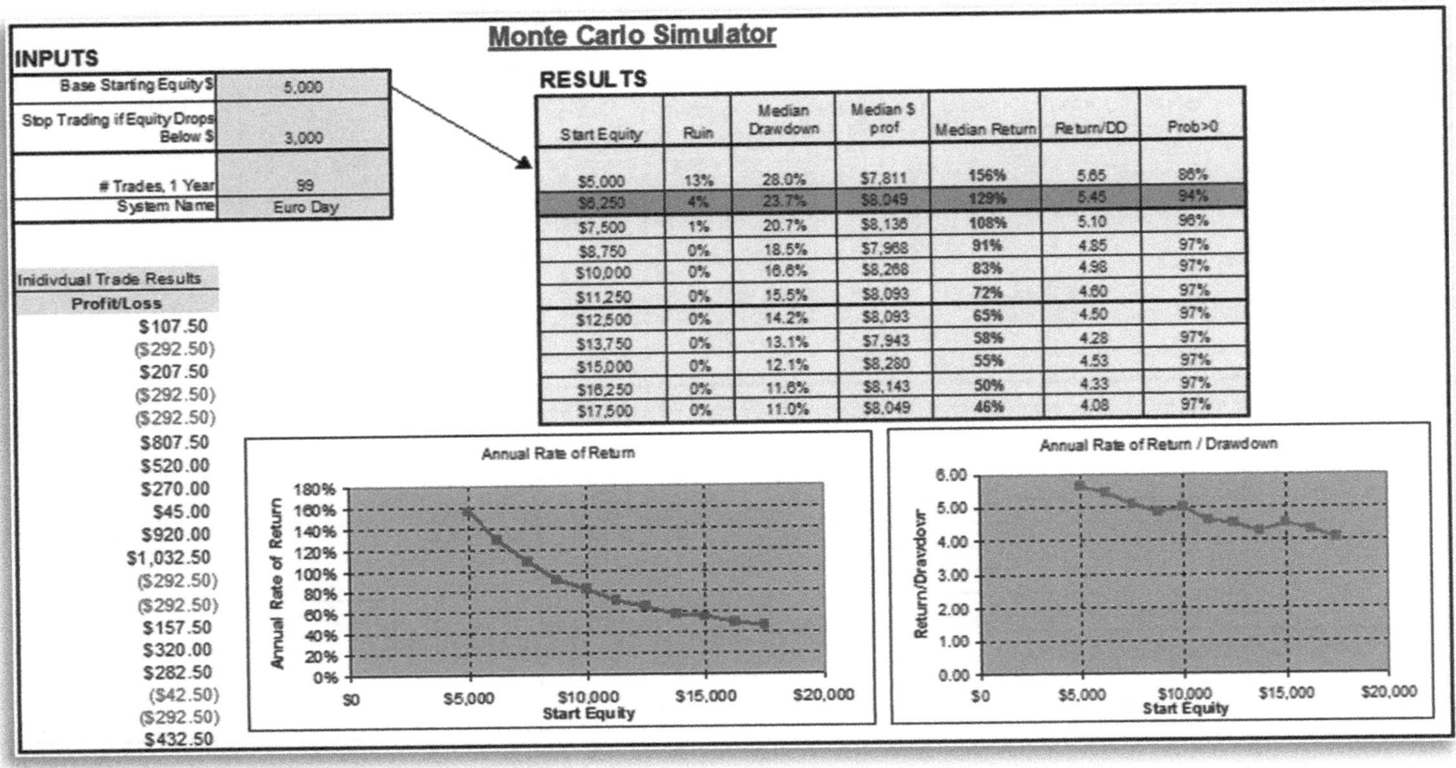

Monte Carlo Simulator

INPUTS

Base Starting Equity $	5,000
Stop Trading if Equity Drops Below $	3,000
# Trades, 1 Year	99
System Name	Euro Day

RESULTS

Start Equity	Ruin	Median Drawdown	Median $ prof	Median Return	Return/DD	Prob>0
$5,000	13%	28.0%	$7,811	156%	5.65	86%
$6,250	4%	23.7%	$8,049	129%	5.45	94%
$7,500	1%	20.7%	$8,138	108%	5.10	96%
$8,750	0%	18.5%	$7,968	91%	4.85	97%
$10,000	0%	16.6%	$8,268	83%	4.98	97%
$11,250	0%	15.5%	$8,093	72%	4.60	97%
$12,500	0%	14.2%	$8,093	65%	4.50	97%
$13,750	0%	13.1%	$7,943	58%	4.28	97%
$15,000	0%	12.1%	$8,280	55%	4.53	97%
$16,250	0%	11.6%	$8,143	50%	4.33	97%
$17,500	0%	11.0%	$8,049	46%	4.08	97%

Inidivdual Trade Results
Profit/Loss
$107.50
($292.50)
$207.50
($292.50)
($292.50)
$807.50
$520.00
$270.00
$45.00
$920.00
$1,032.50
($292.50)
($292.50)
$157.50
$320.00
$282.50
($42.50)
($292.50)
$432.50

FIGURE 19.1 Monte Carlo Results, Euro Day Strategy

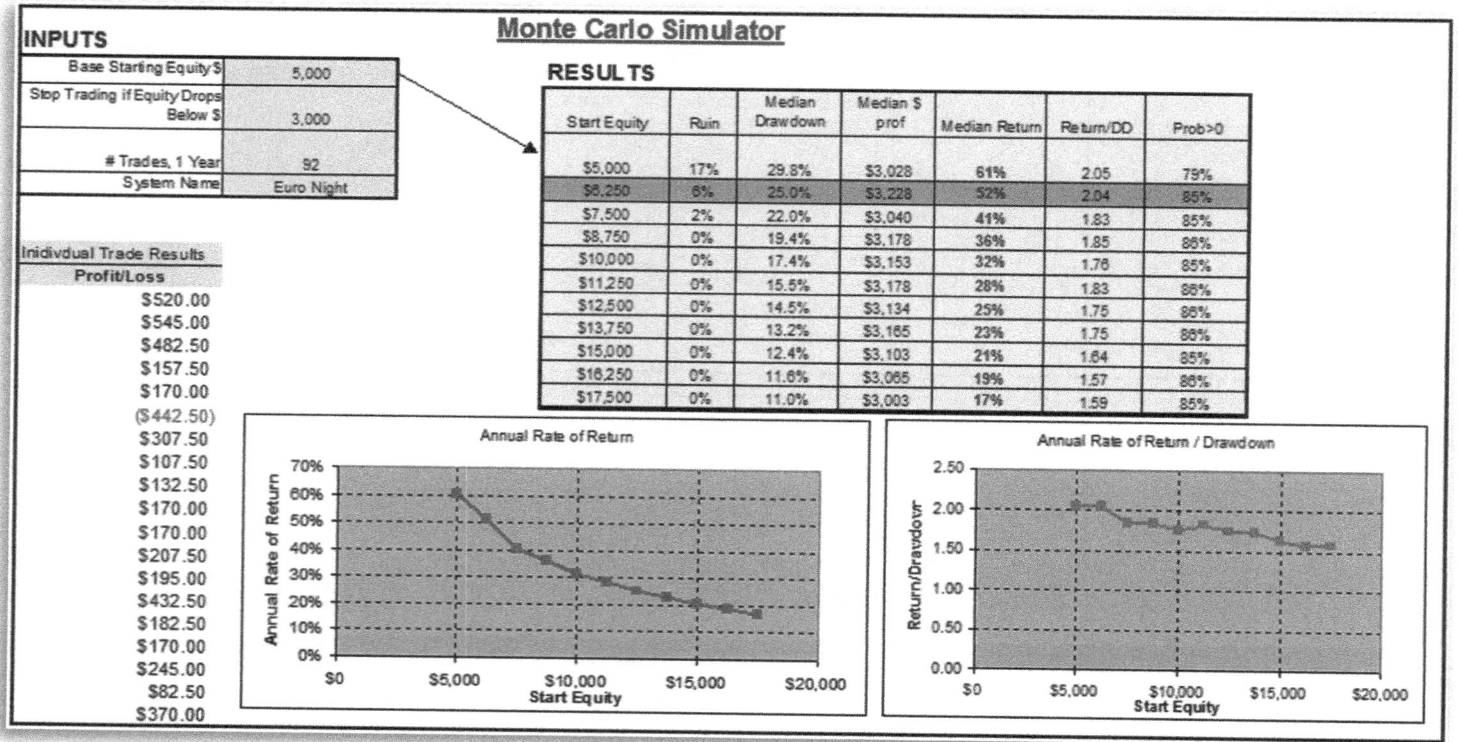

Monte Carlo Simulator

INPUTS

Base Starting Equity $	5,000
Stop Trading if Equity Drops Below $	3,000
# Trades, 1 Year	92
System Name	Euro Night

RESULTS

Start Equity	Ruin	Median Drawdown	Median $ prof	Median Return	Return/DD	Prob>0
$5,000	17%	29.8%	$3,028	61%	2.05	79%
$6,250	6%	25.0%	$3,228	52%	2.04	85%
$7,500	2%	22.0%	$3,040	41%	1.83	85%
$8,750	0%	19.4%	$3,178	36%	1.85	86%
$10,000	0%	17.4%	$3,153	32%	1.76	85%
$11,250	0%	15.5%	$3,178	28%	1.83	86%
$12,500	0%	14.5%	$3,134	25%	1.75	86%
$13,750	0%	13.2%	$3,165	23%	1.75	86%
$15,000	0%	12.4%	$3,103	21%	1.64	85%
$16,250	0%	11.6%	$3,065	19%	1.57	86%
$17,500	0%	11.0%	$3,003	17%	1.59	85%

Inidivdual Trade Results
Profit/Loss
$520.00
$545.00
$482.50
$157.50
$170.00
($442.50)
$307.50
$107.50
$132.50
$170.00
$170.00
$207.50
$195.00
$432.50
$182.50
$170.00
$245.00
$82.50
$370.00

FIGURE 19.2 Monte Carlo Results, Euro Night Strategy

Other points of interest are that I have a 6 percent chance of ruin in that first year, where my equity would drop below $3,000. I also have an 85 percent probability of making money in that first year (i.e., ending the year with more than $6,250).

Note that this strategy is nowhere near as good as the euro day strategy. I expected this because of the goals of the night strategy. If you will recall, I was looking for a higher winning percentage strategy here, not one with necessarily a lot of profit. Even so, the night strategy by itself meets my goals, although the return/drawdown ratio of only 2.0 is on the low end of acceptability. But since it meets my criteria, I can proceed to the final Monte Carlo step.

Euro Day and Night Strategy

While it is nice to know that either strategy, by itself, meets my performance criteria, what really matters to me is how the combined day and night strategy performs. Before I perform the Monte Carlo analysis, however, I have to do some data manipulation. In the previous simulations, I used individual trades for the inputs, which worked fine. But with the combined strategy, how do I ensure that the correct ratio and distribution of trades is taken to reflect what really occurs when I trade both strategies together? Some days, only one strategy will trade, and on other days, both strategies will trade. I want to preserve this with the combined simulation.

The solution to combining strategies into one strategy is to use the daily results, instead of the individual trade results. Then the net results on a given day will be considered as the results of one system. An example of how that works is shown in the "Combined" column of Table 19.1.

By utilizing this technique, we have preserved the characteristics of each strategy's trades, and just combined them into daily trades. A similar approach can be used to combine any two or more systems into one strategy. Simply compile results into daily results, and use that in the simulation.

Once I have the trade data compiled into daily results, I can perform the Monte Carlo analysis on the combined euro day and night strategy. Results are as shown in Figure 19.3. For the combined strategy, if I again keep the risk of ruin below

TABLE 19.1 Combine Daily Results on Multiple Systems to Get "One" Combined System

Date	Euro Day	Euro Night	Combined
9/9/2013	+$100		+$100
9/10/2013		+$600	+$600
9/11/2013	+$100	+$250	+$350
9/12/2013	−$400	−$50	−$450
9/13/2013		+$100	+$100

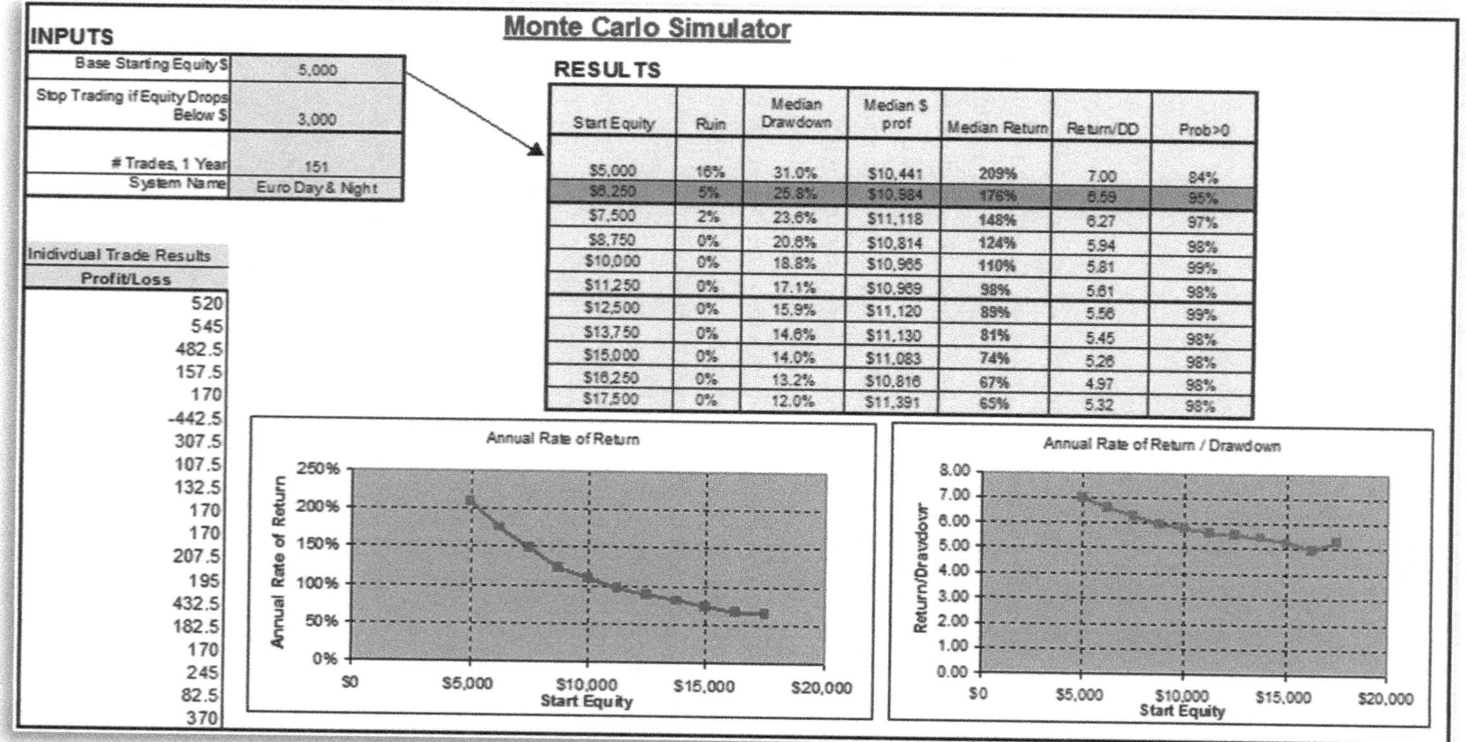

Monte Carlo Simulator

INPUTS

Base Starting Equity $	5,000
Stop Trading if Equity Drops Below $	3,000
# Trades, 1 Year	151
System Name	Euro Day & Night

RESULTS

Start Equity	Ruin	Median Drawdown	Median $ prof	Median Return	Return/DD	Prob>0
$5,000	16%	31.0%	$10,441	209%	7.00	84%
$6,250	5%	25.8%	$10,984	176%	6.59	95%
$7,500	2%	23.6%	$11,118	148%	6.27	97%
$8,750	0%	20.6%	$10,814	124%	5.94	98%
$10,000	0%	18.8%	$10,965	110%	5.81	99%
$11,250	0%	17.1%	$10,969	98%	5.61	98%
$12,500	0%	15.9%	$11,120	89%	5.56	99%
$13,750	0%	14.6%	$11,130	81%	5.45	98%
$15,000	0%	14.0%	$11,083	74%	5.26	98%
$16,250	0%	13.2%	$10,816	67%	4.97	98%
$17,500	0%	12.0%	$11,391	65%	5.32	98%

Inidivdual Trade Results
Profit/Loss
520
545
482.5
157.5
170
-442.5
307.5
107.5
132.5
170
170
207.5
195
432.5
182.5
170
245
82.5
370

FIGURE 19.3 Monte Carlo Results, Both Strategies Combined

10 percent, I find I need $6,250 to begin trading this system, and in an "average" year I can expect:

25.8 percent maximum drawdown
176 percent return
6.6 return/drawdown ratio

Other points of interest are that I have a 5 percent chance of ruin in that first year, where my equity would drop below $3,000. I also have a 95 percent probability of making money in that first year (i.e., ending the year with more than $6,250).

The most interesting aspect of this combined analysis is that the combined system is better than each system by itself. I'll repeat that: *the combined system is better than each by itself.* This is due to the diversification effect, which I discussed in Chapter 15. The return-to-drawdown ratio, my primary metric in Monte Carlo analysis, increases from 5.5 to 6.6, which is a considerable increase. This is because by trading both systems, I get the combined return of the strategies, but on the downside the drawdowns do not combine. Rather, when one strategy is experiencing a drawdown, the other might be hitting new equity highs (or at least not new maximum drawdowns). Diversification, by trading uncorrelated strategies, is what makes this possible.

Looking at the Monte Carlo analysis as a whole, all my performance goals and objectives are met for the combined system. Therefore, I consider this analysis a "pass" and can now proceed to the next step: incubation.

Incubation

At this point, I have 3.5 or so years of walk-forward back-test history. On top of that, I have about 5 months of "incubation" results, watching the euro day and night systems perform real time, with no changes to the original code (other than regularly scheduled reoptimizations).

Walk-forward results: July 2009–March 2013
Incubation results: March 2013–August 2013

If the incubation results of the last 5 months "look" similar to the walk-forward results, I should feel comfortable going live with the strategy.

Are Results Similar?

Here is how I determine if incubation and walk-forward data "match." Keep in mind that I am not a statistician, so I tend to keep things simple, at the risk of not being 100 percent mathematically and scientifically rigorous. What I do passes a common-sense test, though. I use three methods to check for a match:

1. *Student's t distribution test.* This statistical test will tell you if two data groups (the walk-forward results and the incubation results) are significantly different from each other.

   You can pretty easily do this in Excel (with the TTest function), or you can find on online t-test by searching with Google.

   When I run this test, it tells me that there is a 56 percent chance that these distributions are not different. This gives me reasonable assurance that the strategies are performing in real time as they did historically. If, however, the chances of the strategies being different were 0 to 20 percent, I might seriously wonder if I made a testing development mistake.
2. *Data distribution comparison.* I create two histograms of the data. The first one is the actual data, and I lay the walk-forward and the incubation results on top of each other. Do they look like they overlap? The second chart plots a theoretical normal curve histogram, based on the mean and standard deviation. I see a good amount of overlap in Figure 19.4.

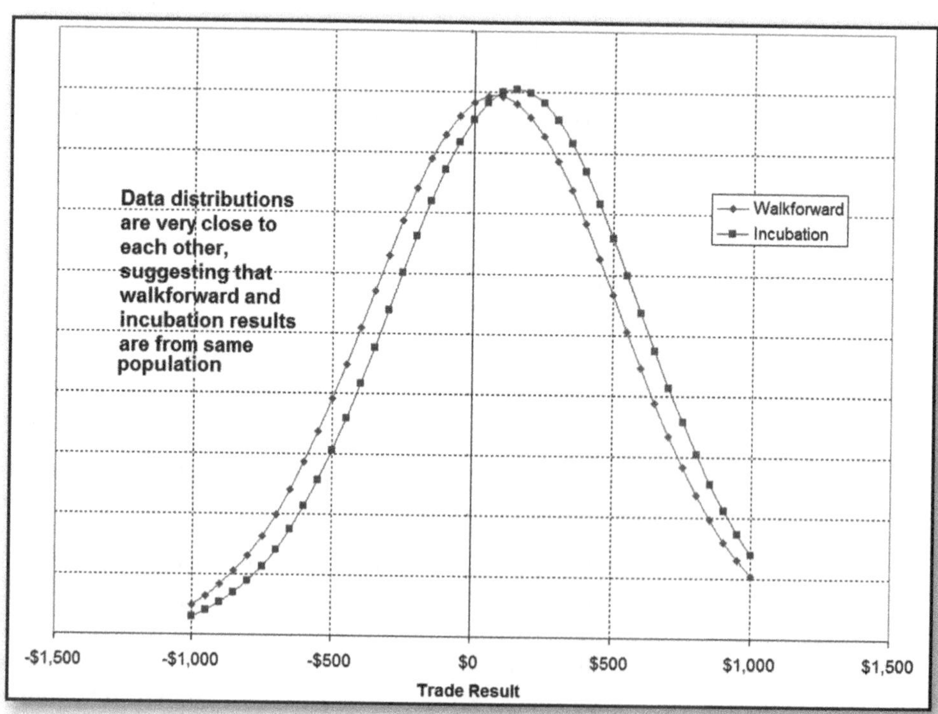

FIGURE 19.4 Incubation Results—Data Distribution Comparison

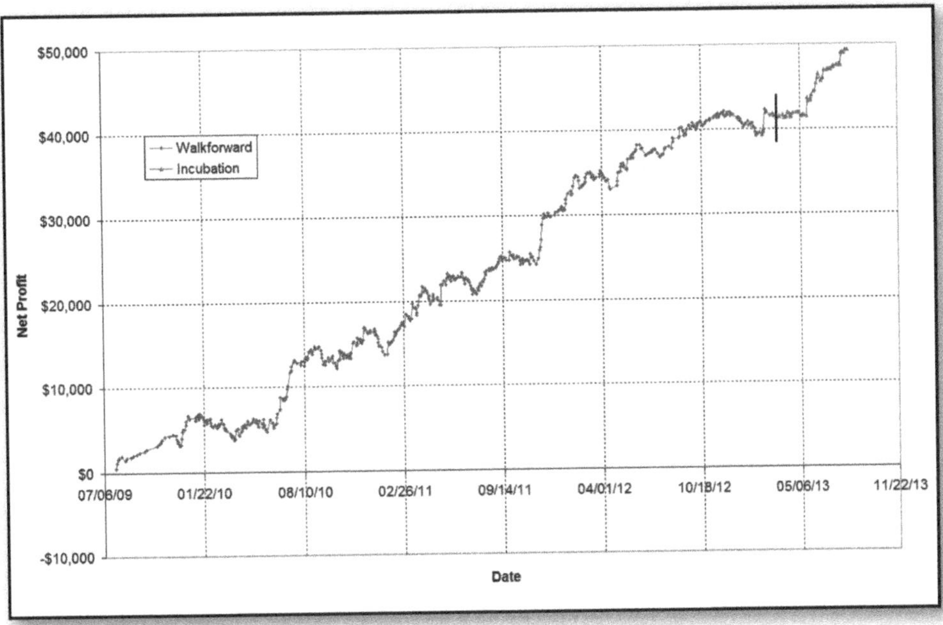

FIGURE 19.5 Incubation Results—Equity Curve Comparison

3. *Equity curve comparison.* This is my favorite method, but it is not very scientific or mathematical. I simply plot all the data and create an equity curve. When I do that, can I see where the walk-forward ends and incubation begins? If I can, that suggests something happened when incubation started, and that is usually a bad thing. If you wonder about this method, just create a strategy with optimized parameters, and then let it run live for a while. Most times, you'll notice a change in the curve. I do not see a radical change in the incubation portion of the curve, shown in Figure 19.5. This is a good sign!

Based on this analysis, I'd say the system is performing in incubation the same as it performed in its walk-forward test. In fact, incubation is better than walk-forward, which does concern me a bit (usually it is the other way around). But it is close enough to give me confidence that I did not screw up during testing in development. It does not guarantee that when I go live, the system will be profitable—that is important to remember.

Final Information

Once all the tests are complete, I can make a decision on whether to proceed with trading the system. Even if the strategy passes all the development steps, I still might decide not to trade it. Position sizing and correlation with other strategies are two possible reasons I might decide not to trade a specific strategy.

Position Sizing

Although I discussed position sizing in more detail in Chapter 16, I did not design the strategy specifically for any position sizing method. Of course, it is an important item to think about before I start trading with real money. A strategy can be great, but if reasonable position sizing cannot be applied to it, it just may not be worth trading with real money. This can occur when single contract losses are too big, and the account size needed to trade the strategy is prohibitively large.

An example of this is a system very similar to one I developed and have been trading for a number of years. This system wins $5,000 per contract on 50 percent of trades, and loses $3,000 per contract on the other 50 percent. The average profit/loss per trade is therefore $1,000, and the Tharp expectancy is 0.33, which is indicative of a pretty good system. But how much money do you need to trade such a system? Assuming the strategy trades 20 times per year, and the quitting equity point is $3,000, you need a $20,000 account to have only a 6 percent chance of ruin. Plus, your maximum drawdown is likely to be 33 percent. That is just too much for many of us. To get a drawdown below 25 percent, one would need a $35,000 account. This probably puts this system out of reach for most traders. Remember, this is trading only one contract. Using any kind of position sizing will make these drawdown and ruin numbers much worse. Thus, in your development process you may end up with a profitable system that you just can't trade.

Correlation with Other Strategies

Before I start trading a strategy live, I always check the performance of the new system with systems I am already trading. I run a simple correlation of daily returns. This will tell me if the new strategy is highly correlated to any of my existing strategies. Obviously, trading two strategies that are highly correlated isn't a good idea unless you cut the position sizing of each in half. Otherwise, you may end up with too much exposure in a particular market or to a particular trading style. Many times, for strategies developed independently, this is not an issue, but it is always good to check.

Monte Carlo—Consistency

One of the interesting side benefits of performing Monte Carlo analysis is that you can get an idea of your profit consistency. Imagine you were manager of a casino. Over the course of five minutes, your casino might make or lose money at the gambling tables. There is some randomness to the results, so even the house could lose money in a given short time frame. As the time increases, your chances of profitability go up, and eventually approach near certainty. Your casino probably makes money every week and almost certainly makes money every month—unless, of course, the criminal underworld is skimming from you!

The concept of a casino got me thinking that I'd really like to be profitable over a week, month, or year with my trading systems. Obviously, that is a function of my "roulette wheel"—my trading system and how much of an edge it provides. If I assume that my historical results will match my future results, I can use the Monte Carlo analysis to determine my odds of profitability. From that number, I can determine how consistently profitable I am over any given time period.

Using this idea, I ran the analysis on my euro day and night system. Before I reveal the results, keep in mind that this system on average will generate $10,000 to $12,000 profit per year. It is a pretty good system. But will it provide a steady return stream? Here is what the results show:

- *Weekly*—59.6 percent of weeks should be profitable. So, within one year's time, I should make money 31 weeks and lose money 21 weeks. That's okay, but not really a great way to try to make a living.
- *Monthly*—74.8 percent of months should be profitable. In one year, three months will be down months. Again, not very steady returns—what if all three down months came in a row?
- *Quarterly*—86.2 percent of quarters should be profitable. I like that.
- *Yearly*—98.8 percent of years should be profitable. One losing year in a 30- to 40-year trading career. That is very nice. The analysis says if I can live with the weekly and monthly uncertainty, then I'll be rewarded almost every year with at least some profit.

Obviously, before I ran this analysis I had to make some simplifying assumptions. For example, on average there are 151 trades per year in my trading system. That equates to three trades per week, on average. However, the actual number in any week could be zero, five, or anywhere in between. Forcing it to be three every week leads to some error. But I don't think it would change the results by much. If I am looking for 90 percent of my weeks to be profitable, then my strategy obviously won't cut it, regardless of the assumptions I made.

The next obvious question is: "What numbers should I require for each time period?" That will depend on the trader and his goals and objectives. A trader used to living paycheck to paycheck may require 95 percent winning weeks, or three losing weeks per year. He might know that more losing weeks than that will lead to eviction. A professional Commodity Trading Advisor (CTA) is measured on a monthly basis, so she might desire 95 percent of months to be profitable. A longer-term trader, though, might care only about winning quarters or winning years. It all depends on the trader's circumstances.

To take the whole analysis a step further, as you add good systems to your portfolio, your chances for profitable periods goes up. Sort of like the casino adding new table games to complement the roulette wheel.

Eliminating Big Days

Eliminating the outlier trades from the history makes a huge difference in the results. In the history, there are 614 trading days represented. There are 20 days of profits greater than $1,000. In one year of trading, I'd expect to see 5 of those "big" days. If they don't come, the system on average becomes only slightly profitable. My conclusion is that I am in deep trouble without those big winning days. The question is: is there a reason why I should not expect these kinds of days in the future? Maybe my system rules and variables basically were curve fit to find these big trades. With 10 to 20 big trades, I suppose that is a distinct possibility. However, it is not like these trades are due to a data anomaly or some back-test issue. Strategy 2 (euro day) was specifically set up to let profits run, and not to cap it. If I saw only a handful of large-profit trades, I might suspect some sort of data or back-test issue.

One other interesting question: since I am relying on these "outliers" to generate most of the profit, how likely is it that I even see many of them in a given year?

Outlier Days

Since I know that the performance of my system is going to be driven by large-winning trades (outliers), it is interesting to see how many of these I could expect in a trading year. Here's what I found:

- In a year's time, I am likely to see four to six large-winning trades. That is only one large-winning trade every other month!
- There is less than a 10 percent (actually, 6.6 percent) chance of seeing eight or more large-winning trades in a year.
- There is a 13.6 percent chance that I will have only zero, one, or two big winners in a year's time.

This analysis is a bit sobering, and it does make one thing crystal clear: if I am to succeed with this system, I have to take every single trade because the one I miss just may be the big winner that only comes around once a year.

Based on this data, my expectation for the system is a lot of flat to slightly up or slightly down periods, punctuated by a large winner every once in a while. Why is this important to know? Having proper expectations is crucial to long-term success. I can't get discouraged or lose confidence in the system when I am not immediately making money. Knowing what to expect will help me a great deal, especially if I see very little happening day to day.

PART V

Considerations before Going Live

CHAPTER 20

Account and Position Sizing

Now that I've developed a strategy, watched it in real time for a while, and decided to trade it with my own money, then what? How do I determine how much to fund the account with? How do I position size? Do I start small or big? Do I have a position-sizing scheme? If things go bad, when do I quit trading the system?

At the end of the incubation period in mid-August 2013, I truly have no idea how this system will do over the next few months. My hope, as always, is that it will do great, but as with any strategy, I am always prepared to cut my losses and stop trading it if need be.

To avoid confusion later on, here is a summary of my strategies:

Two Trading Strategies in Euro Trading System:

Strategy 1: Euro Night. Trades overnight session, has high winning percentage, lots of little wins, and an occasional big loser. Uses 105-minute bars.

Strategy 2: Euro Day. Trades day session, lower win percentage, primary profit generator. Uses 60-minute bars.

Both strategies are independent, and I'll be in only one at any given time.
Market: Euro Currency Futures (6E).

When to Quit

Now that I have decided to start trading my euro strategies live starting on Monday, August 20, 2013, I have to address the question that everyone likes to avoid when starting to trade a new strategy: if things go bad, when do I quit trading the strategy?

There are probably a million different conditions you could use as a basis for quitting a trading system. You could set a dollar amount or possibly wait until you get a margin call, or wait until you run out of money. You could stop after X losers in a row, or X losing months. There is no "one" right or wrong answer.

But there are three keys to setting a quitting point:

1. It should be based on the system you are trading. It makes no sense, for example, to quit after a 10 percent drawdown, if historically the system had 25 percent drawdowns before. This seems obvious, but you'd be amazed at how many people make arbitrary decisions like this, without taking the characteristics of the actual system into account.
2. Write it down. Refer to it often. Remember it. This may save you from disaster one day.
3. Follow it. If/when the written criteria are (unfortunately) met, *stop trading*. This is a simple, but *very* difficult, step to follow.

I don't always use the same criteria for finding my quitting point, but here is how I am doing it for the euro system:

A. Look at walk-forward history, and find the worst drawdown that occurred (daily basis). Multiply it by 1.5, since the worst drawdown is almost always in the future. For my system, that worst drawdown comes out to be $3,265. Multiply this by 1.5 to get $4,898.
B. Use Monte Carlo simulation to find the 95 percent level max drawdown. That means, in a year's worth of trading, 95 percent of the time my maximum drawdown will be less than this amount. This turns out to be $5,082. (If I wanted to be more conservative, I could use the 99 percent level. That drawdown is $6,512.)

I should point out those drawdown figures assume one contract being traded the whole time. Yet, I will hopefully be trading more than one contract as time goes on. This could get confusing—my actual drawdown (with multiple contracts) could be a lot bigger than my drawdown limit (based on one contract). I just have to remember to calculate the one-contract drawdown, and compare than to the $5,000 limit. This will be clearer later, when I set up my monitoring system.

Using results from points A and B above, I will take the average, and stop trading when the single contract drawdown reaches $5,000 (slightly rounded).

I have followed points 1 and 2 above. Time will tell if I follow point 3—I better if I need to!

For this particular system, the only quit point I am considering is the single-contract drawdown. This is simple, and pretty robust. If I am trading the system years from now, with many contracts (my hope, of course), I will still have that $5,000 maximum drawdown per contract limit.

In the past, I have used the Monte Carlo simulation results to help me decide when to quit. I have also examined, but never implemented, a temporary quit point based on market volatility. When the market gets super-crazy, it may be best to take a break. I don't think there is a wrong metric or combination of metrics to use to decide when to quit trading. There is probably no "one size fits all" optimum, either. The key, in my mind, is to select some criteria that you are comfortable with, write it down, and then follow it exactly. Then, if your system fails, there should be no tears. You knew the system could break, and you quit at a preordained spot.

I think where people get in trouble is in not having a "quit point," or their quit point is when their money runs out. Speaking from personal experience in the late 1990's, having to quit trading when your money is gone is not a pleasant way to quit.

What happens when the system performance isn't bad enough to hit your quitting point, and it is not great either, but is somewhere in between? Maybe it is making money, or breaking even, and it is within the bounds of what Monte Carlo simulation says is possible. When do you quit, or otherwise cease trading the system? My general philosophy is to watch the downside and let the upside take care of itself. In this case, I watch the max drawdown and, as long as that is not hit, let the system perform. I do this because I never know month to month or year to year what particular systems I am trading will do good, which will do bad, and which will just tread water. Normally, I'll just let system be and not turn them off or on.

But a couple of times a year I rebalance systems I am trading—add in new ones and cull the underperformers and possibly adjust the position sizing. If capital becomes an issue, I might very well stop trading and swap out a mildly profitable but underperforming system for a system that I feel has more potential. The analysis details are never the same, and I don't have strict rules on this. I might, for example, stop trading a system because I no longer like it for some reason—maybe it just doesn't fit me anymore.

I realize that I am sort of talking out both sides of my mouth here. On one side I say, "Maximum drawdown is my only quitting criteria." On the other side I say, "Unless I come up with another legitimate reason to cease trading it." I rationalize this by saying the maximum drawdown is a hard, solid, worst-case criterion and will not be violated. At the same time, though, other circumstances may arise that cause the system to fall out of favor. These circumstances might cause me to quit earlier. That is a big gray area, as unfortunately most things are with trading.

I can say my plan at the start of trading includes only maximum drawdown as the sole criterion for quitting. With the small size and account size I am using to trade this system, I can't foresee needing the capital for a better system. But I am also flexible enough to realize that circumstances may cause me to alter my quitting point at some time.

Minimum Funding Size

At this point, I have figured out (1) that I will begin live trading the euro day and night system, and (2) I will quit trading if my single-contract drawdown hits $5,000. Now I will determine account size. This point is pretty important. Too little capital to start, and I may run out of money before the quitting point. Too much capital and I will have a lower rate of return, as well as an inefficient allocation of capital. Currently, the exchange initial margin on euro currency is $2,750. So, add this to my "quitting point" drawdown, and I get $7,750. This is the minimum account size I should start with. This will allow me to trade up until my max drawdown is reached.

A few important points to consider:

- I am assuming my broker requires exchange margin, even for day trading. If I had access to day-trading rates, I could get by with less. This is always a risky proposition, though, since many people just increase their size because of the lower day-trade margin rates. This is usually not a good idea.
- Margins can and do change. If the exchange required margin goes up, I may be forced to stop trading before hitting my quitting point.
- I am assuming that I am trading a single contract all the time.

As it turns out, I will want more than $7,750 in my account, for position-sizing reasons. I am going to use $8,500, for reasons that will be revealed later.

Position Sizing

If you have a good trading system, eventually you will want to start trading it with multiple contracts. There are tons of position-sizing schemes out there (Van Tharp wrote a huge book on the topic), so there is no right way to do it. There is no Holy Grail position-sizing technique, though, where you get more reward for no extra risk. The simple way to put it is this way: if you trade more contracts, your reward goes up, but so does your risk.

Here is what I am doing (at least for a while; hopefully, once my size gets big, I'll become less aggressive):

As always, I start out with only one contract. Why? Going live almost always reveals issues that back tests, sim tests, and incubation tests keep hidden. For example, if my strategy is automated, what if some quirk in my code sends multiple orders or otherwise goofs up? Or what if my slippage estimates are way off, and real-world slippage actually makes my strategy unprofitable? My experience is that starting with one contract is the cheapest way to find out and correct any live trading issues.

A second reason I like starting with one contract is that I want to remain emotionally detached as much as possible from the strategy performance. One-contract profit-and-loss swings won't impact me or my emotions. Ten contracts, right off the bat, would freak me out a bit—I'd be watching the system too much and have too emotion invested in it. As profits (hopefully) accumulate, I can add contracts at a comfortable level, and not be emotionally disturbed by it. If things go really well, in six months or even a year or two, trading 10 contracts at a time with this proven system will seem natural to me.

Some people would say, "If you have an edge, exploit it fast and furiously by trading maximum size right off the bat. Edges disappear, so take advantage while it exists." That is a good argument, and I understand the concept. But I also know how I best operate, and going "all in" at the start is not good psychologically for me. Of course, you should choose the approach that you feel most comfortable with.

A final reason I like starting with one contract is that I like the strategy to be self-generating—profits will build the account, leading to more contracts, building it further, leading to even more contracts, and so on. No profits mean no increase in size. That just makes sense to me; why allocate more money to a system that isn't generating profits?

One drawback to this approach is that it can take a long time to add that second contract. For example, if you decide to trade one contract for each $10,000 in your account, you will have to have 100 percent return to add one contract. Then you'll need another 50 percent gain to add a third contract. That can take a long time. Some position-sizing techniques take this into account (fixed ratio sizing comes to mind), but these approaches have some negative characteristics I do not like.

I get around this dilemma by sizing my account for roughly 1.5 to 2 contracts at the start. This would be equivalent to starting with $15,000 in the example I gave just above. Then, I need only a 50 percent gain to add a second contract. This still forces the system to perform well, but at the same time I get contract growth sooner. For me, it is a great trade-off.

With all that in mind, here are the details:

For my euro system, I have decided to use fixed fractional sizing.

$$N_{\text{contracts}} = X * \text{Equity}/\text{BigLoss}$$

where

$N_{\text{contracts}}$ = Integer number of contracts, always round numbers down.
X = Fixed fraction, which I determined through Monte Carlo analysis. For this system, I am using 0.175 (I'll explain later how I got this value).

Equity = Current equity value.
BigLoss = Largest daily loss, $885 for my euro system.

Using the preceding, I can create Table 20.1.

Note that my fixed fraction of 0.175 might seem awfully high. It may be for most people. I determine it based on risk of ruin, annual return, and max drawdown. I use my Monte Carlo spreadsheet to calculate all that. Based on the position-sizing analysis so far, I determined that using fixed fractional sizing with $X = ff = 0.175$ was my best alternative. Please realize that this is my personal preference, based on my personal goals and objectives, and that amount probably would not be right for you.

The question is, how did I arrive at this figure? Why not just trade one contract all the time, or use a fixed fractional value of .01 or .02 or 0.10 or 0.50? To determine the position-sizing scheme that is right for me, I use my Monte Carlo simulator, the basic (one-contract) version of which you can download for free at the web site (www.wiley.com/go/algotradingsystems). For a given trading system, it will estimate the probabilities of risk of ruin, median max drawdown, and median annual return for the first year of trading.

The baseline version of this calculator assumes one contract traded throughout the year, but the macro code can be edited to simulate different position-sizing techniques, which is what I am doing here.

There are four performance numbers I look at:

1. *Risk of ruin*. How likely am I to hit my defined lower cash balance. I want this number low.

TABLE 20.1 Position-Sizing Table

ff =	0.175
Equity	$N_{contracts}$
< $10,114	1
$10,114	2
$15,171	3
$20,229	4
$25,286	5
$30,343	6
$35,400	7
$40,457	8
$45,514	9
$50,571	10

2. *Median maximum drawdown.* I have roughly a 50 percent chance of hitting this maximum drawdown sometime during the year. That of course means my maximum drawdown could be much greater than this value, and it could be less. I want it as low as possible, with a personal upper limit I have determined from doing this exercise a bunch of times.
3. *Annual return.* As with drawdown, I have a 50 percent chance of reaching this annual return, and it could be much higher or much lower. I want it as high as possible, but I have no lower-limit threshold acceptable value (although 40 percent is a good value).
4. *Return/Drawdown ratio.* Astute readers will recognize this as the Calmar ratio, although true Calmar is calculated over three years, not just one year. I want this value as high as possible, and I have a lower limit for acceptability. (Just for reference, for professional Commodity Trading Advisors a Calmar above 1 is considered pretty good. That means if you want 25 percent annual return, you have to be willing to accept a 25 percent drawdown).

Using these criteria, I can try a few different position-sizing approaches, with some different parameter values. Note that this is not all-encompassing; I have not analyzed many other potential position-sizing schemes. Maybe one would work better than what I chose.

Before I reveal the results, I should mention that I played around with the starting balance a bit, although I am not showing those interim results. Basically, by adjusting the initial account size, I was striking a balance between having too much money in the account, being able to add on a second contract relatively quickly (without doubling my account size first), and keeping risk of ruin low. I eventually settled on $8,500 as the start balance, a good trade-off among all competing metrics.

Here are the results, with the one I chose highlighted ("ff" is the fixed fractional amount) (see Figure 20.1).

My selection meets all my criteria, and I am comfortable with it. This position scheme is the right one for me, right now. *But,* depending on how things go, I might change it down the road, either to a different scheme altogether, or a smaller value of ff (i.e., I will become less aggressive as the account grows). I'll let the performance of the system dictate if and when that happens.

With the fixed fractional sizing I have chosen, results say that in an "average" year (meaning, 50 percent of years will be worse, and 50 percent of years will be better), I expect to make $30,735 profit in that year and hit a maximum drawdown of 38.1 percent sometime during the year. That profit number seems a little too good to be true … and my motto is "if something seems too good to be true, it probably is." And that profit number does seem too good to be true—362 percent rate of return in that first year seems too high, and that makes me suspicious. Remember,

Start Equity	Ruin	Median Drawdown	Median $ Prof	Median Return	Return/DD	Sizing Method
$8,500	1%	19.6%	$11,960	141%	7.12	1 contract always
$8,500	1%	37.8%	$31,598	372%	9.64	add at 10K, and every 5K up
$8,500	0%	22.0%	$13,189	155%	6.81	ff = 0.1
$8,500	1%	32.3%	$21,155	249%	7.86	ff = 0.15
$8,500	1%	38.1%	$30,735	362%	9.55	ff = 0.175
$8,500	1%	43.6%	$39,074	460%	10.44	ff = 0.2
$8,500	4%	53.9%	$60,688	714%	13.38	ff = 0.25

FIGURE 20.1 Position-Sizing Results

though, the actual rate of return could be just about anywhere on the spectrum. It is just that the 362 percent is the median value.

I now look at a histogram of possible returns, shown in Figure 20.2. It will be interesting to see if the year 1 results are anywhere close to the median ending equity (black vertical line). If they are, I will be very happy. I'll still be happy if I even hit the 25 percent mark, which is a final equity of about $21,000, or a 147 percent return for the year. Almost in "too good to be true" region, but it is a possibility.

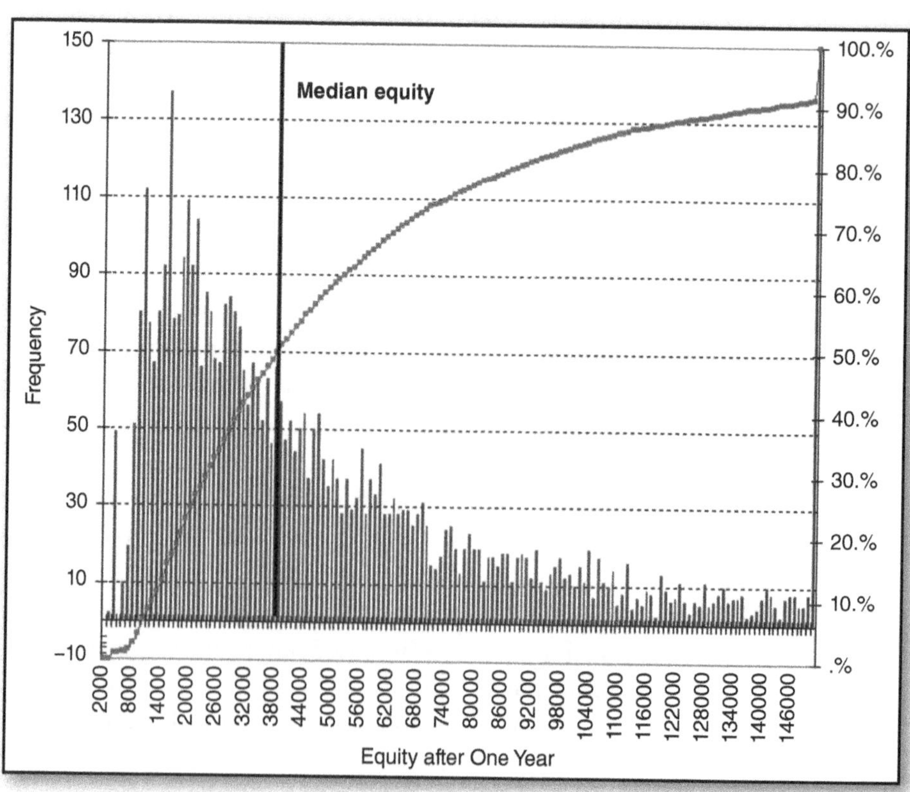

FIGURE 20.2 Histogram of Possible First Year Returns

Unequal Position Sizing

I am using the same position sizing for the two strategies in my euro day and night system, even though strategies 1 and 2 are for the most part different. The only thing they have in common is the stop-loss point, around $425 (34 ticks) per contract. Given their different trade distributions, is the equal position size approach correct? Maybe the position sizing should be different for the two strategies. Possibly, that would improve overall performance metrics.

As with any trading idea or thought that pops up, I reserve judgment on it until I test and analyze it. The numbers will tell me if this is a good thing to do or not. No emotion is the point, I suppose. I'll spare you some of the minutiae of my analysis, but I primarily looked at "trade two contracts of strategy 1 for every one contract of strategy 2."

Results

Current method (identical sizing, both strategies)
Acct size: $8,500
Max DD: 38.1 percent
Annual return: 362 percent
2/1 Sizing method
Acct size: $12,500
Max DD: 38.3 percent (same as current method)
Annual return: 255 percent

Conclusion: I would need more money in the account to trade a 2-to-1 ratio, and my annual return would go down. So it does not make sense.

Note: I performed a pretty simple analysis to conclude this. Really, what I should do is let the fixed fractional sizing for each strategy float, and find the optimum for each.

CHAPTER 21

Trading Psychology

Frequently, I hear from discretionary traders, and the conversation goes something like this:

Discretionary Trader: "I am sick of losing. I am too emotional to trade and make trading decisions at the same time. I want to try algorithmic trading."

Me: "That is good you realized a need to change your losing ways. Why do you think algorithmic trading will work?"

Discretionary Trader: "Because I can be a brain-dead button pusher and just follow the system. Kind of like that episode of *The Simpsons,* where Homer sets up a drinking bird to continuously tap the "y" key on his keyboard, so he would not have to do any actual work. I want to be the drinking bird, just following the system."

Me: "You do realize that the drinking bird eventually stopped and almost caused a nuclear meltdown, right?"

Discretionary Trader: "Huh?"

That pretty much sums it up—many people think there is no emotion involved in mechanical trading. Emotions manifest differently in algorithmic trading, as opposed to discretionary trading, but they are there, in many different aspects of trading. The nice thing about algorithmic trading is that your emotions theoretically should not matter for entry and exit signals. The key word, of course, is theoretically. In reality, emotions can creep in many different areas of mechanical, 100 percent rules-based trading. In this chapter, I'll point out some of these major areas and provide tips for how to minimize their impact because, just as with discretionary trading, emotions can really kill the performance of an algorithmic trader.

When to Begin Trading

Most people, when deciding to go live with an algorithmic strategy, never think about when to actually enter that first position until they do it. But, as I've said before, entering a position in the middle of an open trade can be emotional. Also, what if your system had six consecutive winners—do you wait for a losing trade or two before you start trading? There are really two questions to address:

1. Should you start trading your system after looking at its equity curve?
2. Should you start trading your system in the middle of a trade, or wait for the next new entry signal?

As with most decisions in trading, there is no absolute right or wrong answer. But if you look at the problem beforehand and make consistent decisions, you can eliminate much of the emotion when starting out.

Let's say you've created a trading system with the equity curve shown in Figure 21.1 (it is from an actual system I have traded with real money). This is a pretty good equity curve for a walk-forward test, and it passed the incubation test you just ran for a few months. The system is at an equity peak, and you are very excited (there is the emotional part!) to begin trading.

At first glance, you see the new high and immediately think, "It is a runaway train, I have to get on now!" That is certainly understandable. At some point, though, that

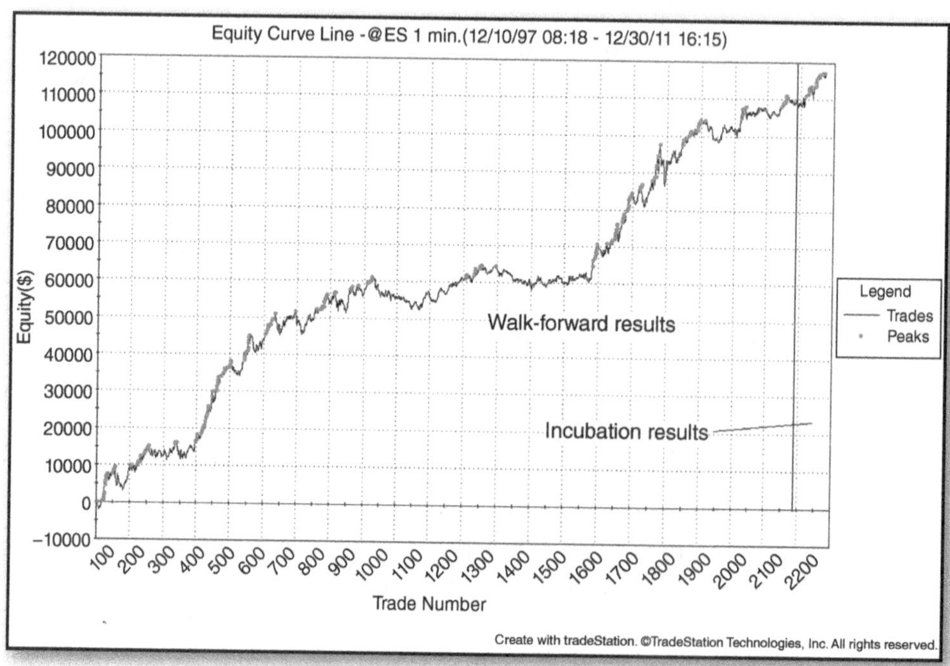

FIGURE 21.1 Sample Walk-Forward Equity Curve

train will slow down or even reverse direction. It is a terrible feeling to start trading a new system at an equity high, only to endure a drawdown right off the bat. So maybe it is better to wait for a small pullback in the equity curve and then begin trading. Of course, you run the risk of there never being a significant pullback, and then think of all the profits you'll miss out on!

Both approaches, starting at or near a new high, or starting after a pullback, have their emotional advantages and disadvantages. On any given system, no one really knows the best approach to take. Over many systems, it probably does not matter all that much—some strategies will continue being profitable right after you start, and other strategies will immediately go into drawdown. For me personally, it seems that most systems go immediately into drawdown, but I think that I forget about the ones whose equity curve takes off and just remember the immediate drawdown systems.

Given the emotional charge inherent in either approach, the simplest thing to do is to make a decision for all future systems you start trading and then stick to it. For example, you could decide to begin trading after four months of successful incubation, regardless of whether the equity curve is at an equity high, recovering from a drawdown, or somewhere in between. That way, sometimes you'll be right, and sometimes you'll be wrong, but it should be an emotionless task to begin trading.

Once you have decided on an approach to start trading, you'll realize that there is an existing position that needs to be accounted for. Should you wait for the next new signal? Or should you enter the current winning or losing position? Again, emotion can enter into this decision. As with the equity curve decision, it is best to decide up front and keep emotion out of it.

Part of the decision to enter an existing trade depends on your software and your trading style. Some automated platforms may have trouble recognizing a manually entered position. This could lead to your exit signal's not being triggered. If this is the case with your software, it is best to just wait for the next fresh entry signal.

Your trading style also plays a role in entering an existing position. In a fast-paced day-trading system, with multiple trades per day, the answer is easy: just wait for the next entry signal. Since they happen often, there will be little to be gained or lost. A different story exists, though, for strategies that have positions on for days, weeks, or months at a time. What is the best approach here? If the position is close to breakeven, just enter it manually. It may cost you or make you a few extra dollars, but in the long run it does not matter.

The decision gets a little trickier with open positions that are currently big winners or big losers. What approach is best here? Some people will want to enter an open winning trade, on the theory that winning trades will keep on winning. That makes sense, except that you may be incurring much more risk to enter a winner. Let's look at an example. Let's say your trade is set up to yield either a $500 profit or a $250 loss, and you never change the profit target or stop-loss. It is now midway through the trade, and you have a $300 open profit. Should you enter? Well, initially you had a 2:1 reward-to-risk ratio, and by entering mid-trade, you have a 200:550 or 0.36:1 reward-to-risk ratio. Although the likelihood of your getting a $200 gain before a $550 loss is much better than the original likelihood of $500 gain or $250 loss, I'd focus more on the downside. Instead of losing $250 on the trade, you could lose $550. Ask yourself whether you want to risk that extra loss.

The same logic applies to open losing trades. In this case, however, your loss would be less by entering midtrade, and your potential gain could be a lot larger. This is the approach I use when starting to trade a new system: if the current open trade is a loser, I enter it. If it is a winning trade, I wait for the next signal, or until the position pull backs in profit to near breakeven. This is the approach that makes me comfortable. I am not emotional about it, I don't worry if I made the right decision, I just consistently execute the plan. To me, that is the important point.

As you can see, going "live" with an algorithmic system leaves you with a few conundrums and questions. Over the years, I have probably fiddled with all combinations of the choices of when to start trading a strategy. I've been through the sheer disappointment of waiting for a pullback in the equity curve, only to see the system go up for months on end. I've also entered open positions and suffered losses right off the bat, when waiting for the next entry signal would have been better. Similarly, sometimes the opposite occurred, and I "won" at these decisions. Overall, I don't think it has improved my situation at all but has definitely led to lost emotional capital. So now I have a plan, known in advance, and I start every system the same way. This eliminates all emotion from the equation.

When to Quit

Once you've settled on an approach to start trading a system, you've completed half the battle. But, do you know when you'll stop following that new system? Emotions can play a huge role here. Whether you are following your own trading system or following an adviser, newsletter, or some other service, if you don't have an exit plan for discontinuing it, you really need to.

Why? Studies have shown that when people are under stress, many times they make poor decisions. Certainly, if you were losing money with your systems, you would be stressed. Consequently, you might make a knee-jerk reaction to the losses, or you may stick your head in the sand and avoid a decision all together. Both scenarios can be dangerous. So the time when you are losing is a bad time to determine when to stop trading a strategy.

Ideally, you determined when to stop trading when you first decided to trade the system. If not, it is not too late. Just determine the metric(s) that are most important to you. They could include such things as:

- Maximum drawdown.
- Consecutive losers in a row.
- Amount lost in a week/month/year.
- Overall profit after X months.
- Overall winning percentage dips below XX percent.
- Significant break in your personal equity trend line or equity moving average.
- New highs, or breaking of another "good" metric (yes, some people try to quit at the top).
- Anything that can be measured and monitored.
- Statistical Process Control techniques—for advanced users only.

The exact condition you select probably is not as important as writing it down and sticking to it. That is the key. It needs to be solid, definitive, and written down. Ideally, you'll also tell your spouse or a friend, too, since it is harder to back out when you make the proclamation public.

I've heard that one money management firm's exit criterion is 1.5 times the maximum drawdown, and a 24-month commitment. Those aren't bad, but the best one is the one that you feel comfortable with—one you can stick with.

You'll definitely worry less about your system's performance if you write down and follow your exit plan.

Once you have decided on an approach to start with real money trading of a strategy, and formulated an approach to cease trading should things go bad, all you have to do is turn on the system and let it run, right? You can sleep well, go to your day job, and just let the system run, without any emotional expenditure on your part, correct? Certainly, that is how the gurus selling automated "robots" or "advisers" make it sound. That's how they lure many people in: the siren song of emotionless trading. Unfortunately, much like the sailors in ancient Greece who lost their lives sailing to the sound, many a trader has been undone by the emotions involved in so-called emotionless algorithmic trading.

Emotions bubble to the surface in mechanical trading in many different ways. The most common time for emotions to come into play is in the decision to take every trade or not. Clearly, if you've tested a strategy and concluded it is worthwhile, then you need to follow it exactly as tested. That sounds easy until a drawdown is incurred, or a number of consecutive losing trades occurs. That is when doubt and fear creep in. "The last five trades have been losers, and that only happened two times in the walk-forward back-test historical testing," says the little voice in your head. "Skip this trade, and wait for a winner first." Unfortunately, this is how the mind works, at least for me. It takes nerves of steel sometimes to overrule the voice in your head. But for any chance of long-term success, you need to keep taking signals without question. Otherwise, by picking and choosing which trades to take, and which to reject, you have completely invalidated all the testing and analysis behind the system. In other words, you are just gambling, and that almost never ends well.

Once you get a good feel for your strategy, you'll begin to know ahead of time when a signal is likely to be triggered. For example, at the close of each bar if you are expecting a buy on an upward moving average cross, if the current bar is trending higher, you'll know the cross will occur at the close of the current bar. Greed can take hold here—why not enter now, before the bar closes? Extra profit might be yours, with no real additional risk. But just like "cherry picking" certain trades, this "jumping the gun" scenario is a really bad idea. There will be times where it doesn't work out, and times it will. You can waste a lot of emotional capital stressing over whether to enter (or exit) early or not. Just remember, though, that when you don't take the entries and exits exactly as your system says, you should not rely on historical results at all. What you've created is a new strategy, with no real historical basis.

In both of the preceding scenarios, emotions can come in when you make decisions contrary to the strategy rules. So in both of these cases, the emotions can be eliminated by strict discipline—following the rules of the system without question, without fail. This discipline takes time to develop, especially if you are trading only one strategy. Your tendency will be to watch that strategy carefully, think about it often, and inevitably ponder overruling the strategy. My advice in this case is to trade multiple strategies if you can. Once you are trading three or more strategies, it becomes hard *not* to follow the rules. This is akin to the serial liar, who tells so many lies to so many people that eventually the truth comes out. You'll get so confused by what you are actually doing and what you should be doing that just following the rules will be much, much easier.

In automated trading, I occasionally have to deal with emotions at a stressful time—when something goes wrong. It could be an Internet connection lost, a manual order placed incorrectly, a broker issue, forgetting to roll over, or one of a thousand different "gotchas" that can spring up. Once you notice the issue, or the position mismatch, your stress level goes through the roof. At least mine does. What should I do—exit everything, wait for a better price and reenter, do nothing, run around the room babbling like an idiot? These are all possible reactions to an unforeseen problem; heaven knows I've done my share of incoherent screaming and shouting at times. Emotions can take hold, and terrible decisions can be made in the heat of the moment.

The solution to eliminating emotions at stressful times like this is surprisingly simple, yet many times tough to implement. Simply sync your real-world position and your strategy's position as quickly as possible. Don't try to get a better price, finesse the order, or any nonsense like that. Just get back in with market orders. Don't think about this decision, don't react to any external stimuli—just execute and get positions to match. Sounds simple, yes, but in reality it can be impossible to do. Just keep it unemotional, and in the long run you'll be much better off.

I've mentioned it before, but it bears repeating: the key to successful algorithmic trading is discipline. You need to be disciplined enough to follow signals without fail. You have to avoid the temptation to enter early or jump the gun and exit early. Plus, when things go wrong, you absolutely need to get your system back in line with its rules as soon as possible. Your ability to do this will be determined by the amount of discipline you have. Just remember, though, when your emotions take over and you do not follow the rules, you are basically just gambling. Gamblers in the market usually lose.

CHAPTER 22

Other Considerations before Going Live

In addition to starting with the right account size, knowing when to quit, and setting up a position-sizing scheme, there are other considerations that you must think about before going live. The list of potential items is long, so here I just highlight some of the issues I have found most important when going live.

Accounting, Trading Brokers

I trade multiple systems live right now, and I use various accounts at various brokers. I do this for a few reasons. First, doing all the bookkeeping and accounting gets confusing when multiple systems are all lumped into the same account. More than once, "orphan" positions that I forgot to close pop up. Having one trading system per trading account makes things a lot easier from a management standpoint.

The second reason I use multiple brokers is that sometimes brokers go belly up or walk away with your money. I lost some money when PFG Best went out of business in 2012, when its founder revealed he had been forging bank statements for years. I still have only gotten back about a third of my money, and I doubt I'll ever see it all. I'm no longer mad about it, but when I go back and look at the interview I did on Fox Business Channel right when the scandal broke (http://video.foxbusiness.com/v/1729212213001/pfgbest-victim-unable-to-trade-with-account-frozen), it is clear to me I was in a pissed-off state of mind. I do not need that aggravation again. To me, spreading my risk around will keep me trading even if one broker fails.

The drawbacks to my approach are obvious. If I am worried about brokers failing, having more accounts with more brokers just increases the chances of my running into a bad broker, right? My approach may not be better than finding the best broker and just putting all my eggs in that basket. The second drawback is that using multiple brokers leads to a less-than-optimal use of capital (margin) situation. This leads to less return, since more of my money is not put to use. That, to me, is an acceptable trade-off.

So, for my euro day and night system, I will open a new trading account.

After looking at my automation requirements, and the fact that all my code is written in TradeStation Easy Language, it makes the most sense to either use TradeStation as the broker or a NinjaTrader broker. For the Ninja option, there is a neat little feature in NinjaTrader that will take TradeStation-generated signals, run them thru NinjaTrader, and then send the signals on to a Ninja Broker. I've used it before with success, so it is a good option. The TradeStation option is the cleanest and easiest, of course.

Automation, Unattended, VPS, Where Are Orders Kept?

Here are some other topics I had to consider when taking my euro day and night strategy live:

Backup Plans

In an ideal world, computers never crash, Internet connections never go down, your broker always is up, and so on. In the real world, lots of things can go wrong. Some things to consider—do you need any of these?

- Backup PC
- Backup data storage (offsite and onsite)
- Backup Internet provider
- Backup power supply
- Backup phone line
- Backup broker
- Backup trading desk

There is more, I know, but having backups (and possibly even backups for the backups) for everything on this list will get you a long way.

To Automate or Not to Automate?

During incubation, I manually traded my strategies in simulation mode for a while. I had to have TradeStation alert me, after which I would manually place orders in another platform. Over time, I missed a few trades, made a few mistakes, forgot to cancel open orders, and so on. Overall, I don't think these mistakes cost me any simulation "money." In fact, they may have saved me a few bucks. But that isn't the point. The point is that I want to trade the system as I developed it. So, automation makes the most sense for me. Therefore, I will trade it automated.

Attended, Unattended?

TradeStation always warns its clients that "automated trading does not mean unattended trading." This is pretty sound advice, since issues pop up from time to time, Internet connections go down, orders get missed, and so on. I plan on usually being around the PC when this strategy is running, so I'd say it qualifies as "semiattended." If my account grows and my contract size gets significant, I'll revisit this approach.

VPS

Many people use virtual private servers (VPSs) for their trading, to keep the downtime and data lag to a minimum, and their reliability high. I personally do not use any VPS services currently, but I am always monitoring my situation for reasons to use it. In the past year, I've lost Internet connection only twice, and once was on a weekend. If my systems traded more than a few times a day, or if I were running a high-speed scalping strategy, I'd definitely use a VPS.

Where Orders Are Kept

I bring this up because many people don't know where their orders are. When your automated strategy fires an order, is it kept on your machine? On the broker's servers? At the exchange? Plus, different types of orders (limit, stop) may have different routing. For example, limit orders might be sent directly to the exchange, but stop orders may be held at the broker.

My point in bringing this up is that you should know where your orders are and have plans in place in case something goes wrong. You might think you have an order at the exchange, but after your Internet goes down and a fill was missed, you might realize it was really held on your PC. Emergency situations are not a good time to find out answers to these questions.

Rollover Considerations

Many traders have difficulties accounting for rollovers. They wrongly assume they'll have to "eat" the premium between the old and new months, or that they'll pay multiple spreads to accomplish the roll. If you do it correctly, you don't have to pay a premium, but you may have to pay two bid/ask spread costs instead of one, and you'll have to pay the equivalent of one round turn commission. A lot of people are under the mistaken impression that they always lose or gain premium during a rollover. While this might be true for strategies such as scale trading, it does not have to be true for algorithmic systems with a simple rollover. I'll explain all of that with a real-world example.

First, it is worth explaining *why* a rollover is necessary. For intraday traders, where positions are closed at the end of each trading day, rollover should never be an issue. On the day of rollover, those traders simply start trading the new front contract month. For swing traders, however, the situation is a bit more complicated. Before first notice day or last trading day, whichever comes first, the trader must "roll" his position from the old contract month into the new contract month. For instance, if you are long September euros, you'll want to sell the September euros, closing you out of that position, and buy the December euros. Not surprisingly, the devil is in the details, and an example is the best way to show the process.

Let's say I have a system that trades the euro. I use the back-adjusted continuous contract to calculate all parameters for the strategy. I am currently trading the September contract, but let's say I roll to December this afternoon

Based on the signal from my continuous contract chart, I bought the September contract at 1.3272 a few days ago. At that time, September was the front month; the continuous contract thinks I entered at 1.3272.

This system has a $625 stop-loss, and a $1,250 profit target. So my stop loss is at 1.3222, and my profit target is at 1.3372. Both of those are based on the September contract, which is what was the lead contract at initial entry.

Now, a few days later, I have to roll the position into December. Let's first look at the math, and what happens to the continuous contract, and why I don't lose the premium (difference) between the two contracts when I roll over. Right at rollover, let's say December was at 1.3303, while September was at 1.3299. This is a difference of .0004, which is what the back-adjusted continuous contract needs to know. To adjust the continuous contract to have December as the front month, you simply have to add .0004 to each price point in the existing continuous contract. So we do this and now have a continuous contract, with December as the front month.

Now, if you have your trading strategy applied to the updated continuous contract, the strategy will think you bought at 1.3276, with a stop-loss at 1.3226 and a profit target of 1.3376. "But wait!" you say. "I didn't buy at 1.3276. I somehow got screwed!" Here's the math, neglecting the bid/ask spread and the commission costs, just for this example.

Real World—What Your Actual Trading Account Sees

You bought September at 1.3272. You sold September at 1.3299. Profit = $337.50.

You bought December at 1.3303. Current price is 1.3303. Profit = $0.

In the real world, you have a closed profit of $337.50, an open profit of $0.

If your new stop-loss gets hit, you will lose (1.3226 – 1.3303) * 125,000 = –962.50. Add that to the previously closed profit of $337.50, and your total loss is $625.

If your new profit target gets hit, you will gain (1.3376 – 1.3303) * 125,000 = +912.50. Add that to the previously closed profit of $337.50, and your total gain is $1,250.

Strategy World—What Your Strategy, Acting on a Back-Adjusted Continuous Contract, Thinks Is Happening

For the original continuous contract scenario, the continuous contract thinks I entered at 1.3272.

This system has a $625 stop-loss, and a $1,250 profit target. So my stop-loss is at 1.3222, and my profit target is at 1.3372.

For the new rolled-over continuous contract scenario, the continuous contract thinks I entered at 1.3276.

This system has a $625 stop loss, and a $1,250 profit target. So my stop loss is at 1.3226, and my profit target is at 1.3376.

As you can see, the profit and loss from the real world and the strategy world is exactly the same.

Suppose you are long the September euro contract at 1.3222, and it is getting to the time in mid-September when you must roll over to the December contract. When you have to perform this rollover in an algorithmic strategy, how do you actually accomplish it? I usually do it one of three different ways. Each one has its advantages and disadvantages.

Method 1: Quick Roll (Most Expensive Typically)

In this approach, you enter a sell order at the market in September euro, and enter a buy order at the market in December euro. Since both orders are market orders, they will be immediately executed. Using the prices above, here is the math:

Sell September at 1.3299 (bid price)

Buy December at 1.3304 (ask price)

Closed profit = $962.50 – $5.00 commission = $957.50

Open profit = Long from 1.3304

Advantages: Guaranteed fill, quick, easy

Disadvantages: You pay two bid/ask spreads, and if you are not quick with second order, market could run away from you, costing you money.

Method 2: Leg in Roll (Cheapest Method Typically if Done Correctly)

In this approach, you enter a sell order at the market in September euro, and try to work a buy order at the bid price in December euro. The sell is immediately executed, and the buy is a limit order, which hopefully will get filled at the price you want. You could also do this in reverse: sell on a limit order, and then when you are filled, immediately buy with a market order. You probably should use the limit order on the side with the biggest spread, and the market order on the tight spread. Using the prices above, here is the math:

Sell September at 1.3299 (bid price)
Buy December at 1.3303 (bid price)
Closed profit = $962.50 − $5.00 commission = $957.50
Open profit = Long from 1.3303

Advantages: You save yourself $12.50 by getting in the December contract one tick better than you did with method 1.

Disadvantages: More complicated, plus you may have to chase the market up to get the December fill. You can easily lose more than one tick by trying to be too greedy with your limit order.

Method 3: Exchange Supported Spread Roll (Cost Usually between Methods 1 and 2)

The exchanges have a great tool to help spreaders—a dedicated quote feed and tradable symbol for executing spread orders, which is what a rollover is. In this case, you are buying or selling the spread, not the individual legs. You get simultaneously filled on both legs at the same time. Using the prices above, here is the math:

Buy spread at 4.5 (ask price). Note that this doesn't tell you the actual execution prices. You'll see these on your statement, and they are really irrelevant. So, we will just assume some prices, keeping the spread fill price correct:

Sell September at 1.3329
Buy December at 1.3329 + .00045 = 1.33035
Closed profit = $962.50 − $5.00 commission = $957.50
Open profit = Long from 1.33035

Advantages: Simple, no chance of only one leg executing, cost usually in between methods 1 and 2.

Disadvantages: Some brokers don't support this. For example, TradeStation's main platform for automated trading does not allow this. You can do it manually in TradeStation Futures 4.0 platform, but that platform is not made for algorithmic strategies. It is also easy to screw up the order, and buy the spread instead of selling it. You have to be careful. Also, don't think that just because you are trading the spread symbol, you'll pay only one commission. Some people think this is true, and I guess those folks don't read their statements very closely. When the brokerage does its accounting, it splits the spread into a separate buy and sell fill for each leg. When this happens, commission is charged for each. There is no free lunch, commission-wise, with this method!

You can see from the above example there is $12.50 cost difference between all three methods, with method 1 being the most expensive, method 2 being the cheapest, and method 3 in between the other two. This is not always the case, but is true in general.

One method I did not mention above is to use limit orders on both sides of the spread. Astute readers have probably already thought about this method, and how it could save the spread on each side of the rollover. There is a reason I have not included it, and that is because it is a *terrible* thing to do. In theory, the approach saves you two spreads, but in reality one spread will be filled and the price will more often than not run away from your second limit order, leaving you with half a rollover (in other words, flat). Thus, the times this approach does work are completely overshadowed by times the approach does not work. In the end, it will cost you much more to try and save a few dollars in spread costs. Therefore, I recommend one of the three methods above, completing the rollover quickly, and then moving on to other trading endeavors.

That is how a rollover is actually accomplished. Whenever I can, I use the exchange-supported spreads to do my rollovers. I can do this with systems where I enter orders manually. For my fully automated systems, I generally use method 1, even though it is the most expensive. When I use method 2, I sometimes find myself chasing the market with my order, or worse yet, I forget about the rollover for a while, leaving me temporarily doubly exposed, until I fix it.

PART VI

Monitoring a Live Strategy

CHAPTER 23

The Ins and Outs of Monitoring a Live Strategy

In factories, when a machine makes parts, the operations are closely monitored and the dimensions closely checked. The idea is to ensure that the part-making process is going smoothly, and to give an early warning signal when things are beginning to go bad. The same process holds true in evaluating live trading systems. I use a variety of tools to monitor strategies I am trading or that I am incubating.

The first chart I use is what I call a "bird's-eye view" chart, as shown in Figure 23.1. It tells me, at a glance, how my strategy has performed historically and in real time. To keep consistency, I use the same data source for all the data. In my case, it is the Trade List provided by TradeStation. You can get similar data from just about every trading platform. *This is* ***not*** *actual real money data,* which will be covered in later charts and metrics.

The point of this chart will be to gauge the general overall effectiveness of real-time performance (the portion of the curve on the right). Are the real-time data consistent with the historical test and the incubation period data? If not, there may be something amiss. Maybe the strategy has stopped working correctly, due to market conditions, for example. Or maybe the assumptions made in the strategy about limit order fills are not realistic. This could especially be true in scalping-type strategies, although really you may need actual real-money results to check that. Bad assumptions or strategy development technique up front may not show up in

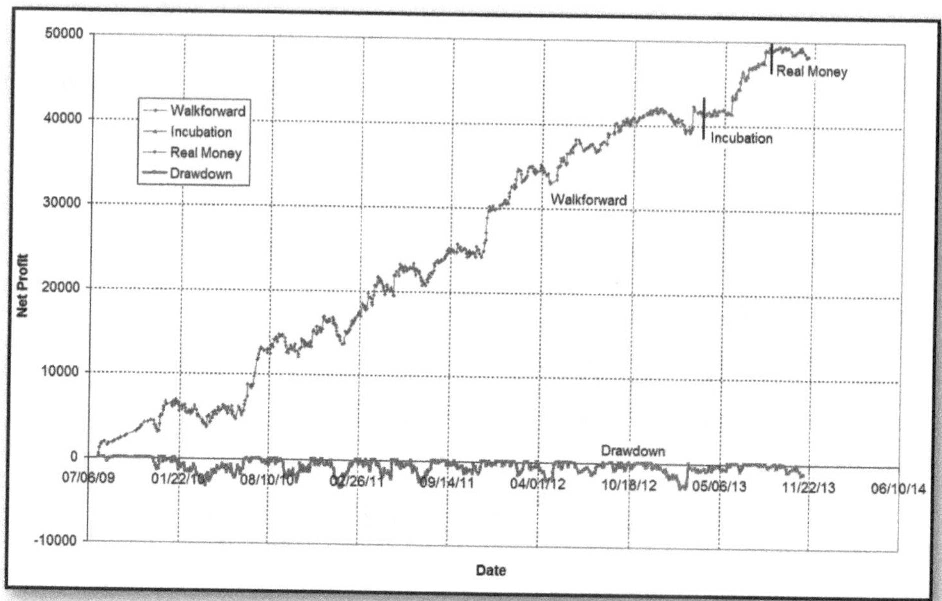

FIGURE 23.1 Bird's-Eye Equity Chart

historical or incubation tests, but they certainly will be revealed when real money is on the line.

I update this chart every few weeks and quickly review it. This gives me a general feeling whether my strategy is performing as expected. If it is, I can quickly move on to the next chart.

If you don't know how to create an equity chart as shown in Figure 23.1, here is how to create it.

How to Build an Equity Curve (and a Drawdown Curve, Too!)

Sometimes, after 20-plus years of trading, some tasks become so rote and routine to me that I forget that I had to learn them at one point. Such is the case with creating equity and drawdown curves. It is simple to me, but to someone who has never done it before, it can be a daunting task. So, I'll go through the math behind creating an equity curve and a drawdown curve.

Equity Curve

The equity curve can be built on a closed trade-by-trade basis, or on any time scale you wish. I like using a daily equity chart, in part to eliminate the noise from intraday price changes. You can use your daily account statement to get your current equity balance.

Here is exactly how to build an equity curve based on daily data:

Day 0 equity = Initial starting balance
Day 1 equity = Day 0 equity + Change in equity during day 1
Day 2 equity = Day 1 equity + Change in equity during day 2
And so on ...

Then, you simply plot the day X equity values, and you have your equity curve.

Drawdown Curve

The drawdown curve is the difference, on any given day, between that day's equity, and the *maximum* equity up to that point. So, let's say an account starts out with $10,000 on day 0. On day 1, it hits a new equity high of $10,500. The drawdown on day 1, since it is a new equity high, is $0. On day 2, let's say the equity falls to $9,700. Now, the drawdown on day 2 is $10,500 – $9,700 = $800. And so it goes through the rest of the days. On days where a new equity is reached, the drawdown will simply be $0. On all other days, the drawdown will be the difference between that day's equity and the maximum equity up until that point.

Day X drawdown = Minimum of $0 or (Day X equity – Max equity from day 0 to day X)

A spreadsheet to create equity and drawdown curves is included at the web site (www.wiley.com/go/algotradingsystems) and the resource web site for this book.

Monthly Summary Chart

When I used to work in aerospace (or the "real world," as I sometimes refer to it), our small company ($250 million annual sales) would have a weekly sales and production meeting called "How We Doin'." Incorrect grammar aside, it was an excellent way for the managers of the company to quickly see how sales were for the month and quarter, what quality and production problems were occurring, and just a general sense of where the company currently stood.

Now, fast-forward a few years. I am trading full time, working alone. But I still want to see at a glance "how I'm doin'" with my strategies and trading. Obviously, my account statements and equity curve tell the overall story, but that is not enough detail for me. What strategies are doing well? Which are underperforming? Of strategies I am incubating, how do they look? Should I make some changes in what I am trading? This "how I'm doin'" report can help me answer all of these questions.

		Expected Ann Return	Actual Ann Return	Notional Capital	Expected Annual Gain	Actual Annual Gain	Return Efficiency	Worst Drawdown	Actual Monthly DD	Drawdown Efficiency	Expected Return/DD
59	System 1	64%	125%	$12,500	$7,956	$15,625	214%	-4,812	-4,538	6%	1.7
60	System 3	40%	70%	$150,000	$59,976	$105,576	198%	-15,000	0	100%	4.0
32	System 4	88%	74%	$25,000	$21,996	$18,472	146%	-20,205	-11,330	44%	1.1
3	System 6	253%	121%	$15,000	$37,932	$18,130	88%	-30,143	-13,691	55%	1.3
64	System 5	144%	108%	$8,500	$12,268	$9,211	83%	-1,700	-1,028	40%	7.2
35	System 2	63%	23%	$12,500	$7,884	$2,826	45%	-14,205	-4,159	71%	0.6
Sub	TRADED REAL $	66%	76%	$223,500	$148,012	$169,840	115%	($86,065)	($34,746)	60%	

FIGURE 23.2 Monthly Summary Chart

I developed a spreadsheet to help me with this task. It tells me at a glance how my strategies are performing, and I can easily drill down and see detail if I need to.

First, there is a summary page, shown in Figure 23.2. I include every strategy I am trading live on this page. I also include, in another section, the strategies I am currently incubating. This summary sheet collects all the data I am interested in (of course, if you did this yourself, you'd likely pick different metrics than I did). This summary sheet gets the data from the individual sheets, which I will describe a bit later.

To keep things simple, I base everything on one contract being traded, even though that is usually not what I am actually trading. Why? My goal with this spreadsheet is to see how my strategies are doing compared to how I thought (calculated) they'd be doing. If I included position sizing, it would muddy up the view for me.

Of all the numbers on this sheet, I am primarily interested in two columns:

1. *Return efficiency.* How am I doing, compared to my expectations? That is how I define return efficiency, and it is simply my actual return divided by my expected return. If my strategy is performing exactly as I had calculated, it will be 100 percent. Obviously, I want this to be close to or above 100 percent. Typically, when I take all the strategies together, I find my efficiency is somewhere between 70 and 100 percent. So this says that if my historical testing says I should make $10 a year, I am actually making somewhere between $7 and $10.
2. *Drawdown efficiency.* This is how I am doing with regard to drawdown. Just like with return efficiency, I calculate this as my actual drawdown divided by my expected drawdown. I then subtract the result from 1, to make the number 100 percent the ideal value. It is a bit backwards to do this, but I do it that way so that both efficiency numbers have 100 percent as their ideal value. Then, the closer the efficiencies get to zero, the worse off things are.

Once a month, I go through and update each of the individual system sheets with performance data, and that automatically updates the main sheet.

The monthly summary sheet reveals my current performance for all strategies. It gets data from the individual strategy sheets. I have one page of my spreadsheet for each of the strategies I am currently trading or incubating. Figure 23.3 shows the individual strategy summary sheet. It is pretty simple, yet pretty effective. I can see at a quick glance how a strategy is performing, compared to my expectations (which,

Name:	Euro D&N
Strategy Name:	2 strats
Workspace Name:	2013-02 EDandN
Subscribers at:	
Real Money Traded:	TradeStation
Real Start Date:	8/20/2013
Expected Monthly Profit:	$1,022
Max Intraday Drawdown:	($1,700)
Notional Capital:	$8,500
Walk-forward Type:	StratOpt WFP
Actual Data Source:	TS reports, acct stmt

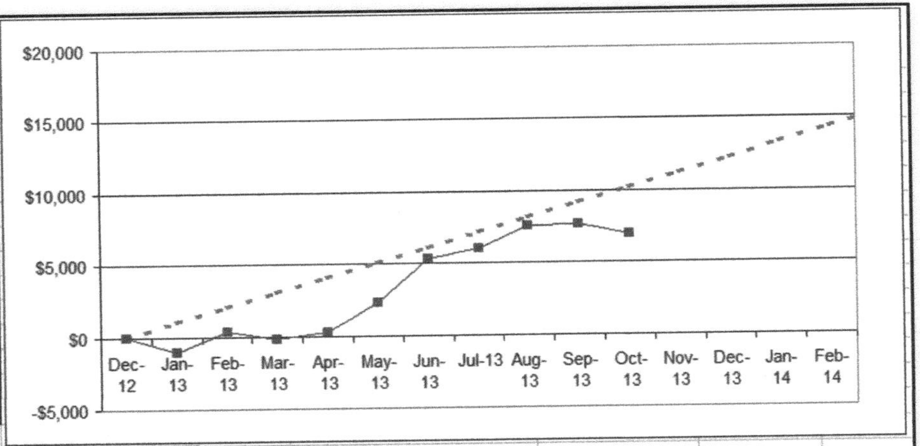

Month	Cum Expected	Actual	Cum Actual			
Dec-12	$0	$0	$0		Expected Ann Return:	144%
Jan-13	$1,022	($1,028)	($1,028)	1	Actual Ann Return:	98%
Feb-13	$2,045	$1,359	$331	2		
Mar-13	$3,067	($500)	($169)	3	Expected Annual Gain:	$12,268
Apr-13	$4,089	$418	$249	4	Actual Annual Gain:	$8,318
May-13	$5,112	$2,031	$2,280	5	Return Efficiency:	68%
Jun-13	$6,134	$3,021	$5,301	6		
Jul-13	$7,156	$755	$6,056	7	Worst Drawdown:	-$1,700
Aug-13	$8,179	$1,503	$7,559	8	Actual Worst Monthly DD:	-$1,028
Sep-13	$9,201	$118	$7,676	9	Drawdown Efficiency:	40%
Oct-13	$10,223	($745)	$6,932	10		
Nov-13	$11,246			11	Min Ann Gain, 1,2 yrs, all	$7,562
Dec-13	$12,268			12	Notes:	

FIGURE 23.3 Individual System Monthly Chart

of course, are based on historical performance). When you have 30 to 50 strategies to keep track of, a quick summary like this is really invaluable.

For many strategies I trade, that is all the information I need—a quick view at performance. If something catches my eye, I can always dig deeper.

On a monthly basis, the only number I have to update is in the "actual" column. This represents the actual profit or loss for the strategy for that particular month. It can be taken from trading statements, after adjusting for the number of contracts, or it can be taken from the strategy performance report. I typically do the latter. The expected numbers can all be obtained from walk-forward historical testing.

The max drawdown is obtained from the strategy report. Note that this is an intraday value, where the drawdown the spreadsheet calculates is on a monthly basis. This obviously is not totally correct, as ideally you would want to compare drawdowns over the same length of time. But for my purposes it is adequate.

One way that the individual monthly performance chart can be of great assistance is by identifying strategies that are performing too well. Too well? Yes, performance that is too good can be a bad thing.

An example is shown in Figure 23.4. I started incubating this strategy a while back, and it took off.

It was "too good to be true"—way above its historical norm. For that reason I decided to keep incubating it. The next few months are shown in Figure 23.5.

Now the strategy is in line with historical norms, but the standard deviation of monthly performance is a *killer* (look at the down-month performances). I looked into it further and saw that the system was not acting normal. So I decided to keep incubating. Figure 23.6 shows what happened.

This is a good example of (1) performance that is too good being a bad thing, (2) standard deviation of results (high degree of variability seen from visual inspection) being an early warning sign that things were not quite right, and (3) the monthly performance

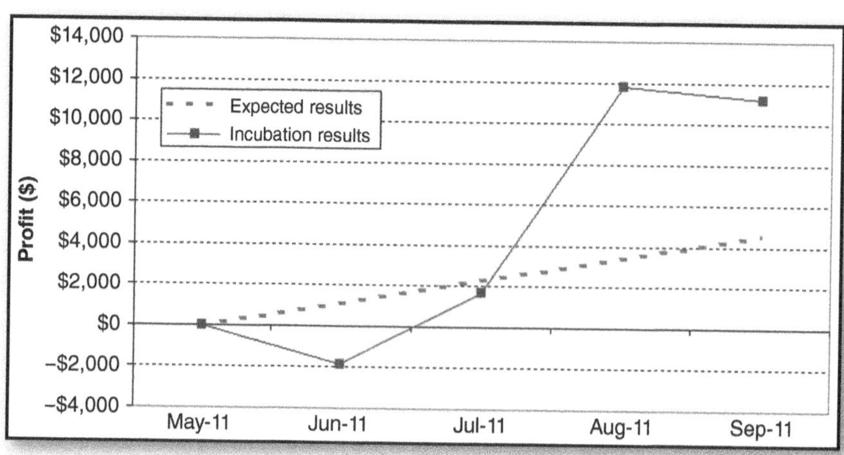

FIGURE 23.4 Superb Incubation Performance

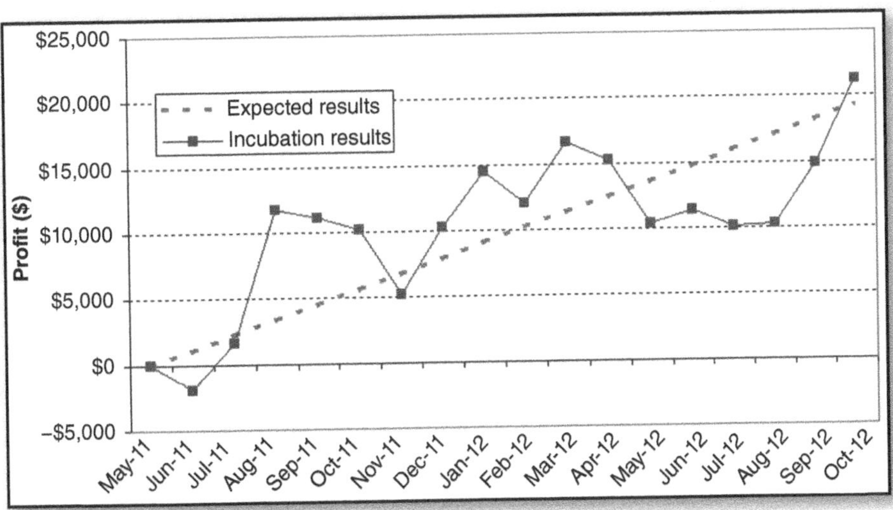

FIGURE 23.5 Most Strategies Eventually Revert to Their Mean

report showing all this information in an easy-to-digest format. As an epilogue: I am still incubating this particular strategy but have not traded it with real money.

So far, I have discussed a few different ways to track the performance of a strategy. These tools are excellent for assessing the longer-term performance of a system—over a significant period of time (months to years), is the strategy performing as it should? While this "view from 35,000 feet" is useful to have, you also need to have measurements at the weekly or daily level. This helps answer the question: is my new strategy performing to expectations? I use a couple of different methods to review the shorter-term performance. There is a simple way and a complicated way. First, I'll look at the simple way.

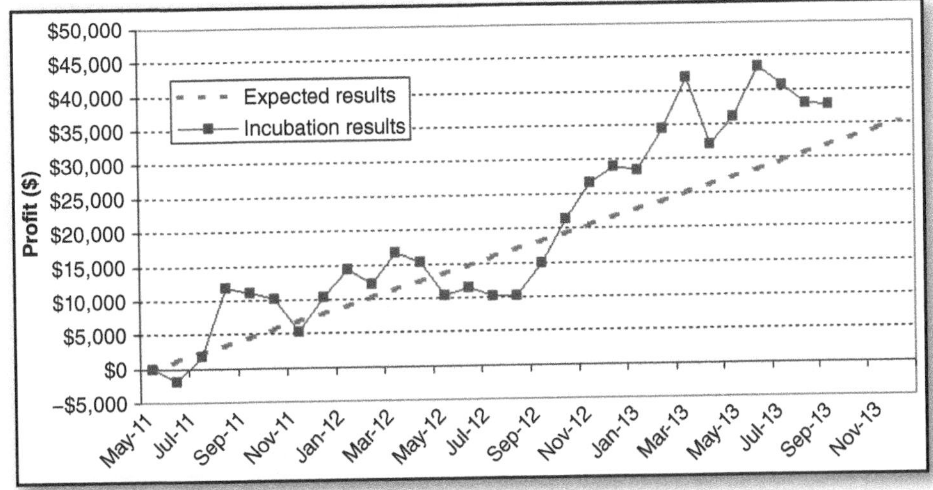

FIGURE 23.6 Incubating Even Longer

The only data you need for this is the average trade or average daily result. If you have the standard deviation of this value, then you can do even more.

All you do is plot your results, along with the equation "$n * avg$" where n is the trade number/day, and "avg" is the average value. You'll get a chart like the one shown in Figure 23.7.

If you are above the average line, your strategy is doing better than you thought. If you are below, your strategy is worse.

This chart becomes really useful as time goes on. Over 30 or more periods, you'd expect the strategy to be right around the average line. That is how I use it. Then, at a quick glance, I know the general state of the strategy. This chart is very similar to the monthly tracking chart shown earlier. It is nice, but it doesn't convey a lot of information, especially early on in the life of a live strategy. To get more insight, add two lines for the +/− standard deviation curves:

$$\text{Upper curve: } n * avg + sqrt(n) * (std\ dev) * X$$

$$\text{Avg curve: } n * avg$$

$$\text{Lower curve: } n * avg - sqrt(n) * (std\ dev) * X$$

where

n = The trade number
avg = The average profit per trade
$std\ dev$ = Standard deviation of the avg trade
X = Standard deviation multiplier

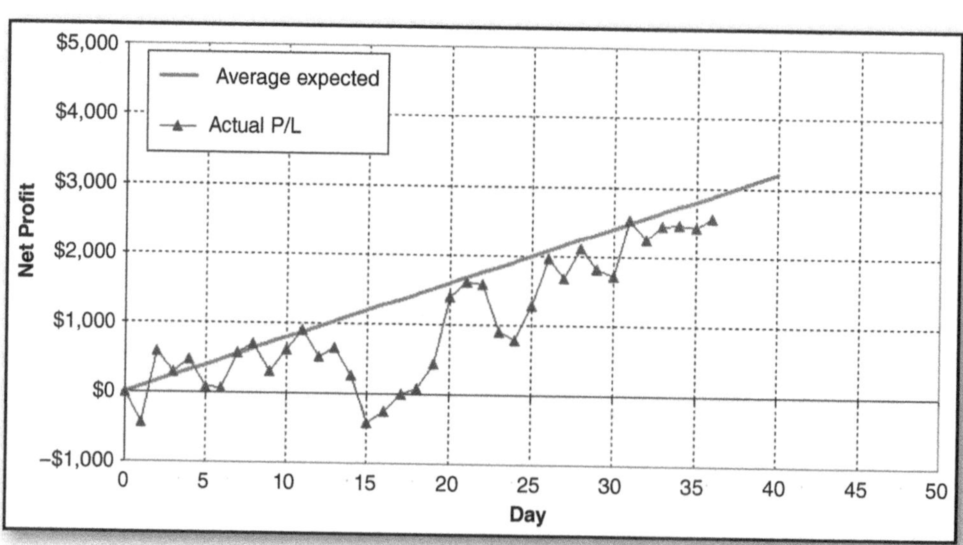

FIGURE 23.7 Daily Performance Review

What this tells you is that roughly 68 percent ($X = 1$) or 95 percent ($X = 2$) of the time, your equity curve should be within the upper or lower bands. Most well-performing strategies will have their equity curve within the standard deviation bands. If the equity curve is outside of those bands, maybe there is something wrong with your strategy.

Figure 23.8 shows a sample strategy, with $X = 2$ bands. The most interesting point here is the bottom curve, the −2 standard deviation line. Look as it starts negative and stays negative. Imagine that! A winning (positive expectancy) system can still have negative results for quite a while. Pure random chance (the order of trade results) can lead a winning system to appear to be a losing system.

Of course, over time, the positive expectancy starts to dominate, and the lower curve will eventually turn positive. This has *huge* implications for the trader who "tweaks" his method if, after five trades, he is not showing a profit. He may well have just changed a winning system! This lower curve really shows that it takes time for even a winning system to show profits.

Here is a great quote that explains it better than I can. It is from the book *Trading Bases* by Joe Peta (Penguin Books, 2013):

> Well, if you had the opportunity to invest in a venture with a positive expected value, like ownership of a roulette wheel, would you prefer to own it for one hour or nine and a half hours? Funny things can happen in one hour; there is no guarantee of a profit even with the house edge. But over nine and a half hours, the natural fluctuations inherent in the game will smooth out, and the chances of losing money will be very small, approaching zero over time.

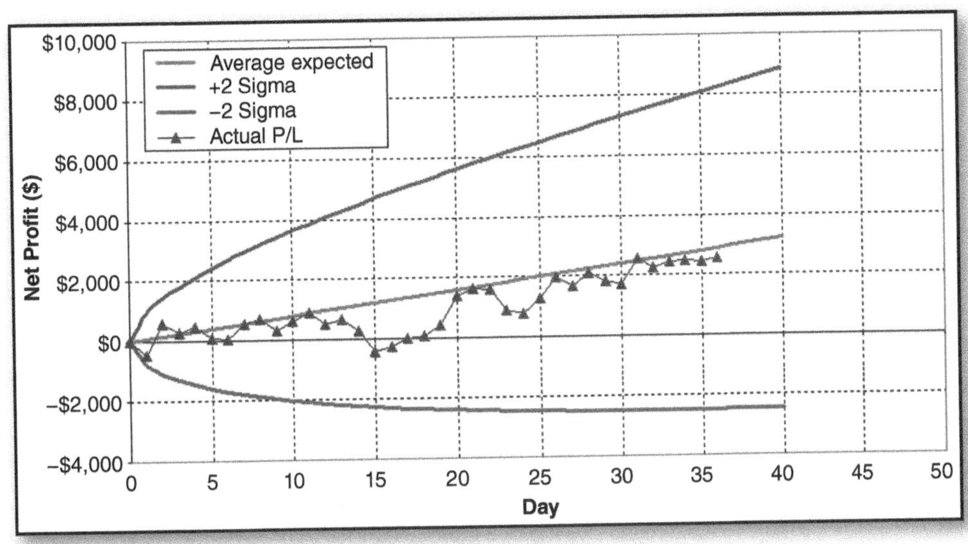

FIGURE 23.8 Daily Performance Review with Performance Bands

Astute readers will recognize that the graph in Figure 23.8 uses standard deviation and therefore assumes the trade results have a normal distribution. In reality, most trading systems do not have a normal distribution. Rather, the distribution will likely have a spike in negative territory, where a stop loss might be placed, and they will have an extended tail on the profit side, or a spike in positive territory, corresponding to a profit target. An example of a real trading system histogram, versus the normally distributed version, is shown in Figure 23.9. Depending on the specifics of the actual trades, assuming a normal distribution may be a bad idea.

To alleviate this concern, we can simply take the Monte Carlo results from numerous runs and use percentiles based on them. This will provide a more accurate representation of the expected bounds of the trading system.

A simple example can help explain this approach, before I apply it to the actual trading data. Assume that we have a trading system that averages $100 per day, with a standard deviation of plus or minus $50. With two standard deviation bands, we expect roughly 95 percent of the values to fall in between the upper and lower curves, or the 97.7 percentile on the upper end and 2.3 percentile on the lower end. If we then run Monte Carlo analysis on a trade-by-trade basis, for each trading day we simply select the values at the 2.3 and 97.7 percentiles. Since these values use the actual data, not an assumed normal distribution, they should be more accurate and representative of the actual trading system. The drawback is that the curves will not be smooth and could change if the simulation is rerun. Such are the penalties for using Monte Carlo analysis.

If we run the day-by-day Monte Carlo analysis on the euro trading system, how do the curves compare? There is a good, but not perfect, match between the standard

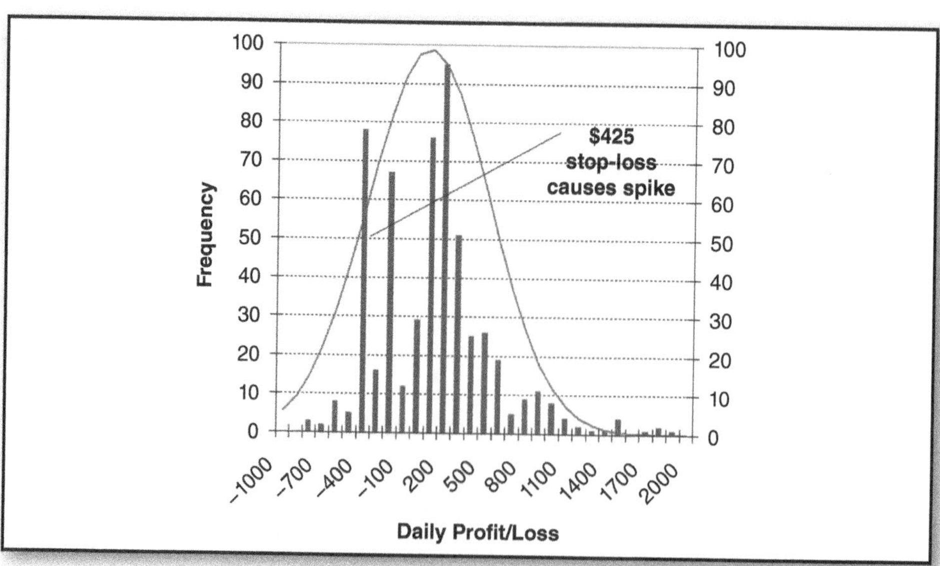

FIGURE 23.9 Histogram of a Typical Real Trading System

deviation and the Monte Carlo lines. Either is probably acceptable for tracking purposes. I personally like the Monte Carlo version, since it does not make any assumptions about the underlying data.

How to Use This Graph

The daily tracking graph can be used to help you quit trading a system. For example, if the real-time performance of your strategy falls below the lower 10 percent line, it could mean that your system is no longer working. After all, the odds were 90 percent that your strategy should be performing better than this. An example of a real-world system should make this crystal clear.

Figure 23.10 shows a sample case of a real-world system I traded with my own money.

Curve 1: The system performance after 140 days. Barely positive, and close to the −1 Sigma line. That means, at that point, only 16 percent of the randomly generated equity curves, based on the historical back-test trades, would have been worse than this.

I'm sure most people would have stopped trading at this point. I did not, since I knew that even with the bad performance there was a chance that the system was not fundamentally broken.

Curve 2: The curve for the next 200+ days (Figure 23.11). I kept the system running, and now it is performing closer to its expected value.

As I explained earlier, I use Monte Carlo simulation to determine if a strategy is performing to expectations. It is basically the same result as with using mean and

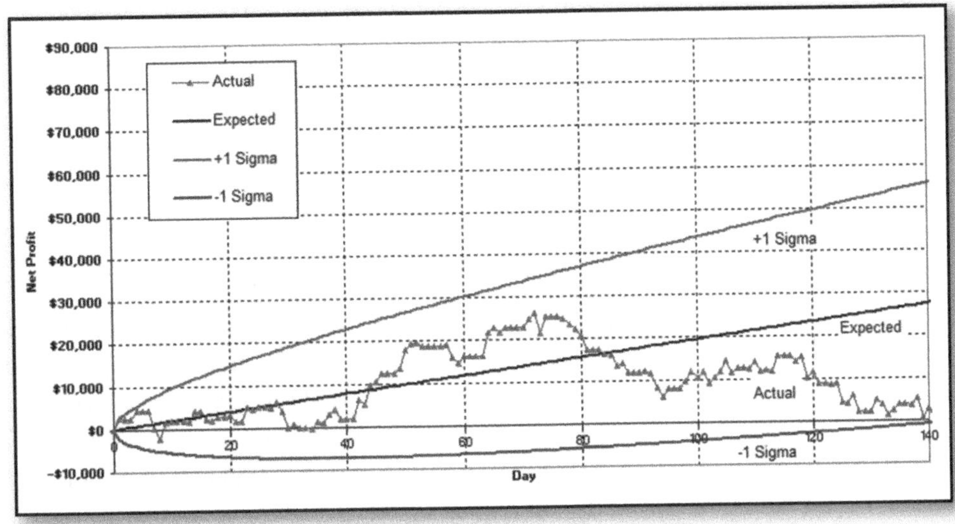

FIGURE 23.10 140-Day Daily Performance

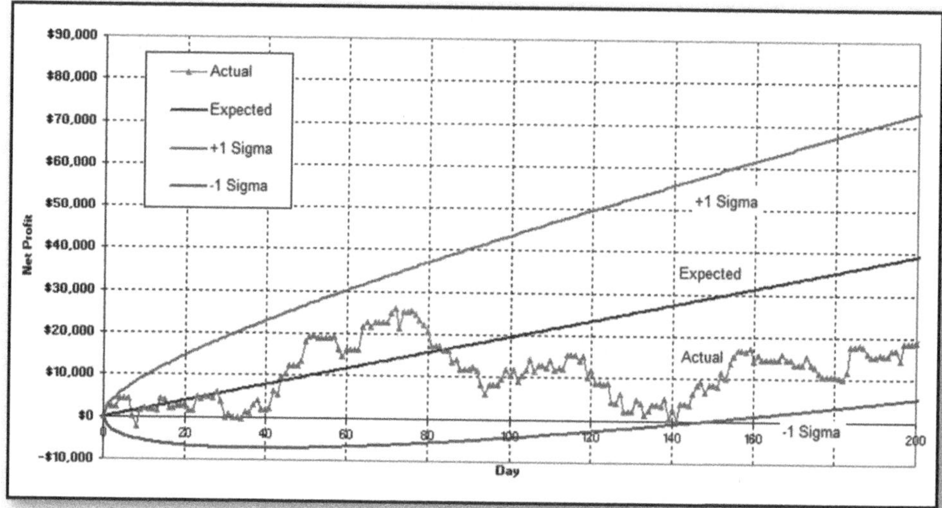

FIGURE 23.11 200-Day Daily Performance

standard deviation, except that you can include "boundary condition" effects with Monte Carlo (like quitting after a certain percentage drawdown or quitting when account gets blown out).

Tracking Expected and Actual Performance

In all the examples I have shown in this chapter, I have used the performance numbers generated by the back-testing software, which was TradeStation in my case. These numbers have built in certain assumptions about:

- Amount of slippage per trade.
- Amount of commissions per trade.
- Fill logic for limit orders.
- "Perfect" trading versus real-world trading.

Depending on your trading system and the values you put in the back-test software, you may or may not have a realistic view of how your system will perform in the real world. I'm sure you've experienced this—you see a terrific-looking equity curve only to find out later that the creator did not include commissions or slippage in the performance data. Or you discovered an unbeatable scalping system for the mini S&P, only to discover, upon further review, that your back-test engine assumed limit order fills as soon as the price was just touched, not when the limit order price was exceeded (this is a very common mistake, especially with many so-called trading simulators out there). Finally, you will have Internet outages, data delays, and all sorts of other little gremlins. The point is that the performance you expect is not the performance that you'll get.

If you are treating your trading as a business, it is imperative that you track actual performance and compare it to predicted performance. After all, when your actual performance is below your expected performance, isn't that akin to something or someone stealing from you? It sure feels that way to me—I fully anticipate to achieve the predicted performance or better, and when I don't, I search for and correct the reason.

I track my actual performance on the daily tracking graph. I also keep a running table of actual versus predicted performance. Most of the time, the actual performance does slightly better than the predicted performance. This is a very good thing, as it shows that my assumptions for commissions, slippage, and the like were a bit on the conservative side. I'd rather be conservative in my estimates and be pleasantly surprised with actual performance, as opposed to underestimating slippage and later being disappointed.

CHAPTER 24

Real Time

When I take a new strategy live, I like to review the performance on an ongoing basis, to make sure things are going more or less as expected. For my euro day and night strategy, which I started live trading in late August 2013, here are my real-time updates every three to four weeks of trading it, for the first four months, along with a discussion of a few interesting events that came up along the way.

Four-Week Review—September 13, 2013, End Date

Week 4 of trading the euro day and night system with actual money is now complete. For the first few months of live trading, every four weeks or so, I review the current performance of the system as shown in Figure 24.1, and answer some standard questions. This information may be useful should the performance of the system become erratic—maybe there was something I could have seen earlier, or something I just plain out missed.

Summary: Well, after four weeks of trading this system live, I am right where I started—breakeven.

Am I surprised at this result? Absolutely not. It is well within expectations.

Am I disappointed in the results so far? Yes. Anytime I start a new strategy I want to make money at the beginning.

Are results in line with expectations? Yes. The current profit is below the average I expect, and it is above the lower 10 percent line. So, while it is underperforming currently, I see no reason for alarm. Also, I have had two winning weeks and two losing weeks. Over time, I expect about 60 percent of my weeks to be profitable, so the performance is just as I expect.

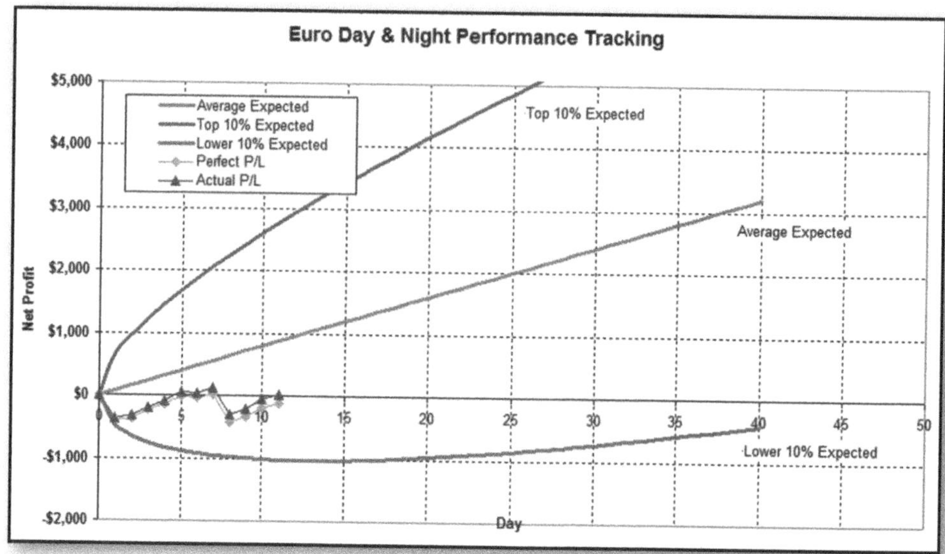

FIGURE 24.1 Daily Performance, After Four Weeks of Live Trading

Are fills and trades live comparable to TradeStation strategy report? Yes, in fact, in most cases my fills are better than what I had anticipated. Slippage is usually less than I had expected.

Do I see any reason to stop trading this system? No.

Do I see any reason to change my position-sizing plan, that is, reduce or increase my risk? No.

Update after Week 7

Seven weeks into trading this system live, and things went bad this week, with a couple of large losing days. The cumulative equity is hovering right around the 10 percent line, which is generally a good warning sign that the system is not working the same as its historical test. If circumstances were different, I might consider stopping trading this system. The things working against the "quit now" idea are:

1. There are only 18 days of live trading data—too short, in my mind, to make a decision to quit.
2. Most important, when I laid out the criteria for stopping live trading, performance relative to the daily performance was not considered (sometimes I do consider this in my "when to quit" analysis). For this strategy, though, I used maximum drawdown as my stopping criteria.

I will keep on trading, realizing that things need to improve.

After seven weeks of live trading, is the system performing as designed? First, let's look at the number of trades it has taken. A sharp increase or decrease in the number of trades, when compared to the walk-forward history, would suggest that the market action is different than the historical market, causing many more, or far fewer, trades to be taken than normal. After seven weeks, the system has traded for 18 days, or 53 percent of possible days. Historically, it trades about 151 days per year, or 60 percent of days. So the system is trading less than the average. But some years it has traded as few as 130 days (51 percent) and as many as 175 days (70 percent). Based on all this, I'd conclude that the number of trades is generally in line with expectations, although at the low end. Anecdotally, I have felt that the volatility has been lower than usual. There have been a handful of days where an entry was missed by only a few ticks (the big Fed move day, September 18, was a case in point). A little more volatility in the hours before the announcement and the system would have entered a big winner.

Second, let's look at average performance versus actual performance. The average historical performance of the system gives $1,441 profit after 18 trading days. Actual performance, however, is at −$746. This is a *huge* discrepancy, and the conclusion obviously is that the system is not performing as well as it should. But here is where is gets tricky. Take a coin and flip it 100 times. If you get 60 heads, do you conclude that the coin is "broken," that is, biased? What if you got 70 heads, or 80, or 90? Even if you flipped 100 heads in a row, could you absolutely conclude that the coin is biased? No! There is a chance, albeit very, very small, that a fair coin could be flipped heads 100 consecutive times.

It is the same way with a trading system. You can ask, "Is it broken?," but the answer will always have some degree of uncertainty. That uncertainty sometimes makes all the difference to your conclusions and decisions. Some people take statistics as gospel, but I'll relate a little secret I learned. Back in my previous career, I had a statistician who worked for me. I assigned a project to him that required a lot of data analysis and then some sort of conclusion. After he reviewed the details of the project, before he even started work, he asked me, "What conclusion would you like? I can make the data support your point of view, whatever it is." I was astounded, but I never forgot the lesson—statistics can be manipulated very easily, so be careful making any conclusions based on them.

Right now, the actual system performance is at the 10th percentile of what was expected. The 50th percentile would be right at the average, so the 10 percent mark is pretty bad. But it is still within the realm of possible outcomes. If it were below the 0 percentile—let's say the system had lost $8,000 through the first 18 days—then the system obviously would not be performing as expected. That would be an easy decision. It is where there is uncertainty that things get tough.

There are statistical tests that could be run to show whether the current trades could be part of the historical distribution of trades, but even such advanced analysis is not definitive. There is always a gray area. So how do I navigate the gray area? First, I try to determine the parameters that will cause me to quit trading a system. I could certainly use the percentile number approach and have a quitting rule that says, "If after X days the performance is below the Yth percentile, I will cease trading." X and Y would be at my discretion, based on personal preferences. As long as I stick to the rule I create at the start, I'd be doing fine. For me, and for this particular system, earlier I decided that I would quit only when I hit a $5,000 drawdown. So I am not using the data in the tracking graph to decide when to quit. Sometimes I do use it, though.

To summarize:

Is the system performing as expected? No, not even close. It is performing much worse than expected.

Is the system "broken?" Maybe, maybe not. It depends on how you define broken. One cannot say definitively it is broken or it is not broken.

Am I going to quit? No. My quit point, established earlier, calls for a single-contract drawdown of $5,000. This was a well-thought-out amount, and I can't just toss it out the window. I'm going to stick to the plan. I realize, though, that sticking to the plan might be akin to the captain sinking with the ship.

Week 8 Review

Week 8 of trading the euro day and night system with actual money is now complete.

Summary: First, let's look at the big picture. I like to do this regularly, because at a glance I can tell if things are going as planned or not. From looking at Figure 24.2, a couple of things are clear:

1. Over the whole course of the system history (walk-forward, incubation, live), the system performance hasn't changed much. I could draw a line from the start of walk-forward to the start of incubation, and then another line from the start of incubation until the present time, and the slopes of those two lines would be about the same. This gives me some reassurance that the system is behaving, subject to point 2.
2. In Figure 24.3, It is easy to see that the live trading (dark gray line with triangles) has not been up to par at all. The performance these past two months has been down, and while it has not crashed and burned, it certainly has been a disappointment.

After eight weeks of trading this system live, I am down about 5 percent from the start.

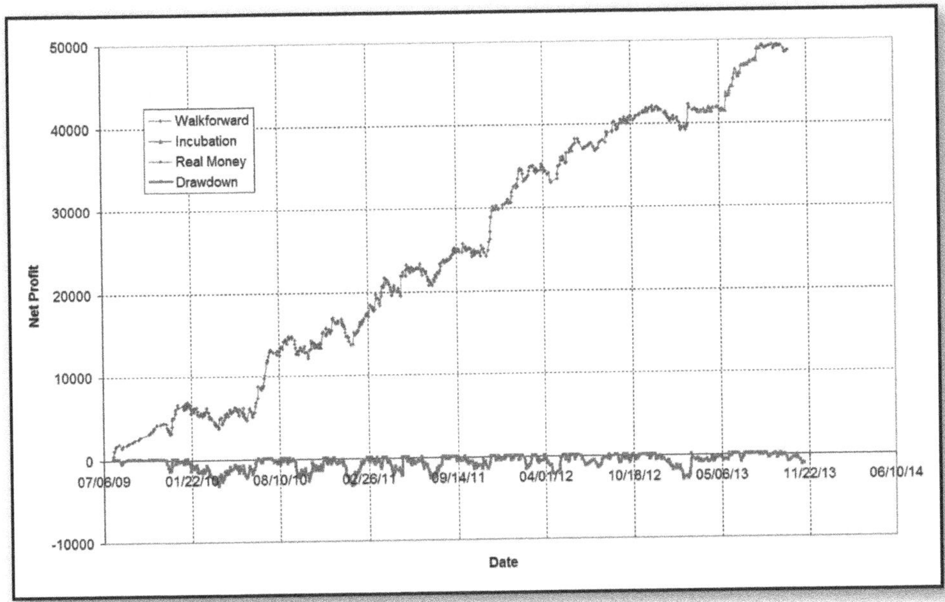

FIGURE 24.2 Big Picture Equity Curve after Eight Weeks

Am I surprised at this result? Absolutely not. It is well within expectations.

Am I disappointed in the results so far? Yes. After eight weeks, I had hoped to be making some money. The performance these past eight weeks is way behind the long-term average, so it is very disappointing.

Are results in line with expectations? Yes. The current profit is below the average I expect, and it is right around lower 10 percent line. So it is

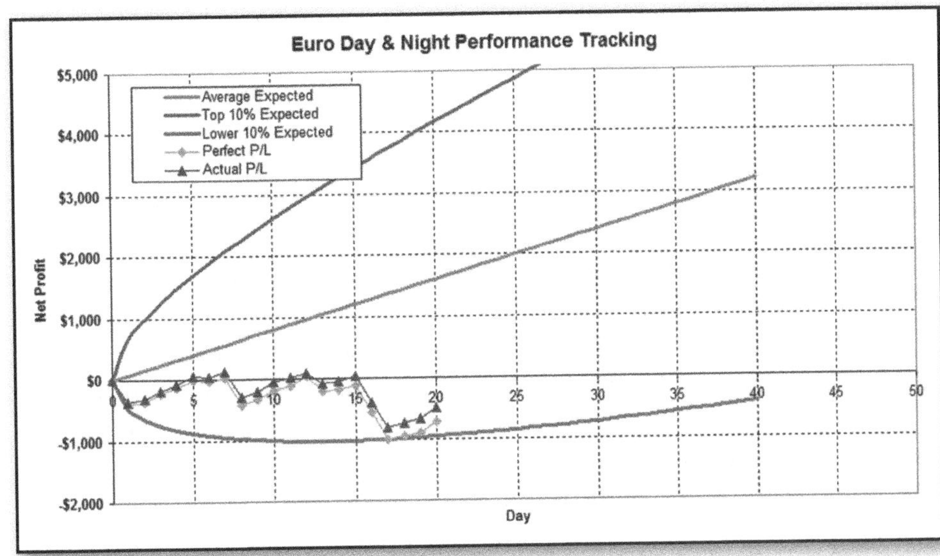

FIGURE 24.3 Daily Performance after Eight Weeks of Live Trading

underperforming currently, and I will be concerned if equity drops below that 10 percent line. Also, I have had four winning weeks and four losing weeks. Over time, I expect about 60 percent of my weeks to be profitable, so the performance is a bit behind in that regard. Plus, one week was really, really bad.

Are fills and trades live comparable to TradeStation strategy report? Yes, in fact, in most cases my fills are better than what I had anticipated. Slippage is usually less than I had expected.

Do I see any reason to stop trading this system? No.

Do I see any reason to change my position-sizing plan, that is, reduce or increase my risk? No.

After eight weeks, I will keep on trading per the plan, but storm clouds are forming on the horizon. I need some sunshine instead!

Week 9—Automated Trading Issues

You've probably heard the phrase "automated trading does not mean unattended trading." You've also probably read all the disclaimers that the brokerage throws at you before they allow you to turn automation on. With TradeStation, for example, there are tons of disclaimers you have to sign when you open an account, and then if you want to automate a strategy, there are two more disclaimers you have to click and accept. The first disclaimer is 397 words, and the second is a whopping 593 words. That is a lot of legalese to wade through just to automate your trading.

But all those warnings are there for a reason. Ignore them at your own risk. That's what happened to me in week 9 of live trading. Let me explain.

My euro day and night strategies enter on limit orders, which are supposed to be active for the current bar only. After the bar closes, any open orders get canceled by the software. Depending on the strategy logic, another limit order may be placed for the current bar.

So, Monday night during week 9, my euro night strategy placed a limit order to buy, well below the market. It did not get filled during the bar, so it should have been canceled. For whatever reason, it was not canceled. This is the first time I have *ever* seen this occur. The success rate of the software auto-canceling orders, from my experience, has to be well over 99 percent. That is excellent, but errors can and do occur. Just look at the airline industry, for example. There are roughly 28,000 commercial flights per day, and if even 99.99 percent had successful takeoffs and landings, two or three planes would crash *per day*. That's where claims of 99 percent plus uptime, accuracy, whatever are meaningless. Anything less than 100 percent perfection runs the risk of costing you money.

The order rested at the exchange until 5 A.M. Tuesday morning, when it was filled. I noticed this rouge position Wednesday morning. Of course, with Murphy's Law in effect here, I noticed it not when the position was profitable, but after it had gone negative. Then, to add insult to injury, while I investigated the issue—before I exited the position—I watched it drop another $125 or so. Once I confirmed that the position was wrong, I exited with about a $550 loss.

Who's to blame here? Well, the software did not do its job, since it should have canceled the order. But, ultimately, I can blame no one, and no thing (software, Internet connection, etc.), except myself for the error. I'll repeat that: I am to blame! I am the caretaker, and if things go wrong, as they occasionally will, it is up to me to be aware of it and fix it. I take full responsibility for this screw up, and I added some steps to make sure it is not repeated:

1. Check statements every day. If I had checked it that first morning, I'd have probably exited with a $300 profit, instead of a $550 loss.
2. Check platform every few hours for uncanceled orders.
3. Improve checking of positions. I normally check my positions every few hours, but somehow this one slipped by me.
4. Make sure filled orders show up on the chart. For some reason, this fill did not—they usually do.

Not a killer loss, but enough for me to getting pretty upset at the situation! Percentage-wise, for this account, the losses were 7 percent, so that is pretty bad. Eventually, I want this strategy to get to 10 contracts, and at that point it would be some serious money.

I noticed the bad trade about 30 hours after I entered it. Then I exited at almost the worst time, with a $550 loss. Now, less than one hour later, I could have exited with less than a $100 loss. Is it just me, or does this kind of stuff happen to you, too? If I did not know better, I'd swear that someone was controlling prices, and watching my positions, and deliberately doing things to maximize my losses! I can definitely see why people feel this way—at times, it surely feels like the market is out to get me personally!

I've thought a lot about this occasional paranoia-type feeling. I know why some of this occurs. I tend to discount—not really notice or dwell on—every good thing that happens to me (mistakes in my favor, excellent news reports right after I enter a position, etc.). Money-making anomalies become just a blip in the equity curve. They are nice, but I don't really remember them too well. But I tend to remember losses due to mistakes and keep them filed in my memory bank. Some of these "losing lessons" might be good to remember—today's automated issue is a good example—but most should be forgotten just as easily as the money-making mistakes. That doesn't happen for me, at least not usually.

Last year I actually did a study of this psychological phenomenon. I added up all my winning mistakes and all my losing mistakes. The net impact, from a monetary basis, was just about zero. But from a psychological standpoint, it definitely was not breakeven. One would think this feeling ("the market is out to get me") would have disappeared after 20-plus years of trading. But it hasn't, and I suspect it never will!

By the end of the week, what should have been a decent winning week turned out to be a losing week, due to the entry "glitch" described earlier. That cost me $550. I have taken some immediate steps to prevent it from happening again, and I think I am in the clear, at least for the time being. My actual performance now lags the perfect strategy performance, and the issue this past week is to blame for that.

The problem ultimately comes down to this: if I am depending on a computer to place, cancel, and replace orders, unless someone is monitoring it at all times, there is always a possibility of something going haywire. The question is how much of my limited resources (it is just me, after all) do I devote to the effort to make the automation goof-proof? Doing the usual amount of effort hasn't worked—since I just lost $550—but at what point will I be confident that those issues will not occur? Plus, it is usually not the issues you know about, but the issues you don't know about. This case was one of them. After thousands of automated trades over the years, this particular issue had never come up before!

Enough about that issue for now. Performance is still lagging, and the euro day system has not had a trade in two weeks (I think I can blame lower volatility for that). Regardless, I will "keep on trading!"

Week 9—Limit Order Fills (October 28, 2013)

One of the tricks unscrupulous system vendors play is to assume that all limit orders are filled as soon as the price is touched. You can recognize this by looking at a price charts of their trades. If the method shows trades being bought at the exact low of a bar, and/or sold at the exact high of a bar, you can bet this game is being played.

Of course, the reality is that it is hard to buy the low and sell the high. My experience is that, depending on the market and when your order is placed, you can probably do this 5–20 percent of the time. The other 80–95 percent of the time, price has to trade through your price to get you a fill at the limit price.

This can be an issue with back testing. If your back-test engine assumes that limit orders are filled when touched, the results will be too optimistic. If the back-test engine assumes price must be penetrated to get a fill, then the back-test results will be a bit too pessimistic. I always go with the pessimistic approach. My actual results can then only be better than the back test.

During trading for week 9, the euro day strategy bought the exact low of the bar on a limit order. Of course, part of the reason I was filled was that I was trading a 1 lot; if I were trading a 10 lot, I probably would have received only a partial fill. The interesting thing is that when I refreshed the chart, the trade went away, according to the strategy engine. Since the price did not go one tick below my limit price, the strategy engine assumes there was no trade. But my real account says there was a trade because I was indeed filled. Since the trade was a winner, it was a nice surprise for once! So this is roughly a $400 trade in my real account's favor, when compared to the back-test engine. This makes up for the order problem that cost me $500 in the previous week.

Week 12 Review

Summary: First, let's look at the big picture, as I always do. From a look at Figure 24.4, a couple of things are clear:

1. Over the whole course of the system history (walk-forward, incubation, live), the system performance hasn't changed much. Just as after week 8, I could draw a line from the start of walk-forward to the start of incubation, and then another line from the start of incubation until the present time, and the slopes of those two lines would be about the same—with the slope from start of incubation to present being a little flatter. This gives me some reassurance that the system is behaving well on a longer-term basis.
2. It is easy to see that the live trading has been lagging long-term performance. The performance these past three months has been down, and while it has not crashed and burned, it certainly has been a disappointment.

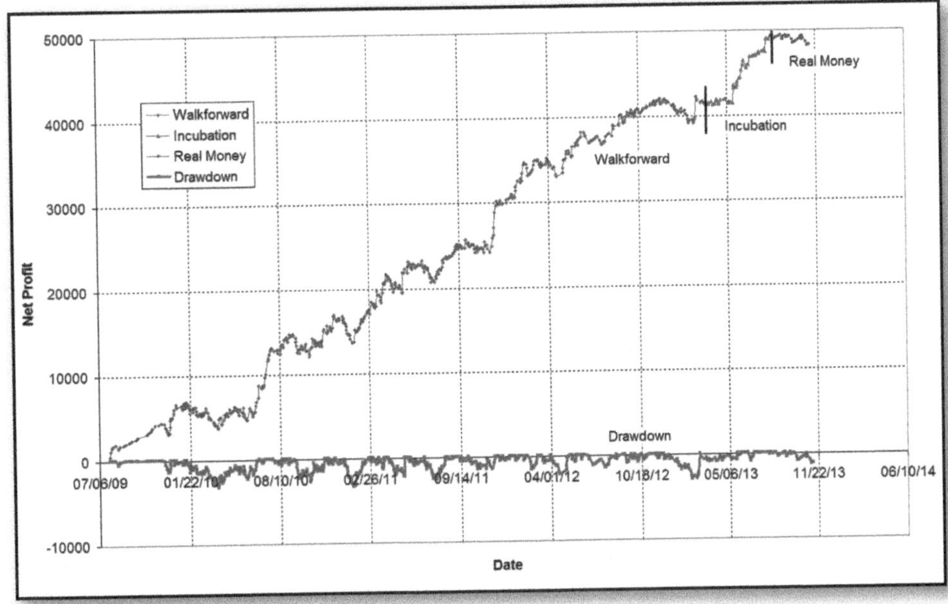

FIGURE 24.4 Big Picture Equity Curve after 12 Weeks

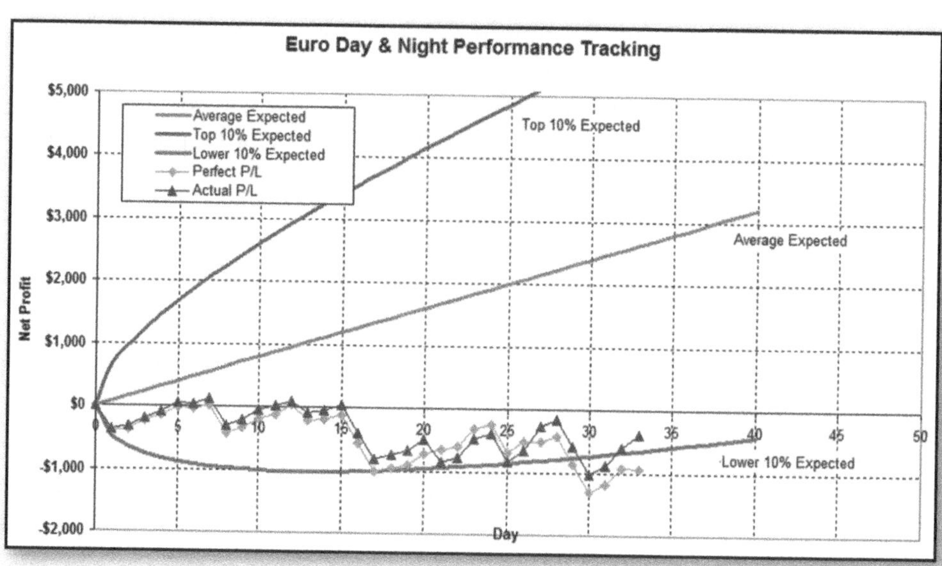

FIGURE 24.5 Daily Performance, After 12 Weeks of Live Trading

After 12 weeks of trading this system live, I am down about 10 percent from the start for the strategy-calculated performance, and about 4.5 percent for the actual performance (Figure 24.5).

Am I surprised at this result? Yes. I had expected better, certainly close to breakeven by now—at the very worst.

Am I disappointed in the results so far? Very much so. The performance these past 12 weeks is way behind the long-term average, so it is very disappointing.

Are results in line with expectations? Just barely. Results are around the lower 10 percent line, which means the system in real time is close to being a different system than walk-forward and incubation. Not quite different yet, but getting close.

Are fills and trades live comparable to TradeStation strategy report? No, but it is a good thing! I am doing about $550 better live than the strategy predicts because of (1) less slippage than I had planned for and (2) a few trades where I was filled in real life when price just touched, but did not exceed, my limit price.

Do I see any reason to stop trading this system? No.

Do I see any reason to change my position-sizing plan, that is, reduce or increase my risk? No.

After 12 weeks, I will keep on trading per the plan, but this system is just kind of floundering. A couple of big winners, which is what the system is based on, are needed.

Week 13—Time Limit Review

As my strategy continues to flounder around breakeven, I start to wonder: how long am I willing to put my capital at risk without any return? The answer for me involves the "next best alternative."

Every six months or so, I look at every system I am trading, and also the systems waiting in the wings (ready to be traded live, but currently not trading live). If I find a better system than the one I am trading, and I don't have enough capital to trade both (or perhaps because of correlation issues I do not want to trade both), I will replace it. Thus, even if the euro trading strategy is performing decently (making money as opposed to its current situation of near breakeven), I still might replace it with the "next best alternative."

I do this exercise only two times a year, in part because it is involved (complicated correlation studies, etc), but mainly because it is only fair to a new system going live to have some time to prove itself. Most people don't have the patience to do this, and they jump from system to system, never giving any system a fair chance. It would almost like pulling a pitcher in baseball from the game as soon as he gives up just one hit. As I showed earlier, even winning systems can be losers for quite a while, until the long-term positive expectancy really shows itself.

Of course, even with this twice-a-year analysis, my original quitting point is still in effect. If I hit that, I am out, regardless of the next best alternative (which may be cash).

Week 15 Review

Summary: After 15 weeks, the euro day and night trading strategies are finally doing better, as depicted in Figures 24.6 and 24.7. By looking at the big picture, it is clear that the performance of the past few weeks is getting the live results closer to the historical back test. The system still has to improve performance, but things are certainly looking better. After 15 weeks of trading this system live, I am up about 1 percent from the start for the strategy-calculated performance and about 9.0 percent for the actual performance.

Am I surprised at this result? Obviously, I was hoping for better, but I am thankful that the system is showing a profit at this point.

Are results in line with expectations? Results are definitely more in line with expectations, especially in the past few weeks. But the strategy as a whole is still underperforming. As stated earlier, this approach relies on a handful of big profit trades per year, and so far in live trading there have not been any.

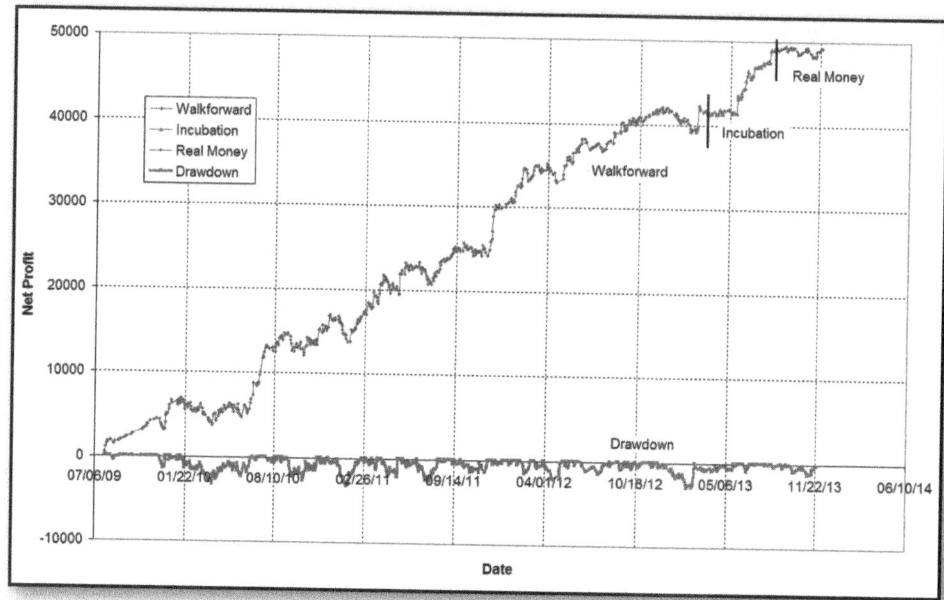

FIGURE 24.6 Big Picture Equity Curve after 12 Weeks

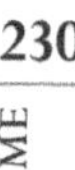

Are fills and trades live comparable to TradeStation strategy report? No, and that is still good! I am doing about $700 better live than the strategy predicts because of (1) less slippage than planned and (2) multiple trades where I was filled in real life but not in the back-test engine (limit price penetration issues).

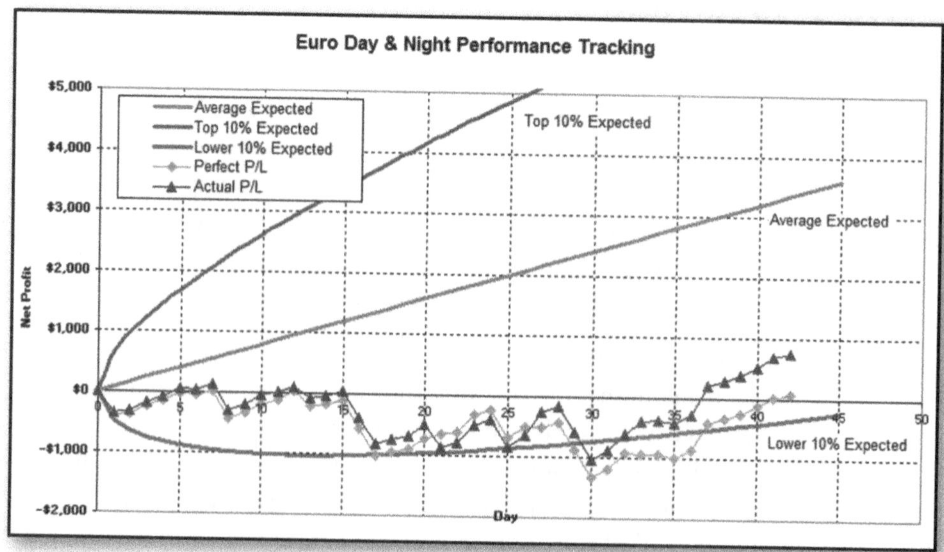

FIGURE 24.7 Daily Performance after 15 Weeks of Live Trading

Do I see any reason to stop trading this system? No.

Do I see any reason to change my position-sizing plan, that is, reduce or increase my risk? No.

After 15 weeks, I will keep on trading per the plan, but this system is still underperforming, compared to original expectations. That is one drawback to a trading approach that requires large, but infrequent, winning trades. It might be a long time before this system really shows its capability.

Future Reviews

This running diary will continue indefinitely, or until I stop trading the euro day and night system, at which point I'll explain any reasons I had to stop live trading. Updates can be found at the web site (www.wiley.com/go/algotradingsystems).

PART VII

Cautionary Tales

CHAPTER 25

Delusions of Grandeur

Winning the World Cup Championship of Futures Trading has made me a (very) minor celebrity in the small world of trading, and that is pretty neat. Both struggling and accomplished traders have gotten in touch with me because of my success, and some great relationships and trading discussions have resulted. I've probably never had a better time talking trading than I did a few years ago in Chicago, as I spent the day with four other World Cup Championship of Futures Trading winners. If only I had a tape recorder for those conversations and discussions—pure gold! Being a top contest performer for three consecutive years opened quite a few doors for me. All things considered, participating in the trading contest has been a very fun ride.

Of course, there is a downside to all the notoriety, too. Trading seems to attract people with what I'd describe as "defective" personalities: these folks possess some personality flaw, something they cannot see (but everyone else can), something that probably impacts their trading. Believe it or not, seeing flaws in other traders can be a big help to improving your trading. So I'd like to present some of the most outrageous characters I've come across while trading, many of whom I've met because of my notoriety. Many of these people I like and have sympathy for, so I have changed names and certain facts so as to not upset any fragile psyches. Or, as they say in movie disclaimers, "names have been changed to protect the innocent. Any resemblance to any person, living or dead, is purely coincidental."

Don Demo

I've known Don for quite a few years, and he is always telling me about his paper money demo account successes. His discretionary trading performance in demo mode is actually quite spectacular; he can rake in probably $1,500 per day trading two mini S&P contracts. Plus, he is consistently profitable, and makes simulator money 9 days out of 10. He'll crow all day and all night about his trading prowess, except when I mention real-money trading to him. Then, he grows silent, and after some prodding, Don will admit that his last foray into real-money trading ended in disaster. I've counted at least five of these disasters over the years, and each one was followed by even better demo account success. Don considers himself an excellent trader who just suffers unspeakable bad luck in real-money trading.

Don's Lesson: Demo trading is not the same as real-money trading. Winning at simulated trading, with a discretionary approach, has practically zero correlation with real-money trading. Don't assume demo success will lead to real-money success, because it probably won't.

Gus the Guru

I've never met Gus. I've never spoken with Gus. I've never e-mailed Gus. But I know a ton about him from struggling traders who've contacted me. According to these people, he is a guru's guru. Gus times the market in exquisite fashion. He takes indicators, trend lines, Fibonacci numbers, and any other technical tool and paints an almost mystical story of market action. He easily explains why prices do what they do (note the past tense here). When I first heard about Gus, I thought, "He must be rich from trading, since everyone says he is top notch at analyzing the markets." Well, not quite. It turns out that right now Gus isn't trading at all. It seems his last account ran down to zero. Broker malfeasance, he claims, but it is not the first time he has had no money to trade with. Either he must run across a lot of crooked brokers or the story is more involved. In any event, now he sells his advice on the Internet. His pupils, enamored with their guru, got very confrontational with me when I suggested that maybe Gus wasn't such a great trader. More than just on the hook, Gus has these fish on ice, in the cooler, on the boat, filleted, and ready to toss on the grill.

Gus's Lesson: Beware of gurus who don't trade. The reason most don't is that they can't.

Paul the Predictor

If I gave out "outrageousness" awards for people in this chapter, Paul would take first prize. Over the past six years, I probably received 1,000 e-mails from Paul, as many as 20 in one day. Paul is convinced he has some innate ability to predict the direction of the market—any market. And he had no qualms about telling me about his greatness, over and over and over again. His super ability was detailed in many e-mails, when he wasn't trying to partner with me, trying to borrow money from me, or trying to get me to pay him for his trading "advice." Paul was amazed that Goldman Sachs wasn't pulling out all stops to hire him (even though he never applied for a job there, and had no real-money trading experience), and he really got upset when popular trading forums banned him because of boastful posting. For the forums that did not ban him, Paul left on his own accord after realizing members were apparently too dimwitted to appreciate his alleged greatness. As far as I can tell, he may have at one time traded a $5,000 account, but it did not last too long. I haven't heard from him in a while, but my guess is he is a snake oil vendor in the making.

Paul's Lesson: No one can predict the market. Beware of those who claim such abilities.

Cal the Complication King

If I ask you what two plus two is, you'd quickly and correctly answer four. But if you ask Cal the Complication King the same question, he'll give an answer like this: "Two is the base of all exponential derivations, and when one puts it upon itself in the Euclidean number space—disregarding irrationality effects, of course—the parameter space will increase by the same amount." Huh? If you are like me, this guy makes no sense at all. Amazingly, though, answers like this have earned Cal a cultlike following on one or two popular Internet trading forums. He pops up in all sorts of trading topic threads, spews his unintelligible nonsense, and then leaves his sycophants to interpret and defend his "answers." I've never been able to figure out if this nut actually trades, but if he does, I'm sure it is unprofitable—and complicated.

Cal's Lesson: KISS—Keep It Simple, Stupid. Simple concepts sometimes work best in trading. Just because someone talks in riddles doesn't mean he or she knows more than you. In fact, many times it means they know less than you!

Pay Me Peter

I always like talking to system vendors, to see what they have and what they know. Occasionally, I'll find some actual value behind the person. Typically, though, there is nothing behind the curtain with these people. Just smoke and mirrors, and double talk. So it was with Pay Me Peter. He was offering a system for sale, so I asked for details. He was selling his system for $2,500 outright, or $500 up front and $100 a month. With those high prices, I assumed it had to be "Holy Grail" good. So I asked for the performance report. I can usually smell the fake reports a mile away, and that is what I suspected to receive: $100,000 profit per year, no drawdown, 90 percent winning trades—in other words, typical ridiculous results. What he sent me was a shocker: a five-day back test that showed $290 net profit! This seemed crazy, so I asked for a longer back test. Peter then replied that if I wanted to ask more questions, his rate was $100 per half hour, and if I sent money via PayPal he would gladly answer my questions. Who in their right mind thinks this way?

Peter's Lesson: An inflated sense of worth almost always spells doom in trading. The best traders I know are the humblest ones.

Frank Five Hundred

Frank e-mailed me a few years ago and explained he was new to trading. He wanted a forex robot that worked, and had only $500 to trade with. "What do you recommend?" he asked. I replied as I do to all new traders with limited cash. "Your best bet is to study all you can, and do whatever you have to in order to get $10,000 or more to start trading. Anything less than this, and chances are you'll lose it all. Take your time; the market will always be there." Sage advice, if I do say so myself. I wish someone had given me that advice way back when. Frank, though, did not see it that way. He proceeded to swear up a blue storm at me, calling me every name in the book, claiming that I was trying to keep him from making money, and that he'd bankrupt me through his soon-to-be large-scale trades. He was probably the angriest wannabe trader person I have ever come across. After burning all bridges with me, he just ended up buying a robot from some Internet site. I found this out a few years later, when he admitted that he lost his $500 and a bunch more afterward.

Frank's Lesson: If someone gives you general trading advice (not stock tips), and it does not involve buying something from them, listen to them. They are trying to help you. Also, don't start trading with only $500.

Billy the Boaster

Where do I start with Billy the Boaster? He probably has every conceivable mental disorder around. Paranoia? Yes, he believes government agents follow him constantly, trying to steal his trading secrets. Egomania? Yes, he constantly tells me how brilliant he is, how he won a scholarship in high school for being a math whiz, how he was accepted to both (two!) colleges he applied to, and so on. Addictive personality? Yes, a doobie-smoking fiend, his pro-marijuana videos were well received by potheads on YouTube, although not by potential investors. Delusional? Yes, he told me he did not want to enter a real-money trading contest because his strategies would turn $15,000 into over a billion dollars within a year, so "what's the point of entering?" Oddly enough, he could be a decent trader once he cures himself of these issues. He'd rather live in a fantasy world, I guess.

Billy's Lesson: Live in reality. You are just another trader struggling to succeed. Accept the truth, embrace your lot in life, and then success may just come your way.

Connie the Compounder

Seven or eight years ago, I first ran into Connie over at Collective2.com, which, like any other trading site, has its share of delusional folk hiding among good traders. Connie's big thing was compounding. She'd go on and on about compounding, and how great compounding was with her trading systems. The problem was that her depth of knowledge ended at compounding. She knew nothing about investing or trading, besides knowing she wanted to pursue that as a career. So Connie did what most unethical system vendors do: she posted hypothetical results that showed enormous growth due to compounding. She claimed she did the same thing with her own money. Wrong! Unfortunately for her, she was exposed as a fraud when someone found an IRS tax court case against her, where the judge decreed that to write off trading business expenses you actually have to do some trading (go figure!).

Connie's Lesson: Compounding is a great thing, but it is not the only thing. Learn about all aspects of trading before trying it yourself.

Ian versus the Illuminati

The so-called Illuminati (or some other such group) are out to get Ian, who runs a small trading web site. Apparently, Ian figured out that these people have rigged all trading in the world, and he knows all their secrets. Of course, he'll share these secrets with you for only a few hundred dollars. Instead of getting rich by trading his so-called secret code, Ian prefers to harass and be harassed by all manner of online people, starting fights in every trading forum, and being banned from major sites like Facebook, Twitter, and StockTwits. I picture Ian sitting in his grungy little apartment, wearing a tin foil hat to block radio signals from the Illuminati. Even though I believe he peddles garbage, I really feel sorry for Ian, as I think he is truly mentally ill and desperately needs professional help.

Ian's Lesson: Stay far away from vendors who want to fight with you. They probably have many issues going on, and chances are their product is worthless anyhow.

Suki the Spinner

I met Suki on the TradeStation support forum. He was offering a strategy switch—his great strategy for one of my strategies. Unfortunately, I could never give him a walk-forward strategy (that actually worked well with real-money trading, by the way) that was anywhere close to his. I felt deflated—how could I not develop a strategy as good as Suki's? Suki repeatedly berated me and my trading skills. He wondered, "How can you, Kevin, have such poor strategies, while I, Suki the great, have such fabulous ones? Perhaps you need a different career." Well, a few months passed, and then Suki let slip that all his strategies were back tested up to the present day. No walk-forward, no out-of-sample, no real-money results. Naturally, he was a simulation millionaire, and even shared screenshots attesting to his simulator balance. No wonder I could not match him—everything was a play-money game to him.

Suki's Lesson: Beware of back tests. Unless you developed them or fully trust the developer, assume the back test is a steaming pile of . . . garbage. Treat it appropriately.

Paolo the Plagiarizer

Some mental miscreants don't actually trade but just provide advice. Paolo was such a character. A respected journalist for a forex trading web site, Paolo attracted a lot of views and comments to his articles. He seemed very knowledgeable, and I'm sure he earned a good living dispensing trading advice. The only problem was that most of his writing was someone else's. He plagiarized at least a half-dozen trading writers, including myself. This wasn't an "oh, I forgot to include quotation marks"–type offense; it was plain out copy and paste of another's work, passing it off as his own. What is even worse is that he told me it was perfectly acceptable, since most of the articles he stole were free anyhow. He had a big mental block that stealing is wrong.

Paolo's Lesson: Before you become enamored with a trading expert, make sure he or she is the real deal first. Scam artists come in all shapes and sizes.

Slick Sam

Slick Sam is a combination of every slimy system vendor and trading room operator out there. Sam will lure you in with a free pass to his trading room or a complimentary webinar. Then, he'll slowly tighten the noose, getting you to buy expensive "educational" materials. You'll hear about his trades, but you'll never see him take any trades live. Even if you are watching him live, he'll be flat in an uptrend and then suddenly announce, "I just got out of my long position for a profit." Or he'll claim that he can't show you his trades, but you should still believe his fantastic results. Once in a while, Sam will mess up, and you'll see his trading platform says "demo." Of course, whoever exposes that fact will quickly be banned from the room.

Sam's Lesson: Assume that each vendor you encounter is selling his secrets because he needs money, not because he is a do-gooder philanthropist, dedicated to helping newbie traders. This doesn't mean he isn't legitimate, but if you realize his true motivation (transferring your money from you to him), you'll at least enter any transaction with your eyes wide open. In 20 years of trading, I've probably purchased less than 10 systems, courses, consultations, and so on. I am very picky, and I've never been blatantly ripped off. I'm proud of that fact.

The Delusion Conclusion

No one is perfect, but many times even the slightest personality issue can stop your trading success dead in its tracks. The best advice I can give is to look at yourself in the mirror and be totally honest about your trading. Chances are that you are not the greatest trader ever, you probably cannot predict the market days in advance, you probably have not made millions of dollars trading and secret agents are not trying to steal your trading strategies. If you think you are invincible, real-money trading will certainly put an end to that thought. Trading is extremely tough, and you must be mentally sharp to compete. If your nonperfect personality gets in the way, the best thing to do is to get professional help, or just stay away from trading.

CONCLUSION

We've now reached the end of my trading journey. Twenty-some odd years in the making, you've seen some extreme downs, some extreme highs, and a lot of time spent in between both floundering around. First and foremost, I hope this book serves as a warning to all the new traders out there. Learn from my experience:

- Trading is tough. Exceedingly tough. Part-time folks trading from their home are up against professionals. The professionals are really great at taking your money.
- There is no "Holy Grail" out there—no magic trading strategy that you can buy for $100, $1,000, or even $10,000. There are decent ones for sale, but none is perfect.
- Where there is potential reward, there is potential risk. The results equity curve might only show the reward side of the equation, but remember that risk is always there—it just may be hidden.
- The best road to profits is to find your own trading strategy, one that meets all your goals and objectives. Just don't expect the process to be easy.

I learned all of these lessons, and many more, before I really understood how to trade. Even today, I still struggle. No trading strategy lasts forever, and I find myself constantly reinventing my trading, and creating new strategies, in an attempt to stay ahead of the pack. If I relax for a while, I inevitably find my performance suffers.

The majority of this book has focused on developing trading strategies. While I certainly value the contribution of trading psychology and position sizing and money management, I view them as icing on the cake, with the trading strategy as the cake. I look at trading this way for two reasons:

- All the positive trading psychology in the world will not make you profitable if your strategy is a loser. Positive thinking, detailed journaling, breathing exercises to calm your mind, and all other mental-type activities are great, but they still do not take the place of a solid strategy. Many people, and many trading psychology coaches out there, seem to think that having the proper mind-set ensures profits. It is just not true.
- Proper position sizing and money management are important if you have a winning strategy, but conversely if you have a losing strategy, no position sizing or money management method will ever make you profitable. It might help you burn through your account more slowly, but a losing strategy is a losing strategy, no matter how you dress it up. Just think of trading like casino gambling—the house wins because it has an edge, and gamblers lose because they don't have an edge. Changing bet sizes doesn't alter the irrefutable fact: without an edge, eventually you will lose.

For long-term success, you really need to find a winning strategy. This entails a lot of "grunt" work—finding ideas, testing them, refining them, and hopefully eventually trading them. A few years ago, I kept track of my trading strategy development. I found out that I had to test about 100 to 200 trading ideas before I found something worth trading with my own money. Most people would likely abandon trading long before testing 100 ideas. Others would say, "Yes, it takes Kevin 100 ideas, but he is a dullard. I am much smarter, so it will only take me less than 10 ideas." Those same people, unfortunately, usually take shortcuts or cheat to get what appears to be an acceptable trading system. Shortcut takers, in the long run, usually lose.

In the last sections of this book, I put everything together, and walked you through the development of two trading strategies for the euro currency futures. As of this writing, I am trading these with my own money, but I keep a close eye on their performance. In the long term, they hopefully will succeed, and as they do, I'll increase my position size accordingly. If they do not succeed, then I'll eventually swap them out with other strategies. Although I hope that every strategy I create does well, I also know that is not always the case. Surely, the performance of these two euro strategies so far bears that out. They are currently making money but underperforming, and maybe they will continue to do so, or maybe they will return to their long-term averages. One never knows, so I usually prepare for the worst, and hope for the best. Many times, the end result is somewhere in between.

In closing, I'll leave you with one thought: if you put your mind to becoming a good trader and follow that up with proper effort, you can be successful. I am living proof of that, although hopefully your journey will not take as long as mine did. But, to succeed long term, plan on dedicating a lot of time, effort, and money to the cause. Trading is like anything else good in life; if it is good, it is worth working for. Don't be tempted by those offering shortcuts, easy fixes, magic formulas, or Holy Grail systems. Those folks will only sidetrack and derail your effort. Put the time in, follow an approach that other successful traders use, and you'll be much better off. I wished I had taken that approach back in the late 1980s, when I first learned about futures trading from the Cowboy Trader.

Good luck, and happy trading!

Monkey Trading Example, TradeStation Easy Language Code

Strategy 1: Baseline Strategy (No Randomness)

```
input: nContracts(1);
var:ssl1(1);
var:ssl(2000);
    if date >= 1070316 and date < 1080314 then
    begin
        ssl1 = 0.75 ;
    end ;
    if date >= 1080314 and date < 1090311 then
    begin
        ssl1 = 0.75 ;
    end ;
    if date >= 1090311 and date < 1100310 then
    begin
        ssl1 = 0.75 ;
    end ;
    if date >= 1100310 and date < 1110309 then
```

```
    begin
        ssl1 = 0.5 ;
    end ;

    if date >= 1110309 and date < 1120310 then
   begin
        ssl1 = 0.5 ;
    end ;
    if date >= 1120310 and date < 1130308 then
   begin
        ssl1 = 1.25 ;
    end ;
    if date >= 1130308 and date < 1140308 then
   begin
        ssl1 = .75 ;
    end ;



   if date >= 1070316 then begin






if close<close[1] and close[1]<close[2]  then begin
buy ncontracts Contracts next bar at market;
End;

if close>close[1] and close[1]>close[2]  then begin
SellShort ncontracts Contracts  next bar at market;
End;



SetStopContract;

setstoploss(minlist(ssl1*BigPointValue*avgtruerange(14),ssl));

end;
```

Strategy 2: Random Entry, Baseline Exit Strategy

```
input:
iter(1),percentlong(.400),holdbars(2.5),exitclose(0),oddstradetoday(.47),be
gindate(1070319);
var:posstradetoday(0);


//entry is random

input: nContracts(1);
var:ssl1(1);
var:ssl(2000);
    if date >= 1070316 and date < 1080314 then
    begin
        ssl1 = 0.75 ;
    end ;
    if date >= 1080314 and date < 1090311 then
    begin
        ssl1 = 0.75 ;
    end ;
    if date >= 1090311 and date < 1100310 then
    begin
        ssl1 = 0.75 ;
    end ;
    if date >= 1100310 and date < 1110309 then
    begin
        ssl1 = 0.5 ;
    end ;

    if date >= 1110309 and date < 1120310 then
    begin
        ssl1 = 0.5 ;
    end ;
    if date >= 1120310 and date < 1130308 then
    begin
        ssl1 = 1.25 ;
    end ;
    if date >= 1130308 and date < 1130501 then
    begin
        ssl1 = .75 ;
    end ;
```

```
    if date >= 1070316 then begin



if close<close[1] and close[1]<close[2]  then begin
sell ncontracts Contracts next bar at market;
End;

if close>close[1] and close[1]>close[2]  then begin
buytocover ncontracts Contracts  next bar at market;
End;




SetStopContract;

setstoploss(minlist(ssl1*BigPointValue*avgtruerange(14),ssl));

end;









posstradetoday=random(1); //random number for today's trade







If  date>begindate then begin

If posstradetoday<=oddstradetoday then begin //trade will occur today

    //enter trade
    If random(1)<percentlong then buy this bar at close
     Else sellshort this bar at close;
  end;
end;
```

Strategy 3: Baseline Entry, Random Exit Strategy

```
input:
iter(1),percentlong(.400),holdbars(2.5),exitclose(0),oddstradetoday(.47),be
gindate(1070319);
var:posstradetoday(0);



//exit is random


input: nContracts(1);
var:ssl1(1);
var:ssl(2000);
    if date >= 1070316 and date < 1080314 then
    begin
        ssl1 = 0.75 ;
    end ;
    if date >= 1080314 and date < 1090311 then
    begin
        ssl1 = 0.75 ;
    end ;
    if date >= 1090311 and date < 1100310 then
    begin
        ssl1 = 0.75 ;
    end ;
    if date >= 1100310 and date < 1110309 then
    begin
        ssl1 = 0.5 ;
    end ;

    if date >= 1110309 and date < 1120310 then
    begin
        ssl1 = 0.5 ;
    end ;
    if date >= 1120310 and date < 1130308 then
   begin
        ssl1 = 1.25 ;
    end ;
    if date >= 1130308 and date < 1140308 then
   begin
        ssl1 = .75 ;
    end ;
```

```
      if date >= 1070316 then begin

  if close<close[1] and close[1]<close[2] and marketposition=0  then begin
  buy ncontracts Contracts next bar at market;
  End;

  if close>close[1] and close[1]>close[2] and marketposition=0   then begin
  SellShort ncontracts Contracts  next bar at market;
  End;

  end;

  posstradetoday=random(1); //random number for today's trade

  If barssinceentry>=random(2*holdbars) then begin
    Sell this bar at close;
    Buytocover this bar at close;
  end;

    If exitclose=1 then setexitonclose;
```


■ Strategy 4: Random Entry, Random Exit Strategy

```
input:
iter(1),percentlong(.400),holdbars(2.5),exitclose(0),oddstradetoday(.48),be
gindate(1070319);
var:posstradetoday(0);

  posstradetoday=random(1); //random number for today's trade
```

```
If  date>begindate then begin

  If posstradetoday<=oddstradetoday then begin //trade will occur today
    //enter trade
    If random(1)<percentlong then buy this bar at close
     Else sellshort this bar at close;

  end;
end;

If barssinceentry>=random(2*holdbars) then begin
  Sell this bar at close;
  Buytocover this bar at close;
end;

  If exitclose=1 then setexitonclose;
```

Euro Night Strategy, TradeStation Easy Language Format


```
vars: FirstTime (1800),
      LastTime (2359),
      ATRmult (3),
      TRmult (.5),
      Nb (10),
      NATR (60),
      Stoplo(275);

      FirstTime = 1800 ;
      LastTime = 2359 ;

  if date >= 1090721 and date < 1100104 then
  begin
      Nb = 9 ;
      NATR = 93 ;
      ATRmult = 3.15 ;
      TRmult = 0.51 ;
      Stoplo= 425 ;
  end ;
  if date >= 1100104 and date < 1100617 then
  begin
      Nb = 9 ;
```

```
        NATR = 93 ;
        ATRmult = 2.55 ;
        TRmult = 0.66 ;
        Stoplo= 375 ;
    end ;
    if date >= 1100617 and date < 1101129 then
    begin
        Nb = 14 ;
        NATR = 83 ;
        ATRmult = 2.75 ;
        TRmult = 0.71 ;
        Stoplo= 425 ;
    end ;
    if date >= 1101129 and date < 1110515 then
    begin
        Nb = 14 ;
        NATR = 83 ;
        ATRmult = 2.75 ;
        TRmult = 0.66 ;
        Stoplo= 425 ;
    end ;
    if date >= 1110515 and date < 1111026 then
    begin
        Nb = 19 ;
        NATR = 93 ;
        ATRmult = 3.15 ;
        TRmult = 0.56 ;
        Stoplo= 425 ;
    end ;
    if date >= 1111026 and date < 1120412 then
    begin
        Nb = 14 ;
        NATR = 83 ;
        ATRmult = 2.95 ;
        TRmult = 0.61 ;
        Stoplo= 425 ;
    end ;
    if date >= 1120412 and date < 1120924 then
    begin
        Nb = 14 ;
        NATR = 93 ;
        ATRmult = 2.95 ;
        TRmult = 0.61 ;
        Stoplo= 425 ;
    end ;
```

```
if date >= 1120924 and date < 1130310 then
begin
    Nb = 19 ;
    NATR = 73 ;
    ATRmult = 3.15 ;
    TRmult = 0.71 ;
    Stoplo= 425 ;
end ;
if date >= 1130310 and date < 1130826 then
begin
    Nb = 14 ;
    NATR = 93 ;
    ATRmult = 2.95 ;
    TRmult = 0.51 ;
    Stoplo= 425 ;
end ;
if date >= 1130826 and date < 1140101 then
begin
    Nb = 14 ;
    NATR = 93 ;
    ATRmult = 2.55 ;
    TRmult = 0.71 ;
    Stoplo= 425 ;
end ;

Var:   LongPrice(0), ShortPrice(0), LongTarget(0), ShortTarget(0);



//limit entry prices
ShortPrice = Average(Low, Nb) + ATRmult * AvgTrueRange(NATR);
LongPrice = Average(High, Nb) - ATRmult * AvgTrueRange(NATR);


{code to ensure only 1 order is entered at each bar - order closest to
price}
var:diff1(0),diff2(0),EntrytoPick(0);
EntrytoPick=0;
diff1=absvalue(close-LongPrice);
diff2=absvalue(close-ShortPrice);
If diff1<=diff2 then EntryToPick=1;
If diff1>diff2 then EntryToPick=2;


if date >= 1090721 and MarketPosition = 0 and EntriesToday(Date) < 1  and
Time >= FirstTime and Time < LastTime then begin
```

```
If  EntryToPick=1 then begin
  Buy("Long Entry") next bar at LongPrice limit;
end;

If  EntryToPick=2 then begin
 Sell short("Short Entry") next bar at ShortPrice limit;
end;


end;


If MarketPosition=-1 then begin
  ShortTarget = EntryPrice - TRmult * TrueRange;
  Buy to cover("Short Exit") next bar at ShortTarget limit;
end;

If MarketPosition =1 then begin
  LongTarget = EntryPrice + TRmult * TrueRange;
  Sell("Long Exit") next bar at LongTarget limit;
end;


Setstopposition;
setstoploss(stoplo);

SetExitOnClose;
```

Euro Day Strategy, TradeStation Easy Language Format


```
var:xb(2),xb2(50),pipadd(1),Stopl(400),proft(5000);
  if date >= 1091118 and date < 1101025 then
  begin
      xb = 4 ;
      xb2 = 70 ;
      pipadd = 2 ;
      Stopl = 275 ;
  end ;
  if date >= 1101025 and date < 1110929 then
  begin
      xb = 4 ;
      xb2 = 72 ;
      pipadd = 5 ;
      Stopl = 225 ;
  end ;
  if date >= 1110929 and date < 1120904 then
  begin
      xb = 3 ;
      xb2 = 74 ;
      pipadd = 8 ;
      Stopl = 425 ;
```

```
   end ;
   if date >= 1120904 and date < 1130812 then
   begin
       xb = 3 ;
       xb2 = 74 ;
       pipadd = 11 ;
       Stopl = 425 ;
   end ;
  if date >= 1130812 and date < 11400101 then
   begin
       xb = 5 ;
       xb2 = 80 ;
       pipadd = 8 ;
       Stopl = 425 ;
   end ;

var:cs(0),tradestoday(0),startprof(0),starttrades(0),stoplo(0);

cs=currentsession(0);

If cs<>cs[1] then begin
  tradestoday=0;
  startprof=NetProfit + OpenPositionProfit;
  starttrades=TotalTrades;
  Stoplo=stopl;
end;

If totaltrades<>starttrades or marketposition<>0 or startprof<>NetProfit +
OpenPositionProfit then tradestoday=1;




If tradestoday=0 and time<1500 and date >= 1091118 then begin


//entry rules

If (high>=highest(high,xb) and close<close[xb2] )   then begin
  sellshort next bar at high+pipadd/10000 limit;
end;

If low<=lowest(low,xb) and close>close[xb2]    then begin
  buy next bar at low-pipadd/10000 limit;
end;
```

```
end;


//exit rules

Setstopposition;
setstoploss(stoplo);
setprofittarget(proft);


setexitonclose;
```

ABOUT THE COMPANION WEB SITE

Building Winning Algorithmic Trading Systems comes with a companion web site at www.wiley.com/go/algotradingsystems (password: davey14).

You will find five supplementary spreadsheets and other information to help you on your trading journey:

- Daily Tracking Worksheet
- Development Worksheet
- Equity and Drawdown Curve Builder
- Monte Carlo Simulator
- Monthly Summary Sheets

In addition, readers will find quarterly performance updates for the strategies described in this book. (For more frequent performance updates, go to www.kjtradingsystems.com/bookupdates.html.)

For updates and additional resources, go to www.WileyTrading.com. Click on "Free Trader Resources" and register to get access.

INDEX

E

F

G

H

I

L

M

N

O

P

Q

R

S

Printed in the USA
K072164SCI120117 01S29053000000002536